RSAC

ACTIVATION OF ENERGY

PIERRE TEILHARD DE CHARDIN

ACTIVATION
OF ENERGY

Translated by René Hague

A HELEN AND KURT WOLFF BOOK
HARCOURT BRACE JOVANOVICH, INC.
New York

First American edition 1971

Originally published in France under the title *L'Activation de l'Energie*

ISBN 0–15–103276–9

Library of Congress Catalog Card Number: 75-142104

Printed in the United States of America

A B C D E

Contents

Note

As pointed out in the note at the beginning of *Human Energy*,[1] the writings still to be published (including this volume) were never revised by Père Teilhard de Chardin with a view to publication. There are a number of passages which, following his usual practice, he would no doubt have expressed more exactly or would have modified.

This collection, running on chronologically from *Human Energy*, progressively develops the title-theme of that volume. As Père Wildiers wrote in the introduction to the latter, the papers it contains 'are perhaps some of the most original and valuable' of Père Teilhard's writings.

The notes to this volume are intended to prevent any danger of erroneous interpretation. For the most part they consist simply of summaries of some of Père Teilhard's more elaborately worked out passages.

[1] *Human Energy*, Harcourt Brace Jovanovich, New York, 1971, p. 17.

'Hypothesis: a very poor choice of word to designate the supreme spiritual act by which the dust-cloud of experience takes on form and is kindled at the fire of knowledge.'

Père Teilhard de Chardin

The Moment of Choice

A possible interpretation of War

THIS will be the second time, then, in the span of one human life that we shall have known War. The second time, did I say? Is it not, rather, worse than that? Is it not the same Great War that is still raging, the same single process: a world being re-cast – or disintegrating? In 1918 it seemed all over and done with, and now it is beginning all over again.

The same anguish, then, is making itself felt deep within each one of us, and there is not one of us but heaves the same deep sigh. We thought that we were rising up in freedom towards a better era: and now it would appear that we were quite mistaken, that some vast determinism is dragging us irresistibly round and round, or down to the depths. Is it not, we ask, a diabolical circle of incessantly renewed discords: is not the ground sliding back from under our feet at each step we take? The whirling wheel or the giddy slope? Were our hopes of progress, then, no more than an illusion?

Like everyone else, I felt the horror of this shocking trial when I landed in the Far East – flooded by nature and laid waste by an insidious invasion – and learnt that the West was ablaze.

Once again, therefore, I drew up the balance sheet of all I knew and all I believed, and examined it again. As unemotionally as possible I compared it with all that is now happening to us. And here, to put it frankly, is what I thought I saw.

*

First and foremost: no, a thousand times no – however tragic the present conflict may be, it contains nothing that should shake the foundations of our faith in the future. I wrote this in this very journal[1] and I shall repeat it with all the conviction I felt two years ago. Where a group of isolated human wills might falter, the sum total of man's free decisions could not fail to find its God. Consider: for hundreds of millions of years consciousness was unceasingly rising up to the surface of the earth – and could we imagine that the direction of this mighty tide would be reversed at the very moment when we were beginning to be aware of its flow? The truth is that our reasons, even our natural reasons, for believing in a final triumph for man are of an order that is higher than any possible occurrence. Whatever disorder we are confronted by, the first thing we must say to ourselves is that we shall not perish. This is not a mortal sickness: it is a crisis of growth. It may well be that the evil has never seemed so deep-rooted nor the symptoms so grave; but, in one sense, is that not precisely one more reason for hope? The height of a peak is a measure of the depths of the abysses it overtops. If, from century to century, the crises did not become more violent, then, perhaps, we might have cause for anxiety.

Thus, even if the present cataclysm were impossible to understand, we should still, on principle, have to cling tenaciously to our belief and continue to press on. It is enough, surely, for us (particularly if we are Christians) to know that from the most distant reaches in which life appears to us, it has never succeeded in rising up except by suffering, and through evil – following the way of the Cross.

But is it really so impossible for us to understand the meaning of what is going on?

At the root of the major troubles in which nations are today involved, I believe that I can distinguish the signs of a change of age in mankind.

It took hundreds of centuries for man simply to people the earth and cover it with a first network: and further thousands

1. *Etudes*, 20 October 1937: 'La Crise présente' (published under its original title 'Sauvons l'Humanité' in the *Cahier III de l'Association des Amis de P. Teilhard de Chardin*, Ed. du Seuil, Paris. Ed.).

of years to build up, as chance circumstances allowed, solid nuclei of civilizations within this initially fluctuating envelope, radiating from independent and antagonistic centres. Today, these elements have multiplied and grown; they have packed themselves closer together and forced themselves against one another – to the point where an over-all unity, *of no matter what nature,* has become economically and psychologically inevitable. Mankind, in coming of age, has begun to be subject to the necessity and to feel the urgency of forming one single body coextensive with itself. There we have the underlying cause of our distress.

In 1918 the nations had tried, in a supreme effort of individualism, in an obscure instinct for conservation, to defend themselves against this mass-concretion which they felt was coming. At that time we witnessed the terrifying upsurge of nationalisms – the reactionary fragmentation of ethnic groups in the name of history. And now once again the single fundamental wave is mounting up and rolling forward, but in a form made perilous by the particularist enthusiasms with which it is impregnated. So it is that the crisis has burst upon us.

*

What, then, do we see?

At a number of points on the earth, sections of mankind are simultaneously isolating themselves and drawing themselves up in readiness, logically impelled by 'universalization' of their nationalism to set themselves up as the exclusive heirs of life's promises. Life, they proclaim from where they stand, can attain its term only by following *exactly* the road it took at the very beginning. Survival of the fittest: a pitiless struggle for domination between individual and individual, between group and group. Who is going to devour whom? . . . Such is the fundamental law of fuller being. In consequence, overriding every other principle of action and morality, we have the law of force, transposed *unchanged* into the human sphere. External force: war, therefore, does not represent a residual accident which will become less important as time goes on, but is the first agent of evolution and the very form in which it is expressed. And, to match this, internal force: citizens welded together in the iron grip of a totalitarian regime. All along the road we find coercion, continually obliged to turn the screw tighter. And, as a climax, one single branch stifling all the others. The future awaits us at the term of a continuous series of selections. Its crown is destined for the strongest individual in the strongest nation: it is in the smoke and blood of battles that the superman will appear.

It is against this barbaric ideal that we have spontaneously rebelled: and it is to escape slavery that we too have had to have recourse to force. It is to destroy the 'divine right' of war that we are fighting.

We are fighting. But at this point we must take heed. In what spirit, quite fundamentally, are we taking up arms? In a spirit of immobility and quiescence? – or in a spirit of conquest?

There might well be, I fear, a degraded and dangerous way of our making war on war: it would consist in defending ourselves without attacking – as though in order to become fully men we ourselves did not have to grow and change. To fight simply from inertia; to fight in order to be left in peace; to fight so that we may be 'let be' – that, surely, would be to dodge the essential problem presented to man by the age he has reached in his life. 'The other side', I am as convinced as any man, are making a mistake in the violent methods they are using in order to unify the world. On the other hand they are fully justified in feeling that the time has come to dream of a new earth: and it is even in virtue of this vision that they are so formidably strong. One thing, then, we must clearly appreciate: we shall succeed in counterbalancing the current they represent, and then in reversing it, only by overcoming their religion of force by one that is equally wide in its embrace, equally coherent, and equally attractive. Within us, and directed against them, a dynamism must be at work which is as powerful as that by which they are animated. If not, our armament falls short of theirs, and we do not deserve to win. On their side, they are introducing war as a principle of life. If we are to answer them effectively, what shall we, on our side, direct against them?

*

The more one considers this infinitely urgent problem of finding an over-all plan for building up the earth, the clearer it becomes that if we are to avoid the road of brute material force, there is no way out *ahead* except the road of comradeship and brotherhood – and that is as true of nations as it is of individuals: not jealous hostility, but friendly rivalry: not personal feeling, but the team spirit.

Unhappily, this gospel of unanimity cannot be proclaimed without producing a sort of pity in those to whom it is addressed: 'A spineless doctrine – a bleating for a Utopia.' Ah! so we shall find that Rousseau and the pacifists have done more harm to mankind than Nietzsche! Nowadays, seriously to envisage the possibility of human 'conspiration' inevitably raises a smile: and yet, even for the modern world, could there be a more healthy prospect or one with a more realistic foundation?

I recently explained my views on these points in this journal.[2] Racialism defends itself by an appeal to the laws of nature. There is, however, just one thing it forgets when it does so: that when nature attained the level of man it was obliged, precisely in order to remain true to itself, to change its ways. Until man, it is true enough that living branches develop primarily by stifling and eliminating one another – the law, in fact, of the jungle. By contrast, starting with man and within the human group, this is no longer true: the play of mutual destruction ceases to operate. Selection, no doubt, is still at work and can still be recognized, but it no longer holds the most important place; and the reason for this is that the

2. *Etudes*, 5 July 1939: 'The natural units of humanity', in *The Vision of the Past*, Collins, London, and Harper and Row, New York, 1966, pp. 192 ff.

appearance of thought has added a new dimension to the universe. Through spirit's irresistible affinity for its own kind, it has created a sort of convergent milieu within which the branches, as they are formed, have to come closer together in order to be fully living. In this new order of things, the whole balance is changed, though with no diminution of the system's energy. It is simply that force, in its earlier form, expresses only man's power over the extra- or the infra-human. It has been transformed, at the heart of mankind, among men, into its spiritual equivalent – an energy not of repulsion, but of attraction.

Bearing this in mind, the ultimate form to be assumed by mankind should not be conceived on the lines of a stem that is swollen with the sap of all the stems it killed as it grew. It will be born (for born it cannot but be) in the form of some organism in which, obeying one of the universe's most unmistakable laws, every blade and every fascicle, every individual and every nation, will find completion through union with all the others. No longer a succession of eliminations, but a confluence of energies – 'synergy'. Such, if we have ears to hear, is the message of biology.

For my own part, I can find no other doctrine of force to set against that of sheer Force.

In that case, however, we must abandon every illusion and every form of indolence. If such is the horizon towards which duration is leading us, it would be useless for the democracies to dream any longer of one of those incomplete and ambiguous worlds in which the nations, with no mutual love but faithful to some ill-defined, static concept of justice, would obediently respect one another's frontiers but would know one another no better than strangers who live on the same landing. Much more than the permanent threat of a war hanging over us, it is undoubtedly the uncertainty of this situation that has brought about the present explosion in Europe. 'No. Things couldn't go on like that any longer'. Irrespective of our wishes, the age of lukewarm pluralisms has gone for ever. Either a single nation will succeed in destroying and absorbing all the others: or all nations will come together in one common soul, that so they may be more human.

There, if I am not mistaken, lies the dilemma contained in the present crisis. This war is of a completely different kind from other wars, and is something much more: what has now begun is the struggle for the completion and the possession of the earth.

If we can see how things stand, if, I mean, we are aware of the dilemma and, in consequence, of the spirit which our position in the conflict forces us, willy-nilly, to defend – then we, in our turn, will find our strength trebled, and this time on a grand scale.

In the first place, we shall be strong in our hearts: because we shall no longer be simply resigned to fighting, as we would be if we were fighting fire, or storm or pestilence: we shall be fighting for something fine that we have to discover and build – we, too, shall be like conquerors.

Secondly, we shall have intellectual strength: because we shall have grasped the principle that must govern, in its most general conditions, the peace of tomorrow. Tomorrow: shall we not, it may well be, still be thinking covertly of 'after the war' in terms of humiliation and annihilation for the loser? And, in that case, where is our virtue? Are we now going to speak the language of the enemy? And what purpose would be served by restoring any one of the former orders of things, when the whole problem is precisely to leave them all behind?

Finally, we shall be strong against those we have to overcome. This is the direct corollary and conclusion of all I have just said. We commonly speak of it as an economic war, a war of attrition. But, if my view is correct, it is much more a war of conversion, because it is a war of ideals. At this moment, under the armoured shell of aircraft, submarines, and tanks, two opposed concepts of mankind are confronting one another. It is, therefore, in the depths of the soul that the battle will be decided. Let us only hope that under the shock of events the passion for unity blazes up in us with more ardour than the passion for destruction that is ranged against us. At that moment, perhaps, our adversary may well come to see, behind our blows, that we respect him and wish to have him with us more than he imagines he hates us. He will recognize, perhaps, that we are resisting him only in order to give him what he is seeking. And then, struck at its source, the conflict will die of its own accord, never to break out again.

'Love one another'. This gentle precept, which two thousand years ago came like a soothing oil humbly poured on human suffering, offers itself to our modern spirit as the most powerful, and in fact the *only* imaginable, principle of the earth's future equilibrium. Shall we at last make up our minds to admit that it is neither weakness nor harmless fad – but that it points out a formal condition for the achievement of life's most organic and most technically advanced progress?

If we did so decide, what awaits us would be the true victory and the only true peace.

In its own heart, force would be constrained to disarm, because we should at last have laid our hands on a stronger weapon with which to replace it.

And man, grown to his full stature, would have found the right road.

Unpublished, Peking
Christmas 1939

The Atomism of Spirit

An attempt to understand the structure of
the stuff of the universe

WHETHER it is a matter of climbing a peak, of cutting up a
diamond, or of unravelling some complex of magnitudes
tangled up by nature, the best way to get on is not generally to
make a frontal attack on the difficulties that stand in our way:
it is much better to look to right and left for the slight crack
that can indirectly lead us without effort to the heart of the
problem.

Ever since man reflected, and the more he reflected, the
opposition between spirit and matter has constantly risen up as
an ever higher barrier across the road that climbs up to a better
awareness of the universe: and in this lies the deep-rooted
origin of all our troubles. In physics and in metaphysics, as in
morals, in social science and in religion, why are we constantly
arguing with one another, why do we never seem to get any
further? Surely the reason is that, being unable accurately to
define the nature of the relationship that cosmically connects
thought with the tangible, we cannot contrive to orientate
ourselves in the labyrinth of things. Which is the top and
which the bottom in our universe? Or are there even a top and
a bottom?

In what follows, I would like to try to show that there is a
roundabout path which has gradually been cleared by a series
(apparently discontinuous) of intellectual conquests; and that if
we take this path we are probably henceforth, without
realizing it, in a position to surmount the reputedly inaccessible
peak behind which, perhaps, the Promised Land awaits us.

As a starting point in our climb I shall simply take the
'ludicrously' evident fact of the plurality of man. There is not
just *one* man in the world, there are any number of men,
countless myriads even. Precisely as with the stars scattered

over the firmament, precisely as with the particles from which are woven the bodies that surround us, number and mass are integral to man. The molecular structure of mankind is a fundamental condition of our lives which we find in no way astonishing – we do not even notice it, so 'natural' does it seem to us. And yet it is surely just this condition which has always been offering us the clew which we despair of finding. Here we have the truth which once again stares us in the face and yet we cannot see it.

Dismissing any scientific or philosophical preconceptions, let us try thoroughly to understand why man, immersed in the multitude, is himself multiple. We shall then, perhaps, be well on the way to having analysed the stuff of the universe, both in its texture and in distinguishing the positive or negative sign of its fibres.

II. FIRST PRELIMINARY OBSERVATION: THE DIMENSIONAL ZONES OF THE UNIVERSE

Like every reality that is synthetic in nature, our perceptions inevitably link together in a particular order. In order to see, as we know, we have to do more than simply open our eyes. In addition, our observation must, as it proceeds, be reinforced by a certain number of auxiliary ways of seeing.

In the present instance, if, that is to say, the meaning that makes human plurality plain to us is to burst upon our minds, two of these preliminary data or intuitions are required: the first of these is what I shall call 'the vision of the dimensional zones of the universe'.

Let us begin by examining the vision.

On either side of the *middle zone* of the world on the scale of which our humanity is busy and active, objects, as presented to our experience, are arranged in two natural series of size – either indefinitely growing larger, or indefinitely growing smaller: towards the nebulae, or towards the atoms. Above lies the immense, below lies the infinitesimal. Since all time man has been vaguely conscious of being imprisoned in this limitless framework: so much so, that after an initial moment of bewilderment we now feel almost at home in between microns and light-years, in the new world of modern physics. What, however, still remains much less familiar to our minds is the *strangeness*, as yet hardly disclosed, of the two abysses between which we float. In a famous passage, Pascal imagined within a cheesemite another universe containing other mites. We are now finding ourselves obliged to think on lines that *contradict* this idea of a space that expands or contracts and yet retains the same characteristics. Just as the brilliance of light and the forms of life are transformed in the eyes of an observer moving along a terrestrial meridian, or descending into the depths of the ocean – so, and even much more radically, we must conceive the universe as changing shape if we try in our minds to change our position either towards the uppermost, or towards the lowest, of its two extreme zones.

As we move towards the latter (if, impossible though it would be, we could so reduce our size without losing consciousness), all sorts of odd forces (capillary attractions, osmotic currents, Brownian movement, magnetic influences, etc.) would soon fasten on us, to paralyse us, polarize us, or drag us into their feverish dance; and the lower we descended, the more we should have to say goodbye to common experience. Entering this realm of the infinitely small, where we would meet unimaginably fantastic speeds, the first thing we would find disappearing would be the chemical distinction of the elements – because we should have travelled *beneath it*. Losing all meaning, heat, light and resistance would vanish in turn: while the very mass of bodies (the foundation, at our scale, of cosmic stability) would become the most fluid and plastic of things.

Moving towards the top (supposing we were able to increase our size indefinitely) other no less radical changes, though of another order, would intervene in their own manner to upset the ways in which we think and see. By its nature the physics of the immense is much more difficult for us to get hold of, or even to imagine, than that of the infinitesimal. Once we are dealing with matter in colossal volumes and with almost infinitely slow speeds, what impact can it still make on our senses and our imaginations? At the same time we know enough about it to suspect that at these extremely high cosmic latitudes we no longer have any guarantee (any more, in fact, than we have 'at the bottom') that the three angles of a triangle will still equal two right angles, as they do in the Euclidean zone of 'middle latitudes'. Most important of all, we know enough to discover, to our confusion, that in the immense something so fundamental and so simple for our practical life as the coincidence (or synchronism) of two events loses practically all definable meaning or usefulness.

In short, and in contradiction of the usual preconception of the ancient philosophies, there is in nature a relationship between quantity and quality. Change the spatial dimensions of bodies, and it is their very properties that are transformed. Whether the transformation be effected (as in the case of 'dissolving views') simply by relative modification of values – owing to the fact that certain effects, imperceptible at the scale of the intermediate, become preponderant at extreme scales; or whether there really does exist, concentrically with ourselves, a certain number of critical spatial surfaces crossing through which physical values are reversed – in either case the fact remains that our universe is not the same at its equator (which is where we stand) as it is at its two ends. Zonally, it is divided into a number of specifically different domains.

III. SECOND PRELIMINARY OBSERVATION: THE COMPLEXITY OF LIVING MATTER

Let us now withdraw our attention from the immense and the infinitesimal, and turn to another scene, apparently of a different order. Leaving atoms and nebulae, let us take a look, in the vicinity of our own middle latitude, at living matter.

Armed with ever more subtle and powerful instruments provided by science, biology is constantly pressing home its attacks on this object, so close to us and at the same time so extraordinary, which is our own flesh. Chemical analyses and syntheses of incredible delicacy; every sort of trituration, under the influence of the 'dead' or 'living' reagents which today make up the weaponry of research; finally, direct observation under the microscope, with magnifications that have now suddenly just risen from two thousand diameters to a hundred thousand – this is not the place to enumerate the exciting results to which these investigations, still hardly begun, are leading. What, on the other hand, does matter in this connexion, is to note that, dominating the vast corpus of experimental data already accumulated by biophysics and biochemistry, one general fact is emerging, which is more important for our intelligence than any particular fact. By this I mean the incredible complexity of organic beings.

First of all, there is complexity in the sheer *number* of associated particles. In a single molecule of protein there is the equivalent of from 6,000 to 20,000 hydrogen atoms; this number rises to 68,000 in the haemoglobin of blood; to four million in the red pigment of the liver; and to seventeen and even twenty-five million in a virus-particle. No attempt has yet been made, I believe, to work out the number for a living cell, nor indeed would it be possible to do so – and there are about a thousand million million in one human body.

Secondly, there is complexity in the *variety* of assembled mechanisms. The multitude of chemical elements concentrated in living or pre-living particles does not represent a homogeneous swarm. On the contrary, practically the whole series of simple bodies gradually becomes involved and used in the building up of organic bodies: and this in a state that entails combinations whose differentiation and hierarchically ordered interlocking are still beyond our methods of analysis and understanding. At the lowest level these combinations are molecular, but at a higher level there are 'micellar', granular, cellular, histological, etc., combinations of every order; and all these arrangements build up on top of one another and combine in geometric progressions the mere idea of which baffles our minds.

Finally (and in consequence) there is complexity in the *general mechanism* that can ensure the functioning of these countless components that are fitted together.

And all this, we must remember, takes place and operates on *an unbelievably minute scale*. A thread of virus (as photography shows) is no more than three ten-thousandths of a millimetre in length; the smallest bacteria are about the same size. There are some thirty million million cells in a human brain . . . Astrophysicists are tracking down stars in which matter would appear to be inorganically so compressed upon itself as to attain a mass far higher than those we are familiar with. In vitalized matter, it is *the organization* that attains an extremely high *density*.

The truth is that if we examine our own substance closely we are amazed at the reappearance, *once again*, *of the abyss* in a new form. It is no longer the lower abyss of fragmentation nor, at the other extreme, the abyss of agglomeration. It lies in a third direction, and it is the *abyss of synthesis* – the mesmeric depths of a matter which, at a minimum volume, contrives limitlessly to build up on itself at the very heart of our own selves.

If, then, we look at this rising whirlpool from which our thought emerges; if we reflect upon this third abyss, we can, I believe, begin to see the universe falling into shape and settling into equilibrium around the human Pleiades.

IV. THE SHAFT OF LIGHT: COMPLEXITY AND
CONSCIOUSNESS

Let us, then, bring together and combine the two facts to which this preliminary essay has introduced us. On the one

hand, as we began by noting, the stuff of things is transformed
– *there is a change in its properties* – when we follow its main axis
in space and either climb up towards extremely great or
descend towards extremely small magnitudes. On the other
hand, as we have just pointed out, there is a second way in
which bodies can oscillate between the infinitesimal and the
immense. While they are capable of becoming extremely small
or extremely big, they can *also* follow another axis which runs
athwart the first, and so become either ultra-simple or ultra-
complicated in their internal structure. We observed, further,
that the high forms of complexity appear in the zone of living
substances.

If we reverse the terms of this last proposition our ideas will
be clarified.

Hitherto life, as life, has seemed to be impatient of incorporation in what we call science or even to be inexpressible in
scientific terms. It is impossible, we are constantly told, to
include consciousness and thought in the constructions of
physics. If we ask whose fault this is, the physicist blames his
failure on nature; but surely the truth is rather that physics,
arbitrarily limiting nature, persists in building up its universe
along a spatial axis, and it is precisely along that axis that life
does not appear? Once a breakthrough has been effected above
ourselves, running across the very large and the very small,
and so allowing the axis of the complex a clear passage, then a
new cosmic milieu is created by the introduction of this
additional dimension; and in this milieu the vitalization of
matter immediately ceases to appear puzzling or inexplicable.
On the contrary it seems as 'natural' as the variation in mass
with high speeds or the appearance at very great distances of
the effects of relativity.

As we were saying, a new dimensional zone brings with it
new properties. Once the special domain or special compartment of the ultra-synthetic is recognized in the universe, life no
longer comes as an explosion into the scientific picture of the
real. It simply fills up what would, without it, remain a gaping

void in our outlook. Life is the property that is peculiar to *large organized numbers*, it is the specific effect of matter carried to an extreme degree of internal structuration, and as such it falls smoothly into the position of an expected phenomenon. Following on the immense and the infinitesimal, the large complex (since it does in fact exist) cannot but have *its own proper character*. What that is, we shall now see.

Consciousness as an effect of complexity

Still standing on the same ground, let us continue to focus the universe from this re-adjusted point of view; it will not be long before we make a further discovery.

To speak of 'complexity' in the true sense we acknowledge in relation to living matter, is necessarily to imply a multitude of *unified* elements. The fantastic structure represented by the smallest animate particle forms a *whole*: in other words, were it not to some degree radially organized, it would fall back into dust. By its very nature an organism would not subsist, as it becomes more complex, nor would it function, if it did not structurally form *a system that is centred*.

And now, to say 'consciousness' is again, just as inevitably, to express the idea of a being folding back and concentrating on itself. To see, to feel, to think is to act or be acted upon as a centre of convergence for the vast fan of things which radiate around us. It is to be *internally centred*.

Consciousness and complexity, therefore, are two aspects of one and the same reality – *the centre* – depending on whether we adopt a viewpoint outside or inside ourselves.

And this can mean but one thing: that by using this new variable it becomes possible for us to express in more fundamental and more general terms the special transformation which the universe undergoes as it makes a further ascent, in the direction of extremely high complexes.

For lack of reflection, we used, perhaps, instinctively to think that when we spoke of centres we were simply dealing with a metaphysical or geometric abstraction. If we attached a physical reality to the word, we either, maybe, attributed to that reality a 'univocal' value, absolute in every context; or again, quite possibly, we even thought that the simpler an element is, the more perfectly centred it is, or can become.

Now, however, these muddled views are being replaced by the emergence of the first outlines of an exact physics of centration.

If we look at things correctly, the 'centricity' of an object does not correspond in the world either to an abstract quality or to a sort of 'all or nothing' with no half-tones or degrees of intensity. It represents, on the contrary, a *magnitude* that is essentially *variable, proportionate to the number of elements and interconnexions* contained in each cosmic particle under consideration. *A centre is the more simple and profound, the greater the density and the wider the radius of the sphere in which it is formed.* A centre does not simply exist, it builds itself up. This is what the facts tell us. In consequence, there is an infinite number of disparate ways in which matter can become centred. Along the axis of complexity, everything around us happens as though the stuff of the universe were distilled into a rising series of continually more perfect centres. From the point of view of physics, this super-centration corresponds to the accumulation in each nucleus of an ever greater number of more varied and better-arranged particles; from the point of view of psychology, this same super-centration expresses itself in an increase of spontaneity and consciousness.

Moving towards the infinitesimal, we meet dispersion; towards the immense, agglomeration; towards the complex, centration and consciousness – in other words, vitalization.

V. MOLECULIZATION AND HOMINIZATION: NOOGENESIS

'Complexity = Centricity = Consciousness' (1)
We have just seen that, under the operation of this structural

formula (which may be read in either direction at will), the universe expands at a point half-way between the infinitesimal and the immense. At its equator it swells out in a layer *sui generis*, on which the distance between two points is no longer measurable in size but in degrees of organization – or, which comes to the same thing, of psychism.

A qualitative scale (but involving a qualitative factor that is still measurable) running across the quantitative scale of cosmic particles. Such is the overall shape assumed by the real around us.

This first view, taken as a 'still', is obviously no more than an instantaneous, infinitesimal, section of the phenomenon we are trying to picture to ourselves. Whether it is a question of atoms, of stars, or of living beings, every natural series immediately and irresistibly makes itself felt, for minds like ours that are awake to the sense of the evolutionary, as a trail of movement.

'Synthesis = Centration = Interiorization' (2)

Our first fundamental relationship (i.e. (1) above) takes this form if we transpose it to the only scientifically real setting of a space that is indissolubly linked with time.

And it is here, I believe, that the light definitely bursts through.

In the 'common-sense' view and even, too often, in that of a certain sort of scientist, the universe is still divided into two water-tight compartments: the domain of matter and the domain of life; the atomic world of molecules and the cellular world of plants and animals.

Now, it is precisely the surface we imagine as separating these two worlds which begins to disappear for us when we apply relationship (2) – just as does the shimmering meniscus between the liquid and the gaseous portions of a body that has reached its point of vaporization.

Beyond the albumens and proteins, but still a long way this side of cells, there are (as we discover every day more unmistakably) certain extremely large particles. From the external, chemical, point of view, we find it of absorbing interest to consider these new objects. Have we, however, given sufficient thought to the fact that if these particles are hyper-complex the reason, necessarily and correlatively, is that they are hyper-centred, and that in consequence they hold a germ of consciousness? Below life, then, there is pre-life. We have the molecular branch and the cellular branch of matter: these two segments, hitherto treated as divergent or hetero-geneous, are now tending to come closer together as we examine them. From end to end they run on in line. And at this point there appears a single curve which expresses the progress of one and the same physico-biological process: *noogenesis*.

Let us follow the phases of the phenomenon more closely.

At the lower stages, when low molecular weights are involved, there is hardly any folding-back of matter upon itself, and in consequence the effects of consciousness can still not be observed in it; they are as impossible for us to apprehend experientially as are the variations of mass that occur in our bodies when we are in motion, were it only in an aircraft travelling at maximum speed. At a higher stage, however, approaching molecular weights of several millions (in the case of the viruses, shall we say?) the differences between the inorganic and the organic begin to loom up. It is at this point that the 'centric' properties of matter begin to become apparent. When we reach the cell (and to do so, I suggest, we pass through a critical point) these properties have definitely emerged, and we feel that we are moving into a different world. However, even if the cell, by reason of its increased dimensions, can use in its construction methods of inter-connexion (capillarity, osmosis, corpuscular chains) which are denied to small atomic assemblies, it is surely evident that it still belongs at least as much to the world of atoms as to the world of living beings – and this in view of its behaviour, its initial smallness, its condition of existing 'in myriads', and its very shape: and so – once the threshold has been crossed – the process continues logically, stage by stage, up to the higher living beings and then up to and including man.

Beneath the superstructure of mechanical and physiological links which evolution has progressively added to the elementary range of intra-cellular links, we do not immediately recognize in man the natural extension of the atom. Nevertheless, once we have drawn the curve followed by a world which is advancing, along one of its axes, towards large complexes, it becomes clear (and dazzlingly clear) that in each one of us the same movement is being continued: however enriched it may be, it is still the same primordial movement from which, millions of years ago, there emerged the first elementary compounds of oxygen, nitrogen and carbon.

Hominization, then, is the particular and final term (so far as we can see at present, remember!) of universal moleculization.[1]

Thus we find a natural, a *genetic*, explanation of the simultaneous presence in man of three fundamental characteristics whose co-existence always used to be inexplicable: extremely high degree of complexity, of consciousness, and (though small, indeed, in comparison with what is found among lower forms of living beings) of number.

At the same time we have an answer to the key-riddle we asked ourselves at the beginning of this essay: why, we wondered, is man plural – plural just as are stars and molecules?

We can now answer, quite simply, because man is precisely the most recently elaborated, the youngest, and hence the most complex and most fully centred, of molecules.

VI. THE CONTINUATION OF THE MOVEMENT: THE SPIRIT OF THE EARTH

To have recognized that in as much as we are men we are

1. Which amounts to saying that mankind today has not yet reached 'the natural term of its development'. Cf. below, 'The Energy of Evolution'. (Ed.)

caught up in a cosmic process of physico-psychic concentration, is thereby scientifically to formulate *the problem of the future*. We now undoubtedly understand, in its main outlines, the internal law of our development, and if we wish to know what we are going to become, all we have to do is to extend it. Apart from accepting the false evidence that there are in the universe two irreducible forms of matter (animate and inanimate), I know and feel that no more obstinate illusion persists in our minds than that of a complete difference between what prepared us and what we now are. Whatever the historical evidence for a movement of life behind us, we almost invincibly argue as though we had been carried along by this tide to a supreme level and were now complete, in other words brought to a halt.

It is this apparent cleavage between present and past (due to the slowness of the current which draws us with it) which we must in future dismiss from our outlook.

No – if we really observe the still extreme absence of organization, and hence of potential organization, in which the thinking portion of the earth is restlessly in movement *here and now* – we have no justification for the belief that the moleculization of matter has reached its ceiling in us. Everything, rather, goes to show that, in and through mankind, the cosmos is still continuing its arduous drift towards increasing states of complexity: of centration, in consequence, and, as a further consequence, of consciousness.

Let us, instead, look around us with an informed eye and see whether, perhaps, something may not be moving in the direction we have foreseen and expected, of an ultra-synthesis.

In the case of human molecules considered *in isolation*, no positive result emerges from this inquiry. This is a point on which I have made my position clear elsewhere. For the last twenty thousand years during which we have known it (for that is all) there appears to have been no appreciable change either in the structure or in the functioning of the brain of

Homo sapiens. When, however, we leave aside the individual and turn to the *collectivity* of man, something new comes to light.

At this moment we have an earth spreading far and wide before us; but its geographically limited surface is being visibly compressed beneath the swelling multitude of a population whose pressure upon itself is continually being increased, not nearly so much by its numerical growth as by the multiplication of inter-connexions of all kinds and the amazing speeding-up of their development. We look at this vast spectacle without understanding it – we are miles from even dreaming that it can have anything in common with the organic processes of life. 'Social relationships', we think, 'an accidental and ephemeral phenomenon: superficial modifications that can be reversed. Once brains have been developed, of course, they change no more. There can be no comparison with collective structures, which are incessantly destroying and replacing one another'.

Habitually we still refuse to see in human civilization anything more than a monotonous series of reversible oscillations.

But is this in fact true? Let us rather weigh up the changes that are taking place, and try to determine the nature and the significance of their successive appearance.

A first result of the 'mass-setting' which mankind is gradually undergoing at this moment is that every one of us, taken in isolation, is becoming less and less materially self-sufficient. A series of new needs, which it would be puerile and anti-biological to regard as superfluous and artificial, is continually making itself felt in us. It is no longer *possible* for us to live and develop without an increasing supply of rubber, of metals, oil, electricity and energy of all sorts. No individual could henceforth manage to produce his daily bread on his own. Mankind is more and more taking the form of an organism that possesses a physiology and, in the current phrase, a common 'metabolism'. We may, if we please, say that these ties are superficial, and that we will loose them if we wish.

Meanwhile, they are growing firmer every day, under the combined action of all the forces that surround us; and history shows that, as a whole, their network (woven under the influence of irreversible cosmic factors) has never ceased to draw tighter.

Thus *a general human life* is irresistibly being constituted around our own private lives. This is not a matter of a vague 'symbiosis' which would simply ensure, through mutual assistance, the continued existence, as individuals, of the members of the community, or even their further development. Certain 'effects' are already emerging from the association that has been formed, and these are *specifically proper* to collectivity. We take no notice of such effects, and yet we can see countless examples of them on all sides. Take simply the case of an aircraft, or a radio, or a Leica: and consider the physics, the chemistry and mechanics such things presuppose for their existence – the mines, laboratories, factories, arms, brains, hands. By virtue of its construction (and this is undeniable) each one of these devices is, and cannot but be, only the convergent result of countless disciplines and techniques whose bewildering complexity could be mastered by no single worker in isolation. In their conception and manufacture, these familiar objects presuppose nothing less than *a complex reflective organism*, acting *per modum unius*, as a single agent. Already we see in them the work not simply of man, but of mankind.

Now, the type of solidarity which impresses itself upon us so palpably in the order of mechanics, is nothing but the tangible reflection of an even more profound psychological 'setting'. Leibniz and his closed monads have no place in today's world. Henceforth man is less capable than ever before of *thinking alone*. We have only to consider the series of our modern concepts in science, philosophy and religion, and it will be obvious that the more general and fruitful any one of these notions is proving, the more it, too, is tending to assume the form of a collective entity: we can, it is true, individually cover one angle of it, we can make a portion of it our own and develop it, but it rests in fact on a vault of mutually buttressed thoughts. The idea of the electron or the quantum, or the cosmic ray – the idea of the cell or of heredity – the idea of humanity or even the idea of God – no single individual can claim these as his preserve or dominate them. In such things, what is already thinking, just as what is already working, through man and above man, is again mankind. And it is inconceivable, in virtue of the very way in which the phenomenon works, that the movement initiated should not continue in the same direction, tomorrow as today, becoming more pronounced and increasing in speed.

From all this we can draw only one conclusion, that the quantity of activity and consciousness contained in mankind, taken as a whole, *is greater than the mere sum* of individual activity and consciousness. Progress in complexity is making itself felt in a deepening of centricity. *It is not simply a sum, but synthesis.* And this is precisely what we were justified in expecting, if, in the domain of the social, the forward march of universal moleculization is indeed being continued (as my thesis maintained) to a point beyond our present brains.

Until man, we may say that nature was working to construct 'the unit or grain of thought'. It would now seem undeniable that, obeying the laws of some gigantic hyper-chemistry, we are now being launched towards 'edifices made up of grains of thought', towards 'a thought made up of thoughts' – travelling ever deeper into the abyss of the infinitely complex.

The synthesis of man – a magnificent enterprise, but at the same time, we must be careful to note, a long and delicate operation; and (like all life's other efforts) it can succeed only through innumerable tentative gropings and after much suffering. In the case of hearts and brains, much more than in that of atoms, we must remember that not every form of combination can be good. For one human stem that has succeeded in forcing the threshold of reflection, how many millions of other 'phyla' are there which have come to grief! Thus the problem which faces modern man, economically and socially (since, irrespective of his wishes, synthesis is his destiny), is to discover which of the various possible forms of collectivization open to him is *the good* form, in other words the form that most directly prolongs the psychogenesis (or noogenesis) from which he emerged. Man must avoid the blind alleys and find where the issue of evolution lies ahead.

I shall have to return to this point in the next section. For the moment I need do no more than note the two following:

1. First of all, when the curve of 'moleculization' is extended into the future, it enables us to foresee the awakening (and it may well be an explosive awakening) of irresistible interhuman affinities that are as yet unsuspected. Hitherto, in spite of external forces whose influence is to bring them together, the relations between spiritual atoms seem to be governed by an inflexible internal repulsion. The more planetary ties tend to force us together, the more do we feel the need to disengage ourselves from one another. Action and reaction: even in the domain of spirit that is how the work involved in every synthesis can be expressed. If, as I am maintaining, it is true that we are all, each and every one of us, no more than the elements of a vast unit still to come, then, once the last forms of resistance have been overcome – once the piston has passed its dead centre – we must expect to sink into that profound zone in which our forces of mutual attraction are dominant. The greatest of the energies the universe still holds in reserve (and certain indications allow us to feel it stirring) is, without doubt, not the energy we are trying to release by breaking up the atom: it is made up by the still dormant affinities that one day will hurl together the most conscious elements of the universe – in other words, *ourselves*.

2. Granting that, we then have the problem of determining, in an initial approximation, the higher term, still to come, towards which we are being led by the transformation in

which, in common with the world, we are involved. We can see it (for any other picture would contradict the law of moleculization) only as a *state of unanimity*: such a state, however, that in it each grain of thought, now taken to the extreme limit of its individual consciousness, will simply be the incommunicable, partial, elementary expression of a total consciousness which is common to the whole earth, and specific to the earth: *a spirit of the earth*.

And at this point we meet a final question, which brings the whole problem back with a new urgency. In just what form are we to picture this spirit of the earth? This thing which is coming to birth in us and from us, through an ascent into the super-complex – is it some sort of super-family, super-team, super-culture, or super-nation, in which no element, however high its position in the hierarchy, will experience or synthesize in itself the totality of the whole? Or is it rather, as has already happened once in nature, some super-individual that is going to appear at the term of our coming together?

When the collective is taken to its upper limit, is it still 'collective' or does it issue in a super-person? Is it a multi-centred or a uni-centred organism? 'Hyper-polyzoic' or 'hyper-metazoic'? Towards what are we moving?

Is it possible to answer that question?

And if it is, what influence will the solution have on the interior orientation of our lives?

VII. THE BREAKTHROUGH AHEAD, AND REVERSAL UPON OMEGA POINT

So long as it is a question of disintegrated and incandescent bodies, we can succeed in penetrating the secrets of astral life. By contrast, when we are confronted with large complexes which are obscure by nature, we are still as helpless as ever. Since, in all the vast expanse of the heavens, the earth is still the only speck on which we can follow the moleculization of matter into its upper limits, we can find no term of comparison outside the earth to give us information about the limit of the phenomenon. We know today how stars are born and die; but if we are to form an idea of the way in which a planet comes to an end biologically, we are obliged to venture into the hazards of an extrapolation.

Once we have recognized and admitted the character and dimensions as 'planetary synthesis' of life on earth, how (in harmony with the internal laws of the phenomenon) are we to conceive its end? By extinction or explosion, in death? Or, again, by ultra-synthesis, in some super-life?

Although this problem is regarded as scientifically insoluble and is accordingly relegated to individual feeling or instinct, I shall try to show that there is a rational answer to it – provided that allowance is made in our calculation for a magnitude that I consider objective and universal: by that I mean the hope, implicit in the vital act, that the world is developing towards a limitless future.

In order to be able to function, life needs, and ever increasingly needs, to recognize that it is in itself irreversible.

At a degree that is still implicit and incipient, this inner demand can already be seen in the persistent impulse that for hundreds of millions of years has unceasingly driven organic beings 'blindly' towards higher forms of consciousness. In an ill-defined but already explicit state, it springs up, at the first appearance of the inevitable fact of death, in the animal that has become capable of *seeing ahead*. From the critical moment when consciousness turns back upon itself and so makes it its business to *foresee*, every being, no matter how primitive, begins to reject as intolerable the idea that it can ever disappear *completely and utterly*. It is only at an even higher level, however, in the upper reaches of a mankind which is in process or grouping collectively upon itself, that it becomes clearly apparent that it is physically impossible for the universe simultaneously to contain in itself both a reflective activity and a total death.

Here, again, there continues to disclose itself to us, under another aspect, the slow interior drift of which we are the unconscious plaything.

The more the centuries succeed one another, as I recalled earlier, the more men are forced against one another on our round planet, and so assume the form of elements within a unit of a higher order, now undergoing concentration. This great process of synthesis has its reaction in the intimate domain of our personal activities. Hitherto (except for the vague instinct that causes them to reproduce their kind) men were able to try at all costs to forget death by engrossing themselves in the cares and joys of an existence to which a definite limit was set. If we consider the matter, we shall find that it is this loophole which is gradually tending to close up for us. At the same time as mankind is forming one single body in space, it is necessarily, in step with that process, doing the same thing in time. The idea of a total *human work* to be accomplished is surely the inevitable corollary to a totalized mankind. As a consequence of this, a radical modification is insidiously altering the balance of our activities. Without realizing it, every man is becoming accustomed to fear, to entertain ambitions, *to breathe* in an atmosphere of universality – as though his sole support were the global success of mankind that lies ahead. Thus the bulkhead collapses which seemed to isolate our human 'career' from that of our descendants. The centre of gravity of our most tangible interests is shifted as though to an infinite distance ahead. Thereby, too, not only does the prospect of a death of man begin to fill our horizon: there is the further threat and horror of a death of mankind.

Superficially, this would appear to be no more than a change of scale; but here again it is precisely a change that had necessarily to be made (as in the case of all the other properties of the infinitesimal, the immense and the complex) if what we were looking for was to become unmistakably clear. We experience no immediate shock at the idea of annihilation applied to a single grain of thought; or if we do, it comes from so nice a process of introspection that we may well be doubtful about the value of our evidence. On the other hand, when the same idea is extended to the planetary dimensions of the 'noosphere', we immediately recognize that it wipes out simultaneously the whole of the world's past and the whole of its present so completely that we have no alternative but to reject it. In a universe which, through the way in which it functions, is continually concentrating the vital interests of its elements on a collective term to be attained ahead, the whole structure collapses if that upper term is found to be precarious or non-existent. Thus, in step with the progress of hominization, a need for the absolute *is born* in man and *grows more pronounced*. If nothing of what we create (or even more, if *all that is best* in what we create) *does not win through* the disintegrations of matter, then evolution, struck at its very heart by self-disgust, automatically comes to a halt in a meaningless universe.

Life – and so reflection – and so foresight – and so the demand for super-life. These four terms are linked together in a biological chain, and they increase simultaneously. In consequence what the future presages for us is neither volatilization nor senescence. The possibilities, therefore, that confront our minds are greatly narrowed. No term can be appropriate to the growing series of molecules which is not, by its nature, positive and a maximum. This means that in one way or another we are able to escape the decrepitude of the star that holds us. Beyond the spirit of the earth, something greater, more complex and more fully centred than mankind is looming up before us.

But what?

In our search for the ultra-terrestrial sequel to the process in which we are involved, we might start (this is the simplest way) by conceiving that psychological relations will one day come to be formed between our planet and other 'thinking' stars: the combined minds of a large number of 'earths'. Among these major units the cosmic synthesis would then get off to a fresh start, carried to a new order of duration and magnitude. Staggering though this phenomenon appears when we imagine it, it is nevertheless in keeping with what we now know of the vastness of astronomical dimensions. After all, is not life co-extensive with matter? It is not enough to invoke against such alliances the fact (however impressive it may be) that no 'elder' planet has as yet intervened to rescue us from our isolation. We must remember that the human earth is still very young. Incapable of 'transmitting' in its present state, can it even 'receive'? We are completely ignorant of the intensity the psychic charge must attain at each pole if it is to force apart in both directions the interplanetary insulation that separates two conscious centres. I shall be chary, therefore, of asserting that, within the universe of our experience, man is irrevocably doomed to remain (or to be obliged to consider himself) the only one of his species. Nevertheless, for a great many reasons this isolation is only too probable – we have only to think of the difficulties raised by the coincidence of two instances of life separated by extremely great distances in space-time: but quite apart from that, I must point out that should, by some chance, this isolation be ended, we would still be confronted by the difficulty with which we are now concerned. As I was saying, the conjunction of thinking stellar units would allow mole-culization to get off to a fresh start; the end of the process would be postponed to a higher stage. However, while the problem of death would momentarily have been dismissed, it would reappear at this higher degree of complexity with even greater urgency. And it is precisely this shadow of a death (even were it still thousands of millions of years away) that we must *now and for ever* banish from our horizon, if we are to be able to continue to act ever more consciously.

What way out, then, can we find?

The more I study these prospects the more I am convinced that the only way in which the spirit of the earth can *come to an end without perishing*, is by disappearing *in depth* through excess of centration upon itself – whether it does this alone or with the support of other spirits it has met during its journeying. When observed in its external mechanism of *complication*, it is possible that the moleculization of matter may come up against some higher value which it cannot exceed (as, for example, a moving mass cannot exceed the speed of light). In any case, this moleculization – an eddy of improbability within a current whose over-all tendency is to bring bodies back to their most simple states – undoubtedly cannot be continued indefinitely: is not the network it weaves made up of the 'perishable'? By contrast, if it is observed in its internal aspect (that is to say, *the rise of consciousness*), the process appears to know no limiting-value to its developments. Every reflective act, by its nature, initiates a higher form of reflection (so that there is no point at which the continuity of the chain can be broken); but what is more, as we have just seen, the very faculty of thought demands, if it is not to be stifled, the existence of a completely free atmosphere ahead of it.

We can draw but one conclusion from this evolutionary conflict between the without (which is limited) and the within (which knows no limit) of the noosphere: that we must foresee an internal break between the two aspects of the phenomenon. We are forced to conceive that beyond a certain critical value, centration can in some way or other continue *independently* of the physico-chemical synthesis that was necessary, in a first phase, for its initiation: the centre throwing off its original shell of complication.

Can it break away like this?

It can – but *on one condition*: that we presuppose at the extreme limit of the axis of the syntheses and of time, the existence of a centre *of the second species* – not emerging and moved – but a centre, already emerged and actively moving, of universal convergence. As soon as we recognize such a centre, which I shall call Omega, it becomes reasonable to conclude that the grains of consciousness produced evolutively by noogenesis (once the 'human' point of reflection has been passed) fall into a new field of attraction: the pull is exercised on the *basic foundation* of the grains, and it now acts not only on the complexity of their structure but directly on their centre, independently of the structure. From this point of view, what we have called 'moleculization' is thus seen to be a more complicated but at the same time more radical process than we thought. In a first stage (up to hominization) there is a succession of fragile units, suspended over the void that lies behind them: there is a rising centration, but no *true* centre as yet perfected in nature. In a second stage (after hominization) there is a mixed state; there is a continued progress of external complexity and beneath this the universe, which henceforth carries grains of thought, begins to be inverted upon itself – like a cone that has reached its apex. An intangible physics of centres succeeds the tangible physics of centration. Lastly, in a third and final phase, there is the complete turning back of spirit (now collectively centred) upon an interior pole of consistence and total unification: hyper-centration following upon centration.

Escape in depth (through the centre), or, which comes to the same thing, ecstasis.

If we look at it in this way, which is an accurate expression of Christian faith and hope, we see that all sorts of difficulties are readily solved.

In the first place, we begin, at least vaguely, to understand how the way out opened for consciousness in the heart of things makes it possible for the spiritual charge still to build up for millions of years without causing the earth to burst asunder.

Next we discover in what perfect form it becomes possible, without falling into absurdity or the unthinkable, to conceive for our beings the natural and irreversible term of their aggregation: seeing it not simply as a polycentric mankind, arrested at the 'colony' stage, but as a mankind, totalized, more perfectly than any known living being, under the influence of a single higher soul – not collectivized man, but super-personalized man.

And by that very fact, we see a third thing: the most important from the point of view of how we act. On an earth that is in process of irresistible compression, we see that the great problem for man is coming to be to find out how to control in himself the inevitable but supremely dangerous work of the forces of unification. As I pointed out, for one form of synthesis that brings freedom there are hundreds of others that lead only to the vilest forms of bondage. We are only too conscious of this; but how can we come together *in such a way as to free ourselves*? In virtue of the laws of moleculization, the problem obviously consists in finding the way of grouping ourselves together not 'tangentially', in the nexus of an extrinsic activity or function, but 'radially', *centre to centre*; how to associate in such a way as, by synthesis, to stimulate deep within ourselves a progress that is directly *centric* in nature. In other words, what we have to do is to love one another – because love is equally by definition the name we give to 'inter-centric' actions. By its nature, love is the only synthesizing energy whose differentiating action can super-personalize us. But just how can one ever contrive to love a multitude? If we set the two words side by side, love and multitude, surely they enclose a contradiction?

The antinomy provides its own solution as soon as we see that in a centre of our own centres it is possible for us to meet together.

What makes collectivity so monstrous is that, being by nature multiple, it has no thinking mind, no heart, no face which we can fasten on to *through the depths of our being*. For all that 'society' may stifle us in its countless arms, it can still not reach us in the core of our beings or bring us closer together. Mankind, so extolled for the last two centuries, has been brought to a halt at the collective, which is now a terrifying Moloch. We can neither love it, nor love one another within it. That is why instead of fulfilling us, it mechanizes us. Once, however, the warm glow of one and the same common soul lights up in each element of the human throng, distinct from each and yet the same in each: then, in this personalizing centre, itself endowed with supreme personality, as each particle strives to fulfil itself it finds itself flung upon all the others. We were saying earlier that a redoubtable affinity, neutralized by great numbers, still lies dormant in the human mass. We now see that under the rays of Omega it must undoubtedly one day waken into activity, no longer rendered powerless but this time multiplied by the plurality of spiritual particles.

The salvation of the spirit of the earth (which is the only thing that really matters to us) is seen to depend upon the developments – now recognized as possible – of a close affective relationship, cosmic in dimensions.

And with this discovery we find that the question moves into a different context. Our having become intellectually aware, when confronted with the plurality of man, of the fact that we represent structurally the natural continuation of the atoms, transposes the problem of cosmogenesis into an interior domain. By themselves the most amazing advances of science and technology are no more than a preparation and a beginning. When all is said and done, the future of the world depends entirely upon the emergence in us of a moral consciousness of the atom, culminating in the appearance of a universal love.

VIII. ATOM-CONSCIOUSNESS AND 'OMEGALIZATION'

Without our noticing it, a disturbing gap is constantly widening between our moral life and the new conditions created by the progress of the world. This does not mean, of course, that as a result of the hard work of the great religions we have not already succeeded in determining certain definite axes of justice and holiness. Nevertheless, however admirable and progressive these codes of interior perfection may be, they generally have the defect of having been developed, and of being kept alive, outside the perspectives of a universe in evolution. From this stems the obstinate conflict between science and religion; and from this, above all, the slowness of Christianity itself to transpose its precepts and counsels to the dimensions of a mankind which has become conscious of the historic vastness, and the collective potentialities or demands, of its development.

In the course of this last section I would like to give some idea of how the most traditional human moral system takes on a new form, new coherence and urgency – how smoothly it is integrated, and so becomes dominant in the great body of cosmic energies, once man, in regulating his behaviour, leaves behind the individualist position 'of the monad' and resolutely adopts, in judgment and action, *the point of view of the atom*. The idea, developed above, of a spiritualizing moleculization of matter does more than throw light on the stuff of the universe, in its internal structure. The same shaft of light correspondingly brings out, in their main lines, a whole new philosophy of life, a whole new ethical system, and a whole new mysticism.

a. Philosophy of Life

With the increase in his consciousness of his collective strength and duration, man experiences an exactly proportionate increase in his need to find a *tangible objective* for his activities. Why, he asks, are we born in chains, bound in the fetters of toil? Why do we have to search ever further afield? Why slave away in our quest? Why continue to build? Why even continue to reproduce our kind? A man does not need to have lived very long to realize how insistently this question confronts even the most humble folk at this moment – how it affects more and more of us, so that it is now becoming acute. The agony of being alive is increasing in intensity in us, given new force and super-stimulated by the recent revelation we have been given of time and space. Now, it is this anxious uncertainty about the meaning and value of existence that the notion of noogenesis enables us to dispel. As soon as we realize that there is an organic relationship between our busyness as elements and the success of the world that bears us – as soon as a God awaits us in his own person at the top of the tower that, held up by him, we can build if we unite – then, indeed, we find the impulse to live, the essential joy of living.

With Omega, it is a supreme goal and a supreme attraction that rise up, to animate and direct human endeavour. And, as a subsidiary consequence, there are three other reputedly insoluble problems that vanish from our horizon.

First, *the problem of evil*. Whether it be physical or moral, evil repels us only in so far as it appears to be useless or gratuitous. Suffering and sin are the expression of the delays, the mistakes, the 'pain and labour', which are *necessary in terms of energetics* for the synthesis of spirit: they become intelligible and acceptable in so far as they appear as the condition of evolution and the price to be paid for it. Provided the peak is actually there and the game is worth the candle what mountaineer is surprised or complains at having to be injured as he climbs, or even at having to risk a fatal fall? Taken as static facts and in isolation, pain and perversity are meaningless. Taken as dynamic factors, in a system that is fluid and feeling its way, they are both vindicated and transfigured.

Secondly, *the problem of inequality*. If the universe culminated in mankind, in the form of isolated or divergent conscious minds, nothing could console a man for not possessing the health, the qualities, or the social opportunities accorded to others more fortunate than he. In such a universe, the more the 'have-nots' or the failures reflected clearly on their inferiority, the more they would be justified in experiencing a mounting fury for levelling-down and destruction directed against their misfortune and against the 'haves'. Here again, there is a complete transformation if, however unequal they may be in strength and status, the different thinking elements of the earth form but one single convergent mass, destined to find communion and equality in a final triumph. When the attack is in full swing, does any soldier dream of envying his commander at the head of the assault wave?

Finally, *the problem of the individual and society*. Is the individual for society, or society for the individual? – an exasperating question, constantly being dinned into our ears: and a bloody question, too, the inspiration at this very moment of a merciless crusade between the opposed forces of marxism and the democracies. At the same time, it is, basically, a non-existent question if only we can apprehend, in its reality and mechanism, the great phenomenon of noogenesis that is taking place around us. In a universe that is in course of centration (provided the centration be carried out in the right way) the individual and the collectivity never cease to reinforce and complete one another. The more the individual on his side associates himself in an appropriate way with other individuals, the more, as an effect of synthesis, does he enter deeper into his own being, become conscious of himself, and in consequence personalize himself. And the more the collectivity on its side concentrates itself, in an appropriate way, upon elements for whose fuller personalization it is itself responsible, the more, again, is it 'humanized' and personalized, and the more does it allow Omega point to be divined. The two terms are equally essential: they are inseparable. When the limit is reached, it is true – at the moment, that is, when the supreme conjunction is effected – the last step will be taken *from* the element *towards* the whole. It is the whole that will have the last word. In the final analysis (or rather 'in the final synthesis') we may say, therefore, that *ultimately* the person is for the whole, and not the whole for the human person. The reason for this, however, is that at the final moment the whole itself has become person.

b. Ethics

Since the preaching of the Gospel it was possible to believe that man had at last found a definitive and exhaustive expression of inner rectitude, and in consequence of salvation. 'Love one another': it seemed as though all that was finest in morality must have reached its peak and be summed up in that precept once and for all. Today, however, after twenty centuries of experience, it would seem that we have acquired nothing from the Gospel formula. As the years go by not only does mankind seem to be as divided against itself as ever; but, what is more, *a new ideal*, the ideal of conquering force, has continually, for the last two generations, been increasing in strength and mesmeric power, in opposition to doctrines of gentleness and humanity.

We cannot help wondering whether, perhaps, we are witnessing the bankruptcy of charity.

It is this anxiety, I believe, that is allayed, both in theory and in practice, by the fact that the human person is rising up to consciousness of his 'dignity as an atom'.

From the point of view of noogenesis, in the first place, it is perfectly clear that if, all together, our cosmic destiny is to become *one*, then the fundamental and operative law of our activity is to encourage this synthesis by associating more closely. The 'Lord's precept' does not disappear under the harsh light of modern criticism: rather does it leave the domain of sentiment, to become the leading instrument of evolution. 'It leaves the world of dreams, to enter into the system of universal energies and essential laws'. We saw, did we not, that a love is the only milieu in which the stuff of the universe can find equilibrium and consistence at the peak of its complication and centration.

This, however, is not all. While charity is today cheapened in our eyes by the factual setback it has encountered, it undoubtedly suffers much more from its futility and its apparent impotence to justify and inspire our impassioned demand for discovery and conquest. The morality we look for can no longer be based on inter-personal considerations, it must be based on progress. What we need is not lubrication but fuel. As preached to us, charity is static and resigned, and that is why Nietzsche's super-man is now eclipsing the loving-kindness of the Gospel. For all the beauty of the Sermon on the Mount, modern man cannot refrain from listening to the words of Zarathustra:

'Charity – resigned and static . . .'

That expresses the fatal preconception which we have to shake off, and the spectacle of a world in process of concentration is at hand precisely to make us do so.

Among fixed and extrinsically associated monads, it may well be that the supreme virtue consists in easing mutual friction. It is a completely different story in the case of incomplete elements that cannot exist fully except by drawing closer together. For such particles, sympathy becomes the driving impulse to force all obstacles and open up every issue that can lead to unity. From the moment man discovers that, as an atom, he has a responsibility towards a mankind and is in solidarity with a mankind in which he is personally fulfilled, he possesses more than a motive and a driving force for loving 'his neighbour'. There is something much more: there opens out wide before him an unlimited domain of tangible operation into which he *can introduce* the things he feels. He has *the whole vast battlefield of the earth* in which to release, to expend and continually to rejuvenate the passion that animates him. To have to fight, *to be able to fight*, throughout our life, in order to create what we love! An astonishing fulfilment indeed, in which force, purified of violence, emerges from gentleness and loving-kindness, as their climax.

Contrary to the current belief, charity is not out of date, not a thing of the past, in this feverishly expanding world of ours. Rather does it reappear, at the head of the most modern, most scientifically satisfying of moral systems, once, having been transposed into a universe that is being spiritually drawn closer together, it automatically *becomes dynamic*.

c. Mysticism

No moral system can hold together without religion. Or, to put it more precisely, no moral system can live without developing a nimbus of worship. The measure of an ethics is its ability to flower in mysticism. From this point of view, dynamized charity is without a rival.

Let us, however, consider in the light of 'moleculization' what happens in the heart of a man who has awoken to a consciousness of his organic relationship with a universe in process of concentration.

In the first place, as we have just seen, such a man develops the sense of a growing affinity with elements of the same order as himself – for the multitude, that is, of other grains of thought with which he must be associated if he wishes to develop his own soul more deeply. That is the first phase.

However, since the construction, the maintenance and further advancement of human unity is in fact the operation and continuation of the whole play of universal forces, the man in question, in a second phase, is soon guided to an ascent to the reasoned sense of a basic solidarity with the whole of life and the whole of matter *in motion*.

Finally, because this vast system, convergent by nature, holds together only through its impulse towards some supreme pole of synthesis, the thinking atom definitively becomes submerged in the omnipresence and omni-action of a supreme consciousness.

Sense of man; then *sense of the earth*; and finally *sense of an Omega*: three progressive stages of one and the same illumination.

Thereby, too, the psychological possibility of an interior act of undreamed-of richness is confirmed for the man-element and is more exactly defined.

On the one hand, in virtue of the dynamic inter-connexion of all things in noogenesis, the least action, however humble and monotonous, is seen to be a way of co-operating in the great task of the universe.

On the other hand, in virtue of the particular, synthetic, nature of the operation that is going on, to *co-operate* means *to be incorporated in* a living reality. Every form of action (provided it be positive, that is, making for unity) is equivalent to being in communion.

Let us make sure that we fully grasp the importance of this transformation.

More or less consciously (and however convinced we may be that life has a meaning) we all experience in ourselves the saddening feeling of the fragmentation and insignificance of our own lives. With the dawn of every new day, the same obligations confront us; their monotony is heart-breaking, their multiplicity exhausts us, their apparent futility discourages us. Dispersion, routine, and above all boredom – if only we could feel that we were doing *something really worth-while*.

Now, it is in fact this very dust-cloud of ourselves which is illuminated and animated under the influence of Omega. At a lower level of consciousness (as long, that is, as we are unaware of our condition and function as individual atoms) we can never do more than one thing or another thing, with one part or another of our body or of our soul. We are eating, or thinking, or working, or loving; and nothing of all that we do, taken in isolation, satisfies us, because nothing seems to be *important*. On the other hand, at a higher stage of initiation (once, that is, we have appreciated the relationship that links the spiritualization of the world to its complication) this multiplicity, without ceasing to be just what it is, is resolved into something new and unique: and into that new thing there flow together, *as they acquire value*, all the results (no matter how trifling they may be) of our efforts, and all that colours (in however intimate and private a way) our activity. At this high level a transcendent form of action begins to emerge, which embraces and fuses together, in one and the same illumination, the whole medley of things which, seen from lower down, appear to us to conflict with and neutralize one another: all that we know under the different names of activity and passivity, renunciation and possession, understanding and love. The truth is that if a man's *vision can extend* beyond the immense and the infinitesimal almost into the complex, a way of acting opens up for him which has the power to synthesize and transfigure every other form of activity: by that I mean the specific act of experiencing and advancing, in and around himself – through the whole expanse and the whole depth of the real – the unification of the universe upon its deep-seated centre, with the consciousness of that unification it acquires as a consequence: the total and totalizing act (if I may so call it, for I can find no other name) of *omegalization*.

And it is this that leads us directly, in 'bliss-as-atoms', to the high peaks of worship.

Already, in the social and biological field, the fact of our recognizing that, as a result of the properties of love, the universe becomes personalized as it concentrates, was enabling us to avoid both fragmentation through individualization and mechanization through collectivism. Now, in the domain of mysticism, the same light shows us the channel between two equally dangerous reefs. Ever since man, in becoming man, started on his quest for unity, he has constantly oscillated, in his visions, in his ascesis, or in his dreams, between a cult of the spirit which made him jettison matter and a cult of matter which made him deny spirit: omegalization allows us to pass between this Scylla and Charybdis of rarefaction or the quagmire. Detachment now comes not through a severance but through a traversing and a sublimation; and spiritualization not by negation of the multiple or an escape from it, but by *emergence*. This is the *via tertia* that opens up before us as soon as spirit is no longer the opposite extreme but the higher pole of matter in course of super-centration. It is not a cautious and neutral middle course, but the bold, higher road, in which the values and properties of the two other roads are combined and correct one another.

From this, as a final summary, I draw the following conclusion. To have become conscious of our condition as 'atoms patient of synthesis' is not merely to have attained a new vision of the general relationship which links matter to thought, and thought to God. It is in addition, and by that very fact, to redefine the line followed by the immutable axis of holiness.

A neo-spirituality for a neo-spirit, in a universe whose convergent nature has been recognized.

Unpublished, Peking
13 September 1941

The Rise of the Other

WE are now witnessing the division of the world at war into two hostile blocs, clashing together and rearing up to attack one another. We are more or less familiar with the immediate, political or racial, causes of the conflict; but the roots of the evil – or, rather, of the phenomenon – are obviously much deeper, and more organic, than any rivalry between nations for influence or self-advancement. Deep below us, something is undoubtedly going on in the very foundations of man's earth: but what?

To listen to people talking or to read the papers, you would think that this whirlwind of war in which we are caught up is no more than a crisis of disruption, of disintegration. Just when we were congratulating ourselves on having made a step forward, we find ourselves once again falling back.

We have only to consider for a moment the degree of intellectual and moral hypertension in which we are living at present, to form a diametrically opposite judgment of the situation. The earth around us is psychically, if I may so express it, raised to a white-hot temperature. Never, since its globe appeared in space, has it vibrated with more spiritual intensity. What we are suffering from, therefore, is not a drop in internal energy but its mounting pressure.

From this point of view, it seems to me, the true cause of what is happening in the world today is to be found not in some collapse of former values but in the eruption, within mankind, of a flood of new being which, precisely because it is new, comes initially as something foreign and hostile to what we ourselves represent. What takes us by surprise in today's events, what so upsets us and terrifies us – but what in fact we must look straight in the face so that we can analyze its mechanism and its phases, and distinguish what good effects it has side by side with what evil effects – is, in my view, the implacable cosmic tide: it is this that, having first raised each one of us up to its own level, is now at work, beating in a new rhythm, to expel us from our own selves: it is the eternal 'rise of the other' within the human mass.

I. FIRST PHASE: THE MULTIPLICATION OF THE OTHER, OR THE RISE OF NUMBER

At the source of all our troubles we can clearly distinguish the irresistible power of proliferation which characterizes living matter. So long as their degree of internal complication remains below a certain critical value, the particles that make up the stuff of the universe show no permanent tendency spontaneously to increase their number. As soon, on the other hand, as they become vitalized as a result of the complexity of their structure, these same elements begin to reproduce themselves: sometimes (in the simplest case) by splitting into two, sometimes (owing to certain improvements in this elementary process) by the slow accumulation, followed by the sudden emission, of a very great number of seeds. From this arises the terrifying numerical increase of centres of consciousness within the biosphere; from this, too, the increase in the volume of multicellular beings; and from this, again, on the scale of the group, the birth and bush-like growth, through ramification, of living species.

All this we know, from having read it in books or seen it outside ourselves in nature. But have we ever realized in our minds to what a degree this biological mechanism of pluralization envelops us and asserts its grip in the depth of our being? – not slackening but drawing tighter and as though exaggerated by our entry into the state of man.

If life were able today to expand (assuming that it could ever have been born and have grown) over an unlimited or indefinitely elastic surface, there would be no disadvantage in the fact that mankind is every day multiplying still further the absolute number of individuals and nations of which it is made up: an increase that is produced either by the physiological effect of the birth-rate or by the psychological awakening of dormant masses. Each increase in internal pressure would immediately be followed by a release of external pressure, so that the balance would continually be restored.

But the fact remains: for physical reasons that are clearly bound up with the 'pan-corpuscular' structure of the universe, life on earth, taken as a whole, reflects, on a gigantic scale, the conditions of the molecular state. It develops on a surface that is rigidly closed. A whole book could be written on the relationship that causes the simplicity of spirit to depend genetically on the roundness of the earth. When, however, we first come to look at it, it must be confessed that this roundness is the source of a very great embarrassment for us. The more, I mean, we multiply in number, in volume and in radius of individual action, the more we divide for each one of us the free space (already much cut down by the area occupied by sea) placed by nature at our common disposal. Only fifty years ago our school maps still showed vast blank spaces, in Africa, in America, in Oceania, where man could find room to expand. In a single generation these lacunae have been filled; and human masses of the same high demographic density and the same high cultural charge, are now in contact along all their boundaries. Statistics indicate that the absolute increase in the most civilized populations has reached its ceiling: whatever the significance of this, and whether it prove more permanent or less, it is a fact that, through numerical increase and still more perhaps through the dynamic expansion of the elements that make it up, the human group is at this moment attaining a degree of super-compression far beyond any it has yet known. It is the crushing together upon itself of a mass proliferating in a closed volume: the repetition (but on a total scale, and in consequence with no way out available spatially) of the phenomenon that was already making Neolithic tribes drive one another out of the Promised Lands. It is mankind 'setting' together in one bloc.

This, surely, is the meaning our world war has for us; this is what it holds for us; this is what is happening.

II. SECOND PHASE: RELATIONSHIP WITH THE OTHER, OR THE RISE OF THE COLLECTIVE

Thus we are beginning to be too numerous to share the earth between us. 'Living space' is running out.

And, in an instinctive reaction against this continual cropping-up of the other on all sides, the first thing we do is to repel or liquidate the intruders who are stifling us.

It is at this point that there appears a further, and at first sight aggravating, effect of the multiplying force which is incessantly being renewed from deep within the flesh of which we are made.

The more we struggle among ourselves to win free, the less we succeed in standing alone. The more, instead, we become involved in one another, and the more we realize, not without anxiety, that a new order – not to say a new *being* – is striving invincibly to emerge from our reciprocal bondage – animated by a sort of life proper to itself, and tending, formed though it is entirely from our individual consciousnesses, to absorb the latter, without assimilating them, in a blind network of organic forces.

This is the collective.

For a long time – in fact, ever since the appearance of the first Palaeolithic groupings – links had begun to be formed between men who were brought closer together by the need to defend themselves, to help one another, and to feel in common. Man benefited by and appreciated this community of effort, and imagined that he could control it. Now, however, and particularly since the rise of the industrial mega-civilizations, the force whose growth we had assisted is tending to emancipate itself from us and take its stand in opposition to us.

There has been a reversal of mathematical sign, with the result that society, which man thought he had made for his own personal advantage, is now showing signs of preparing to round on the individual and devour him. *Relationships are becoming bonds.*

Confronted, then, by this irresistible rise around us of unitary systems – itself a consequence of the irresistible rise of masses – students of biology are coming to ask themselves whether we may not be in this process the impotent actors and spectators of one of life's oldest and most characteristic performances: for life, this consists, once an organic type has been produced, in using it simply as a brick to be incorporated in what it then proceeds to construct. There has been much talk, and with good reason, of the birth, the development, senescence and death of living branches. What has attracted less attention in this life of the species is the tendency they all display, once they have attained maturity, to group themselves in various ways in large socialized units: as though, in colonies of polyps or in the fantastically differentiated associations formed by the insects, a sort of super-organism were trying to establish itself beyond the individual. The more, adopting this mental perspective, we try to interpret the progress of the phenomenon of man, the more the evidence builds up that under the cloak of 'totalitarian forces' that is now being spread over us it is exactly the same biological determinism at work as that from which the hive and the termitary emerged some millions of years ago.

We noted earlier that, looked at from outside, mankind, being now in contact with itself in every direction, is coming close to its 'setting-point' or solidification. It is beginning to form but one single bloc. At the same time, from the inside, may it not be entering its 'phyletic' phase of collectivization (or socialization)? That would explain many things in this paradoxical war, in which the libertarian hostility of nations is so strangely combined with a totalization that, whatever the issue of the conflict, automatically awaits the winner just as much as the loser. And yet it is against this, we feel, that the deep-seated instinct of our own freedom, and with it our sense of our dignity, is in revolt.

'Increase and multiply': that, we have hitherto recognized, was the hallowed slogan of organic being. Is it possible that beyond a certain limit the two terms of the formula begin to be mutually contradictory? If multiplication is pushed further, is it not going to extinguish in us, by mechanization, the spark of spontaneity and consciousness that it has taken evolution three hundred million years of life and twenty thousand years of civilization to kindle in each one of us?

Confronted with the tide of collectivism, what are we going to do?

Is it possible for us to shatter the forces of 'orthogenesis' in us by consciously going on strike against the birth-rate and so putting number to flight? And in any case, would such a gesture be sufficient to push back the walls of the crevasse that are closing in on our individual personalities? Again, would not mankind simply perish under such violent treatment?

On the other hand, supposing we slavishly or stoically surrender to the gradual bogging-down of our persons in an anonymous system – is it possible that that is what life expects from us?

There seems to be no way out of the situation *if* the inflexible logic of number is to lead to the collective machine.

When all is said and done, however, are we really certain that the play of the inter-human forces of cohesion is indeed sucking us down to the ant-hill?

III. THIRD PHASE: THE SYNTHESIS OF THE OTHER, OR THE RISE OF THE PERSONAL

The time has come, to my mind, for every thinking man to force the circle in which our human outlook is by common agreement enclosed, and to envisage the probability of a hypothesis which a growing weight of facts is beginning to impose on our minds.

Earlier, I mentioned incidentally the more and more evident relationship that is coming to light between the degree of consciousness in beings and their degree of complication. Scientifically speaking, everything in the world behaves as though the stuff of the universe (whose properties change, we know, in the two spatial directions of the infinitesimal and the immense) were able similarly to vary (in this case, in time) in a third direction, that of the complex: life being simply the 'specific effect' attaching to extreme complexities. So long as a cosmic particle contains no more than some thousands of arranged atoms, it still appears to be dead. But if this 'corpuscular figure' rises to several tens of thousands, it begins to be animate (as in the case of the viruses). In the cell and, beyond it, among the higher living beings, the mere number of chemical elements involved in the organism (without taking into account their built-up combinations) leaps to astronomical values. This evident variation of life as a direct function of *synthesized* large numbers can readily be explained if we admit that the more matter is organized, the more it is *centred* (and, *in consequence*, the more 'conscious' it is). In the case of simple, or relatively simple, particles the centration is low and the psychism is accordingly imperceptible. By contrast, in the case of high complexities, the centre gains in depth and concentrates, *as an effect of organization*: and thereby, too, the phenomena of introspection and spontaneity appear and become more marked. From this point of view, consciousness would appear to be a physical property linked simultaneously to the centration and complication of matter upon itself. Thus, depending on the side from which we look at evolution, we would see it either (from outside) as a chemical arch-synthesis or (from inside) as a 'noogenesis'.

This fits in perfectly with our experience.

Bearing that in mind, let us confine our attention to man.

Considered individually, man is, both quantitatively and

qualitatively, the most highly complicated of cosmic particles, and in consequence the most fully centred; by that very fact, again, he is the most conscious. But this is not the whole story. Man can never be apprehended in the state of an isolated particle. He is essentially multitude; he is increasing multitude; and above all, thanks to his astonishing power of physical and psychic inter-fertilization, he is *organizable* multitude. We are so accustomed to this spectacle of the plurality of thinking molecules that we never dream of finding it astonishing. Nevertheless, may it not have a profound significance? Why, for example, should we not conceive that, *in conformity with the whole history of past life*, it represents the possibility and contains the potentiality of a further, trans-human, synthesis of organic matter? We habitually look on the human individual as a closed unit, lost in the gregarious throng of other units, equally locked in on themselves. May he not, rather, be the *element*, not yet impregnated, of a natural whole still in the course of organization?

The very first time we meet it, the idea of a super-human organism seems fantastic. We are so thoroughly used to refusing to admit that anything could exist in nature higher than ourselves! Nevertheless, if, instead of rejecting *a priori* what upsets the accustomed routine of our thinking (and in particular the dimensional limits within which we think), we are willing to entertain it, and then begin to examine it more deeply, it is surprising what order and clarity is introduced into our outlook on the universe by a hypothesis that at first seemed crazy.

The first thing we find is that the actual flow of evolution, which, against all probability, was assumed to have come to a halt on earth with the appearance of man, resumes its normal course. If the terrestrial grains of thought can still combine among themselves, man is no longer an inexplicable dead-end in the cosmic process of noogenesis: in him, and through him, the rise of consciousness is continuing beyond man himself.

Secondly, the rise of number all around us loses its disquieting and senseless appearance. Crushed together on the earth's restricted surface, we were looking anxiously for a field in which to expand. We can now see that that field does not lie in the direction of an escape in space, but can be found in the form of an internal harmonizing in which the multiplication of the other ceases to be a threat and becomes a support, a solace, and a hope for the fulfilment of each individual. By divergence, the multitude can only become a greater evil; on the other hand, by unification upon itself it is effortlessly and limitlessly resolved. We were trying to escape through the circumference: it is only through the axis (by convergence, that is) that we can be released from tension.

The third thing to be transfigured is the spectre of rising collectivization. Judging the future of man from the example of the insects and from certain modern experiments on totalitarian lines, we had grounds for believing that we were caught up in an irresistible mechanism of depersonalization. But if it is indeed the law of *centration by synthesis* that continues to operate in us through the advances and under the cloak of human socialization, then we should be reassured. Assuming that an ultra-human synthesis is really being produced, then (provided it be properly carried out – and I shall show how that can be done) it can only end, from physical and biological necessity, in causing the appearance of a further degree of organization, and therefore of consciousness, and therefore, again, of freedom. Whatever may have been the shortcomings or deviations of our first attempts at association, we are hazarding nothing in surrendering ourselves actively and intelligently to the invasion of the forces of collectivization. They are not, in fact, working to mechanize us but to super-centre and so super-personalize us.

If this hypothesis were sound, it is clear that our situation in relation to current events, and in consequence our attitude to them, would be defined and corrected to a remarkable degree. Instead of continuing to waver between the evident necessity of associating with others if we wish to continue to live, and the fear of losing our own selves if we give up our isolation, we would in future be able to devote ourselves wholeheartedly and unreservedly to the magnificent enterprise of building up the earth. A true 'geopolitics' would at last take the place of the wretched parish-pump disputes to which history has been reduced.

In consequence, I can see no more urgent duty for science at the present moment than to verify the reality of what I have called noogenesis and bring out its laws. Even if we assume that this work has been done for the past, how can we succeed in knowing that we are justified in extrapolating it in the case of man and for the future? By what sign can we recognize that the cosmic synthesis of spirit can still be continued – that it is being continued as a fact – through the earth's restless social activities? How are we to decide, before we initiate the operation, whether the nature of the elements confronting one another allows us to count on success?

In this direction, everything depends on the aptitude we can reasonably assume in mankind for developing among its members an appropriate form of 'universal love'.

VI. FOURTH PHASE: SYMPATHY WITH THE OTHER, OR THE RISE OF THE SENSE OF MAN

In its most general form and from the point of view of physics, love is the internal, affectively apprehended, aspect of the affinity which links and draws together the elements of the world, *centre to centre*. This is how it has been understood by the great philosophers from Plato, the poet, to Nicolas of Cusa and other representatives of frigid scholasticism.

Once this definition has been accepted, it gives rise to a series of important consequences.

Love is power of producing inter-centric relationship. It is present, therefore (at least in a rudimentary state), in all the natural centres, living and pre-living, which make up the world; and it represents, too, the most profound, most direct, and most creative form of inter-action that it is possible to conceive between those centres. Love, in fact, is the expression and the agent of universal synthesis.

Love, again, is centric power. Thus, like a light whose spectrum is continually enriched by new, more brilliant and warmer lines, it constantly varies with the perfection of the centres from which it emanates. Man is the only known element of the universe in which noogenesis has advanced far enough to allow the appearance of a closed centre, reflected upon itself; and in him, therefore, we can appreciate that the synthesizing properties of love operate under exceptional conditions and with exceptional effectiveness and clarity. While infra-human beings can converge and associate only in a diffuse common action, at the level of thought it is the psychic nuclei themselves that come out into the open and begin to unite. Organization of imperfectly centred elements gives way to direct synthesis of centres. From this results the extraordinary totality and fullness of vital contact – and from this, in consequence, in conformity with the synthesizing mechanism of the rise of consciousness, the extraordinary growth of personality that can any day be observed in the particular and limited case of a great human affection.

In virtue of his extreme power of loving, combined with his extreme 'centricity' (or, which comes to the same thing, his extreme complexity), man, in so far as he actually loves, is the most magnificently synthesizable of all the elements ever constructed by nature.

If we understand this situation correctly, we can see, as I said earlier, how and why the appearance of a universal human love would be a sure indication that the totalization of mankind in a super-organism, super-personal in nature, is biologically to be anticipated and can be realized in practice.

If men could love one another, if they could reach the pitch of loving, not with the love of husband for wife, of brother for sister, of countryman for fellow-countryman, but of element for element of a world *in process of convergence*, then the great evolutionary law that ever since the beginning of the earth has continually caused more spirit to appear upon more complexity, would operate again with new vigour. It would even be true to say (as our theory enables us to foresee) that it would never operate more vigorously than in this supreme phase of noogenesis, in which the play of vital combinations (until that phase primarily 'functional') would at last have become directly inter-centric. In that case, we could dismiss the bogey of the termitary: there would never have been such colonies if termites had really been capable of mutual love.

It might be objected that it runs counter to the nature of affective powers to be extended to too great an object. The whole of human experience is at hand, it would appear, to prove that love, which reaches its climax in the case of the couple, is broken up and loses intensity with every increase in the number of individuals it brings together. It has often been said that to love everybody is to love nobody. And two thousand years of Christianity have not succeeded, apparently, in providing the facts to give the lie to this pessimistic saying. To introduce universal love into a concrete prospect for the future, it may be urged, is the same as drawing up plans for the reconstruction of the world based on the possibility of squaring the circle or of perpetual motion.

For my own part, I have no illusions about the element of incredibility in my hypothesis. I find it indeed just as difficult as anyone to feel, or even to imagine, what sort of thing inter-human sympathy (between cosmic elements and other cosmic elements) could possibly turn out to be – even though the empirical laws of noogenesis oblige me to regard its appearance as probable, and even inevitable. With that reservation, however, I shall observe that the quasi-impossibility we still find in conceiving the establishment of a unanimity of man may well derive from our overlooking a certain factor which, if introduced into our calculations, is capable of producing entirely different results. By that factor I mean the quite recent sensitizing of our minds to the organic depth and convergent properties of time.

The discovery of time –

From whichever end we now tackle the problem of man, the influence inevitably makes itself felt of a mental revolution which, without our suspecting it, is making us radically different from preceding generations, separated from us by less than two hundred years. When, towards the end of the eighteenth century, the ideas of evolution and progress began to come to the fore – often in over-simplified and naïve forms – it was possible to believe (as some still do) that it was no more than the infatuation of natural scientists with an ephemeral hypothesis. Today the notion of duration has covered the whole horizon spanned by the mind of man: physics, sociology, philosophy, religion – all the branches of knowledge are now impregnated by this subtle essence. In fact, the limited and the static have disappeared from our outlook, and we are already thinking only in terms of space-time. It is not a question of 'hypothesis', indeed! The only way in which we can interpret such an event is to recognize that, like children awakening to a sense of depth and relief, we have just collectively arrived at the perception of a new dimension. As a direct accompaniment of this, a world of new possibilities is opening up, not only for the speculative constructions of our reason but even more (and this is the important point) for the development of human energy.

Until now, one might say, men were living both dispersed and at the same time closed in on themselves, like passengers in a ship who have met by chance below decks with no idea of its mobile character and its motion. They could, accordingly, think of nothing to do on the earth that brought them together but to quarrel or amuse themselves. And now, by chance, or rather as a normal effect of growing older, we have just opened our eyes. The boldest of us have found their way to the deck. They have seen the vessel that was carrying us along. They have marked the creaming of her bow wave. They have realized that there are boilers to be stoked and a wheel to be manned. And most important of all, they have seen the clouds floating overhead, they have savoured the sweet scent of the Western Isles, over the curve of the horizon: it ceases to be the restless human to-and-fro on the same spot, it is no longer a drifting – it is *the voyage*.

Another mankind must inevitably emerge from this vision, one of which we have as yet no idea, but one which I believe I can already feel stirring through the old mankind, whenever the chances of life bring me into contact with another man whom, however alien he may be to me by nationality, class, race or religion, I find closer to me than a brother, *because he, too, has seen the ship and he, too, feels that we are steaming ahead.*

The sense of a common venture, and in consequence of a common destiny: the sense of an evolution in common that we can see with ever increasing clarity to be a genesis (and even a 'noogenesis'): what forms of action, hitherto impossible to realize – what forms of association, hitherto utopian – what revelation from on high, hitherto misunderstood, may we not anticipate in the special richness of this new milieu and in its special curvature! If charity has so far failed to reign upon earth, may not the reason be simply that in order to establish itself it was necessary for the earth first to have become conscious of its spiritual cohesion and convergence? If we are to be able to love one another must we not first *effect a change of plane*?

Everything, in short, locks and knits together in our outlook provided the rising warmth of a sense of man can be distinguished, by certain signs, beneath the fever from which the world is suffering at this moment. This warmth is evidence of a coming together, a concentration, and in consequence of an ultra-centration of the earth's thinking molecules, and it enables us to recognize that the psychic synthesis of the universe is continuing to be effected through the human mass. That being so, there is undoubtedly no longer anything that should alarm us either in the increased pressure of number or in the growing bonds of collectivization: because, in this instance, the irresistible rise of the other all around us, and its intrusion even into our individual lives, is without any possible doubt the expression and the measure of our own ascent into the personal.

Unpublished, Peking
20 January 1942

Universalization and Union

An attempt at clarification

In the course of this essay I would like to try to solve the following twofold problem – a twofold problem which at this moment is the same for all of us, whether 'friends' or 'enemies'.

Looking at the vast upheaval in which, as a result of the war, we are all caught up, can we, in the first place, decide (*quite apart from any private hypothesis*) what is the mathematical sign of the current that is sweeping us along in one body, pell-mell, and all with equal rapidity? Is it positive or is it negative? Secondly, is it possible to determine, within this current, what is the best line of action for each one of us to take, with a view to our common salvation – again *on any hypothesis*: in other words, no matter what particular position each one of us occupies within the hostile masses now confronting one another?

What worries us until we hardly know where we stand, is the feeling that we are out of our depth in a catastrophe of a vastness and complexity that goes beyond 'the stature of man'. And what causes us agonies of anxiety is the impossibility we recognize (if we are sincere) of approving, no less than condemning, *absolutely* any of the human principles or mystical beliefs that are at this moment in conflict.

We are looking for an absolute principle of discernment which will enable us unmistakably to recognize the significance of what is happening today; and an absolute principle of action to enable us unhesitatingly and at every moment to determine the right thing to do: orientation and guidance: a compass and a course to steer.

In the darkness, with the storm raging, these are what we must find.

We must open our eyes and concentrate on discovering whether, perhaps, there may not be (outside all personal considerations, local, emotional or moral) *a certain undeniable aspect of the present war: one that will irresistibly suggest a certain optimistic interpretation* of the crisis we are going through, and thereby impose upon each and all of us, whatever our position and whatever our circumstances, *the infallible line of advance towards the light, for which we are searching.*

I. AN UNDENIABLE PHENOMENON: THE PROGRESSIVE TOTALIZATION OF HUMAN ENERGIES

What makes the present state of the human world seem so difficult to understand is, I believe, that we are trying to appreciate what is going on while still remaining attached to one fragment of mankind in opposition to other fragments. It is inevitable, for the hostile blocs which divide the world between them, that the prevailing note of the moment, in the relation of bloc to bloc, should be uncertainty and confusion. So long as we are lost in the internal turmoil of the elements, it disguises the general trend of the phenomenon. In simpler and more familiar words, we cannot see the wood for the trees.

Let us try, on the contrary, to emerge from the clouds, charged with contrary energies, in which we are plunged. Let us make a scientific and objective intellectual effort to rise above the flashes of lightning and peals of thunder, and observe the general picture of the storm from outside and as a whole. Viewed from these heights, the disorder, if I am not mistaken, falls into an ordered pattern; and what, seen from lower down or inside, appeared to be revolting chaos begins, in three ways, to take the form of 'directed process'.

We used to feel as though we were floating at random in the hurricane, but now we can distinguish a definite movement in the storm. It is true that we are whirling like dead leaves in the gales of war, but it is even more true and more significant that it is in the direction of a simultaneous universalization, organization and intensification of human energies that this great up-draught is carrying us.

a. Universalization

The first fact to have become evident to all observers (though not so fully understood) is that the various human currents on which we are tossed are all manifesting one and the same tendency to swell to the very dimensions of the earth. This trend towards universalization is emphasized massively and with brutal force in the global character of the war – the first war in history in which the totality of the world is effectively involved. It comes out, however, in an even more explicit and unmistakable way in the internal evolution of the various spiritual movements which are striving for self-expansion and for domination through the medium of force. Only five years ago it was still possible to contrast the internationalism of communism and the democracies with the particularism of the axis powers. This distinction would no longer be possible today. Governed by the very nature of the economic and spiritual environment in which they are developing, racialist nationalisms have rapidly evolved into systems or mystiques so all-embracing as to be without limit, with the result that no difference (except in methods of presentation and realization) distinguishes them any longer from the opposite camp. On both sides it has already ceased to be no more than a question of readjusting spheres of influence and frontiers. From west to east, from Berlin, Rome and Tokyo to London, Moscow and New York, what is dreamed of – the web that is being woven – the bone of contention – among technicians of all sorts, is nothing less than plans for a general re-casting, which will hold good for the whole earth: a 'new order', a 'new life'. Anything short of that would appear intolerably unappetizing to our modern palate. Hypocritical propaganda, the sceptics call it, a cloak of grandeur thrown over a materialist egoism. But, right though the sceptics may be in mistrusting it, is it not already a great thing, is it not already everything, that in order to make itself heard and seduce the masses, propaganda is obliged today to speak in terms of totality?

As the basis of this spontaneous widening of human perspectives, or at any rate as its condition, there obviously stands the astonishing progress in material methods of communication which the last century has seen. Since the recent conquest of the air, and even more of the 'ether', the thinking earth forms but a single unit in which the whole influence, originating in each point, is transmitted to, and every shock resounds in, the whole mass. This resonance of the external environment has certainly a great deal to do with the increased scale of all our thoughts and all our acts which we notice today; but it is not the whole explanation, and the vibration would soon die down if it did not find an echo in our own hearts. Underlying the physical amplification of the least of our deliberate acts, a whole world of latent instincts is wakening in us – a 'general' soul which was only waiting for a body in order to disclose itself. There can no longer be any possible doubt. Spiritually, at the same time as materially, through its conscious aspirations no less than through its economic determinisms, at this very moment and before our eyes, the warring earth is heading straight for universality.

That, I repeat, is a first fact to be noted.

b. *Organization*

In itself, the extension of a thing is a phenomenon that may be interpreted in two ways – comforting or menacing according to the nature of the magnitude it assumes. The process may be fruitful; we may look forward to it, as we look forward to the dawn; but it can equally well be as sterile as the sand of the dunes, as treacherous as the waters of a flood, as destructive as fire or pestilence. If we are to decide, with no possibility of doubt, towards what form of universalization, desirable or alarming, events are leading us, once again we have only to consider the most obvious characteristics of the present war. 'Not only universal war', we are all agreed, 'but *total* war'.

What exactly do we mean by 'total war'?

When we say that war has become total, we are thinking primarily of an unscrupulous choice of methods of securing victory – or, again, of an exhaustive employment of the resources of each belligerent country. In reality, however, the expression implies a further idea – one that is qualitative rather than quantitative. It is true, no doubt, that what makes our war 'total' is that every country is fighting with all the means and all the manpower at her disposal. But it is also, and much more, that within each nation at war the life of the nation is concentrating itself and collectively buttressing itself in a calculated and combined effort for defence or attack.

Here again, for the second time, we find what we were looking for: I mean a characteristic that is common to all today's events, considered globally and without reference to particular values and vicissitudes. All around us, under the cloak of war, and encouraged by it, human trends are running deeper at the same time as they are covering a wider surface. As they spread, so they extend their roots. In as much as, and to the extent that each country is caught up in the movement 'towards a new life', it sees itself carried towards a reorganization that is totalitarian in style.

This can mean only one thing: that looking at it as a whole, whatever the details and internal complexity of the conflict, the general result of all our turmoil is continually to stimulate a little more the collective, dynamic organization of the conscious elements of the earth. What we can now observe is the extension to planetary limits *of an order*.

Organization, universal in dimensions: the two characteristics, and the two elements, of an integral totalization in which (as we shall see) lies the explanation of the unparalleled intensification of human energies we are now witnessing.

c. Intensification

Submerged as we are in the human mass, we have a certain difficulty in feeling the changes which are gradually transforming it in its totality. In all good faith, many minds are still unwilling to see any difference between the world of ancient Greece or the Renaissance and our world today. They believe they are still living on the same scale as Plato and St Thomas. Nevertheless, there is undoubtedly an obvious gulf between those thinkers and us, even if we look no further than the global intensity of life covering the surface of the earth.

Let us see if we can find an example that will enable us to appreciate the difference; and, with that in view, let us look at any one of those V-formations of aircraft which daily and practically everywhere – particularly when a great offensive is under way – are launched on either side by belligerent nations. Have we ever tried mentally to reckon up, as we see them pass overhead, the sum of physico-psychic energy (the two come to the same thing) accumulated in each one of these monstrous arrow-heads?

In the first place, the metal – or rather all the metals – in each particular aircraft; and all that this metal armature presupposes – the mines and factories at the four corners of the world, all the metallurgical science and chemistry of alloys.

Then, the fuel: and behind that, the prospecting, the wells, the pipe-lines, the refineries, the tankers, the whole political and financial organization of oil production.

The internal mechanism, again: the design, the calculations, the production of the engine; the complicated and delicate instruments feeding information to dozens of dials.

The external shape, too, with the whole of aerodynamic science behind its final form.

And finally, the power: the tons of explosive, launched at speeds of hundreds of kilometres an hour against precisely determined targets.

So far we have not done more than consider the body of the machine. Turn now to what constitutes the brain and soul of the aircraft. Here we have the pilot: off duty, a marvellous human instrument, chosen and trained physically and morally from among the best of his race, but now, by flying, raised to super-humanity. Try to appreciate the internal tension of this man, who holds concentrated in himself and personifies the passions and ambitions, the pride of millions of his fellow-men. See him, in the intoxication of the colossal forces a pressure of his hand controls; in the excitement of the mission he is carrying out; in the totality of the sacrifice he accepts; in the fullness of a deliberate act in which the whole of his life reaches a paroxysm of realization.

The whole of industry, the whole of science, all the earth's passion, concentrated, as though to their keenest point, in some kilograms of metal and human flesh.

And then take the cube of this, multiply it to the tenth power, to the hundredth, to allow for the number of aircraft not simply brought together in an external association, but vitally fused into one in the unanimity of their common drive!

Simply as a matter of pure energetics, one thing is scientifically incontestable: in the whole history of life there has never been such an accumulation of organized energy concentrated in so small a volume as during the present war.

Supposing we now extend to the entire surface of our human world what we have just learnt from our analysis of the aircraft. At these planetary dimensions, as we might well expect, the details of the phenomenon become difficult to distinguish. Nevertheless, a single note, that same note, emerges, becomes dominant and grows in volume, above what seemed to us to be pure chaos. Imagine an observer, established on some star, who, ever since the beginning of the geological periods, could have followed and measured, in the form of some radiation, the global charge and psychic tension of the star that bears us. Here again, is it not plain that our age would mark the 'peak' on the chart recorded – the spot where the curve leaps to a stupendous 'high'? From being first a vague blur, then red, then green, the biosphere would suddenly have become incandescent.

Let us conclude the first part of our inquiry with that vision. What we were trying to do, you will remember, was to

discover, in the heart of this present crisis, an absolute characteristic lying outside and above any possible discussion: this, we
hoped, would give us a foundation, in the midst of the storm,
for a theoretical appraisal of what is happening and for a rule
to govern our action. Here, then, we have the characteristic we
were looking for: at this very moment, and coincidently with
the global event of war, mankind, taken as a whole, is passing
through a maximum, never as yet attained, of unitary organization and living force.

What, indeed, can be the meaning of this phenomenon?

II. A PROBABLE INTERPRETATION: THE SYNTHESIS
OF THE EARTH

If we are to find a meaning – though it would be better to say
the meaning – of the ever more intense paroxysm to which the
present war (taken as one whole) corresponds, one condition,
I believe, is essential and at the same time sufficient in itself. It is
that when we look at the world we understand and accept the
particular standpoint that is more and more imperatively
dictated to observers such as ourselves by the scientific theory –
or, to put it more exactly, the scientific fact – of noogenesis.

Let me explain briefly what that means.

Until recent years a marked dualism, or even conflict,
ranged physics and biology in opposite camps. On the one hand
lay the world of matter, on the other the world of life; and
science could not contrive to see how one and the same coherent
explanation could cover these two fields of experience, each
equally objective. Now, however, as a result of investigations
and tentative probings into all directions of the real simultaneously, two points are emerging which would distinctly
seem to indicate a way towards a solution of the problem.

The first is the definite relationship of concomitance which
is progressively becoming more evident as existing between
conscious spontaneity and *organic complexity*. So long as a natural
particle (a molecule, for example) contains in its structure no

more than a small number (some tens, or some hundreds, or even some thousands) of organized atoms, no external trace can be distinguished of what we call life. If, however, the number of atoms incorporated rises to several tens of millions (as would seem to be the case with the organic 'viruses', vegetal animals) then the chemical characteristics develop a fringe of biological properties in the element concerned. Under extreme magnification (approaching 100,000 diameters) the virus particles can be seen as minute rods; and even if these rods do not reproduce themselves in the strict sense of the word, they already have at least the remarkable power of multiplying themselves. Are they infra-bacteria, or are they super-molecules? This is something we cannot decide. Raise the number still higher, and we meet the cell (though when I say the number, we still lack precise numerical data – already, however, such data are less important, since *structure* is beginning to take precedence over number). And starting with that point, from the unicellular protozoon up to man (man with the million million cells of his body, and the thirty thousand million cells of his brain) the sheer figures become astronomical, without even so being able to give any idea of the fantastic complexity of the super-imposed physico-chemical mechanisms.

In consequence of this, and independently of any consideration or interpretation that is philosophical in order, life appears to us more and more objectively as a specific property of matter that has been taken to an extremely high degree of ordered complexity – or, *which comes to the same thing*, of complexity *centred* upon itself. Speaking empirically, it is a combined effect of complication and centration.

To arrange beings, as we have just done, according to their analytic degree of centred-complexity is a purely 'spatial' operation. What happens, however, when we try to distribute the same beings in time, in accordance with the presumed date of their formation? A second cardinal fact now emerges, which is sufficiently well established by and large for us to have no hesitation in relying on it. We may express this as follows: *if the chemical and vital elements of the universe are spaced out in astronomical and geological duration, they do not present a random pattern of dispersion: they form a natural series in which their order of appearance coincides essentially with their order of complication.* The phenomenon is particularly easy to follow in the domain of higher life, provided always that we take as the *index* of animal complexity the degree of enrichment and concentration of the *nervous system* in the cranium. Finally, the i is dotted (if I may put it so) by the fascinating case of man – evolution's *latest arrival*, in whom extreme cerebralization (or 'cephalization') of the organism is accompanied by a staggering increase in psychic faculties.

Thus we find a gradual and simultaneous rise of complexity and consciousness.

For my part, I can see only one possible intellectual attitude to this vast fact which a general convergence of all branches of science is gradually forcing us to accept. This is to recognize that the universe is literally *twice* what we thought it was. Until now we used to look on the mass of the cosmos as being animated by a single global movement, the movement that produced the slow dispersal and dissipation of its energies down the gradient of the more probable and of the less demanding of effort. Now a second current is appearing, running in the opposite direction from this first descending current (and yet generated by it): this, too, is cosmic, but in this case it is directed upwards, in the direction of the less probable and the more demanding. It is from this that there gradually emerge, with the passage of time, progressively richer forms of association, forms that are in consequence progressively more organically centred – and, concomitantly, more vitalized.

That is what I mean by noogenesis.

To return from that digression and get back to our subject, let us take a further look at the broiling atmosphere in which the war is today enveloping the earth. Is it an explosion? or a conflagration? or some malignant fever devouring the structure of man? These various diagnoses which, in our trepidation, we suggest to one another, are quite certainly valueless: for, if the temperature around us is rising, it is only doing so, we have seen, in step with an increase in organization.

'An increase in human totalization *and* in human psychic charge' – there we have the two *linked* phenomena whose *simultaneous* appearance and growth in the course of the crisis we have to explain.

Perhaps you are still undecided?

But, after what we have just said about the existence of the second cosmic current, can you not see that the solution of the problem is contained in the very terms in which it is expressed?

When we speak of 'a progress of organization, duplicated by an intensification of consciousness' what are we expressing? A particular effect of the war which calls for explanation? or is it rather the general law in which the genesis of spirit is historically recorded? In either case, the two factors are identically the same.

This can mean only one thing, that if today's intense crisis is restored, as it must be, to the solid, experiential, framework of modern space-time, it assumes, in two successive steps, both meaning and form.

First, in a general and approximate way, confined to its overall effects of spiritual synthesis, it is evidence of a positive bound in the terrestrial development of noogenesis.

What is much more, however, if we consider closely its strange universalist character, it seems to herald the coming of an important critical point in this noogenesis. Until now mankind, both economically and psychically, constituted no more than scattered, or at any rate loosely associated, fragments on the surface of the earth. The time seems to have come when these fragments are going to fuse and coalesce under the irresistible pressure of geographical, biological, political and social determinisms which have reached an accumulation planetary in order: this global operation coinciding with the awakening of a true 'spirit of the earth', which transcends the spirit of the nation which was all we used to know.

A new order of consciousness emerging from a new order of organic complexity: a hyper-synthesis upon itself of mankind.

Taking a completely objective view – looking at it as coolly as a physicist confronted with the worlds beyond measurement that implacably emerge from his calculations – and whatever protest may be raised by a certain sort of common sense – I cannot see that it is possible to interpret the present progress of the phenomenon of man, in line as it is with the general progress of the world, without arriving at a prospect as fantastic as I have just suggested.

But in that case, if 'common sense' has to yield to hard figures – if, in other words, we are well into the phase of synthesis – what remains for each one of us to think and do, at this precise moment when we are confronted by the crescendo of war?

III. A PRINCIPLE OF JUDGMENT AND ACTION: THE VIRTUE OF THE UNIVERSAL

The first and most important consequence of our having been able to reduce the chaos around us to an effect of noogenesis, is general in order: it means that, on scientific grounds, we are confirmed in an atmosphere of unshakable optimism. 'On scientific grounds', I said. This is something that we must fully understand. A man can be temperamentally and emotionally an optimist without any explicit reason for his hopes other than the *a priori* conviction that 'everything will be all right in the end'. It is not this instinct I have in mind, but a considered conviction based on an indisputable fact, and one more general than all the particular reasons for fear or doubt which can suggest themselves. 'How can you imagine', the pessimists keep asking, 'that we are going to emerge from this crisis even greater than before? Month by month, is not the conflict spreading ever more widely, deepening the rifts between us, exacerbating hatred, and preparing new and more terrible wars for tomorrow: wars between continents, as a sequel to wars between nations? The League of Nations, the Atlantic Charter – can you expect us to take these seriously? Whatever man does, how do you think he can escape from the continually renascent forces of violence and money? For the last century we have been brought to ruin by dreamers. To think first of one's own self, to be strong, each to hold his own at home with plenty of troops, and above all to stamp out like a virulent epidemic any idea of universal concord: history teaches us that that is the only wise course for nations'.

When I hear such pessimistic remarks (a thing that happens frequently), all I answer is: 'I cannot, any more than any one else, yet see where and how the skies will clear. I do not know after what vicissitudes, through what miracle, and in what form, we shall emerge from the war, and I have no intention of making a guess. Amid all these uncertainties, however, one thing gives me solid reassurance. It is this: for all the piecemeal evidence an intelligent and pitiless criticism may hour after hour accumulate, to prove to me that mankind is disintegrating or has irrevocably reached its ceiling – for all that, it still remains true that if we look at the world *as a whole* from a sufficiently elevated standpoint, it presents, without any possible doubt, the characteristics of a mass of consciousness in *motion*. Taken as a whole, the phenomenon of the present war (precisely because it can be seen to be total and universal) bears a positive mathematical sign. Whatever you may say, then – whatever appearances may suggest to me – whatever may happen – there remains a *fact* of a higher order than all other facts, in virtue of which I can only answer: after five hundred million years of mankind the earth is still developing its organicity: its psychic temperature is rising. Therefore it is still advancing. *Eppur si muove!*'

With that point settled, we may leave the pessimists to determine among themselves the impossibility for man to make any progress; joining the optimists, we may ask in what direction each of us can take action in order as effectively as possible to support the synthesis of the world at this critical moment of evolution. Simply to say that we must try, by every means, to encourage and develop the forces that make for unity rather than those that divide us, would obviously be true. But this rule of action is too general, or rather it is too much a confusion with the actual objective we have in mind. That, indeed, is to be united; but how, exactly, are we to do so? Where, that is, are we to find a criterion of selection and a principle of attraction which, without doing violence to our own individual inclinations and convictions, will, *in a natural way*, make our roads converge?

Let us put the problem in concrete terms.

All around us at this moment, the human flood is spiritually divided into a small number of wide hostile currents, each one of which claims the right to be 'universal': communism, democracy, fascism, nazism and 'the new order in the east'. Can we say, categorically, whether or not it is possible from the optimistic and constructive point of view of noogenesis to discover an orientation, an attitude, a deliberate course of action *equally* acceptable and valid at every moment for any and every adherent of any of these five mystiques, and one, moreover, whose infallible effect will be to bring us, by synthesis, closer together?

My answer will be that it is possible: provided the universe (as we have already admitted) is convergent in structure, then such a deliberate course of action does exist, in accordance with the capabilities of every man of good will. For each one of us and no matter what the particular current of universalization to which he belongs, this miraculous act consists simply in following and driving *to the very end the most universalist trend* in that current.

If, each from our own angle, we make this our concern what will in fact happen?

In the first place, we find – even though we may stand at the opposite spiritual poles of the world – that we unfailingly, and without deliberately acting in concert, begin to grow closer. In order to meet together at the material centre of the earth, physical bodies have only to follow, each on its own, the direction in which the pull of gravity is strongest. Similarly, if the world is psychically weighted with unity, if, that is, it contains a single point at which *everything* comes together, then we can be certain of making contact with one another simply by following the direction in which the pull of universalization becomes strongest.

At first sight, it might well seem that there is a certain lack of precision in such a method, since there are surely in our human world a number of different ways of attaining universality. Will the result of the synthesis be the same if communist, or nazi, or democratic influence is predominant? Do these various roads truly lead to the same terminal point, or does not each, rather, have a different centre as its objective?

This sort of anxiety seems to me quite unnecessary – because, however contradictory the trends may appear at their starting point, they must inevitably, as they proceed, correct their heading and converge. If the universalization of a human current is obtained by coercion which forcibly imposes, or by suppression which eliminates, or by mechanization which de-humanizes, it is not complete; it neither attains its maximum nor achieves equilibrium. If we really consider the matter, we shall realize that it is entirely through *lack of universalism* that the democratic, the communist, and the axis mystiques are still so violently in conflict – whether the lack be in the number of human elements incorporated, or in the form of contact (insufficiently deep and total) achieved between them. Faithful to the end to the internal law of 'fuller universalization' that they all accept, the followers of these various movements cannot fail in the end to discover that though they may set out on opposite sides they are all tackling the same mountain, and they must inevitably meet at the same peak: and that is the 'personalizing association of the greatest possible number of men, through the heart, in oneness of mind'.

The problem has only one solution – for there is only one centre, and that centre can occupy only one place in the sphere of man.

So much for the theoretical presentation.

But what do the facts tell us?

Here I shall have to introduce my own personal experience as evidence: my evidence may be regarded with suspicion, but it is categorical. On countless occasions life has brought me into close contact with men whose convictions and activities placed them in a camp reputed to be opposite to my own. In the light of the conventions we accepted, there should have been defiance or hostility between those men and myself. Instead, however, of this frigid reaction, what sprang up at our first contact was a profound sympathy, one of those growing and definitive sympathies such as is born among comrades in arms. Labelled as enemies, we immediately recognized one another as brothers. And the reason for this was simply that, to put it briefly, both they and I were only trying, each from our own side, to magnify and unify the earth. No matter that our methods for achieving this result were still at variance: these differences, we felt, were only secondary and temporary, and would ultimately one day be straightened out and solved. The essential point was that meanwhile we should be able to meet in the atmosphere and light of one and the same ideal.

The fact is that while the quest for the universal can infallibly direct and 'automatically' correct our course towards union, it has in addition the mysterious virtue of directly producing that union. At the extreme *upward* limit, when a democratic, a communist, an axis ideology (and, I might well add, a Christianity)[1] *are universalized*, both the theoretical and the actual opposition between them disappears. Universalization

1. If, in what I have said here, I were not trying to confine myself strictly to the field of experience, this would be the place to develop the subject of the astonishing conformity between the prospect of a world in a state of synthesis and the dogmatic properties of a Christ who is himself also fully *universalized*.

causes the four currents to converge; and, I think, from their confluence there must emerge the new order, as yet impossible to imagine, in which we shall wake up tomorrow.

That is why I believe that if there were a voice sufficiently powerful to be heard above the turmoil of battle, it should proclaim to the warring world:

'Let each one of all you who are fighting *and are still too divided to be able as yet to know one another for what you are*, guard his faith in the cause he believes to be just. But, in the very name of that faith, never cease to widen your ideas and ambitions to the real dimensions of the earth. Cling to your own race, indeed, and your own nation: for a sound synthesis calls for strong and sharply defined elements. But if you wish fully to realize yourselves, beware above all of everything that isolates, that refuses to accept and that divides. Each along your own line, let your thought and action be "universal", which is to say "total". And tomorrow, maybe, you will find to your surprise that all opposition has disappeared and you can "love" one another.'

Unpublished, Peking
20 March 1942

Centrology

An essay in a dialectic of union

INTRODUCTION

In spite of all the theoretical objections that would seek to discourage the belief, our minds remain invincibly persuaded that a certain very simple fundamental rule lies hidden beneath the overpowering multiplicity of events and beings: to discover and formulate this rule, we believe, would make the universe intelligible in the totality of its development.

The instinctive tenacity with which man's thought tries to reduce the world to unity, combined with the fact that all the efforts hazarded in this direction by the greatest philosophers, one after another (Aristotle, Spinoza, Leibniz, Hegel, Spencer), coincide in following this line, surely this is in itself an indication that the problem is patient of solution? Carried, then, on the shoulders of our predecessors and, at the same time, in a better position than they were to perceive the mechanism of a universe whose structure and dimensions modern science is beginning to form an idea of, are we not both justified and well placed to resume their attempts, if only, at least, in order to take one more forward step?

I believe that we are: and that is why I am so bold as to offer here, in the form of a series of linked propositions, an essay in universal explanation – not an *a priori* geometric synthesis starting from some definition of 'being', but an experiential *law of recurrence* which can be checked in the phenomenal field and can appropriately be extrapolated into the totality of space and time.

It is not an abstract metaphysics, but a realist ultraphysics of union.

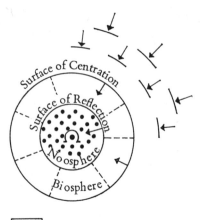

Figure 1. Diagram symbolizing the principle phases of centrogenesis (convergence of the universe along its axis of centro-complexity or personalization).

Note the concentric system of isospheres (surfaces of equal centro-complexity), subdivided into three zones by the two critical surfaces of centration and reflection (cf. sections 9 and 13).

Omega point is at the centre.

 Eu-centric (Thought)

Phyletic (Life)

Pre-centric (Matter)

(⟶ attraction *ab ante* (finality)

⟶(impulse *a retro* (chance)
(cf. section 30)

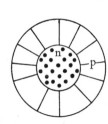

Figure 2. Diagram illustrating the condition of fragmentary centres (segments of centres) in the pre-centric zone. As yet there are no closed 'withins' (section 8).

Figure 3. Diagram illustrating the structure of a phyletic centre in the phyletic zone. *p:* 'peripheral ego', divisible and transmissible; *n:* 'nuclear ego', incommunicable (cf. section 12).

Figure 4. Diagram illustrating the structure of a eu-centric element. *p:* 'peripheral ego'; *n:* punctiform nucleus, reflective and personalized (cf. section 13).

1. Centres and centro-complexity

1. As the foundation for the whole edifice of propositions that follow we have an intuition and two observations:

a. *The intuition:* In the swarming multiplicity of living elements (monocellular and polycellular) which make up the biosphere, we find an authentic continuation of the granular (atomic, molecular) structure of the universe. In consequence, if the human body is restored to its position in the cosmic corpuscular series, it is simply a 'super-molecule': once we see it in this light, we are in the happy position of being able to distinguish in that super-molecule, the properties, in a 'magnified' state, of *every* molecule.

b. *The observations*: Man, the final product of planetary evolution, is both supremely *complex* in his physico-chemical organization (measured by the brain), and at the same time, viewed in his psychism, supremely *free and conscious*.

2. Taken in sequence, these three primary evidential data immediately bring out the three following derived data:

a. At every degree of size and complexity, cosmic particles or grains are not simply, as physics has recognized, centres of universal dynamic radiation: all of them, in addition (rather like man), have and represent a small 'within' (however diffuse or even fragmentary it may be; cf. section 8), in which is reflected, at a more or less rudimentary stage, a particular representation of the world: in relation to themselves they are psychic centres – and at the same time they are infinitesimal psychic centres of the universe. In other words, consciousness is a universal molecular property; and the molecular state of the world is a manifestation of the pluralized state of some potentiality of universal consciousness.

b. Consciousness increases and grows deeper throughout the series of cosmic units, in proportion with the *organized* complexity of those units. While it is completely imperceptible to our observational methods below an atomic complexity of the order of 10^5 (the virus),[1] it can be plainly detected when we reach that of the cell (10^{10}); but it enters into its major developments only in the brains of large mammals (10^{20}), in other words when we have atomic groupings astronomic in order.

c. From this it follows that the most essential, the most significant, characteristic of any of the units whose association makes up the universe, is distinguished in those units by a certain degree of interiority – that is to say of centricity (soul), which is itself a function of a certain degree of complexity (*body*, and, more particularly, brain). This *coefficient of centro-complexity* (or, which comes to the same thing, of consciousness) is the true absolute measure of being in the beings that surround us. That, and that alone, can be the basis for a truly natural classification of the elements of the universe.

3. Now that we have a clew to guide us through the baffling multiplicity of things, we see them fall into order in what can be measured, not along the line that leads from the infinitely small to the infinitely large, but along the axis that rises up from the infinitely simple to the infinitely complex. Further, within this particular space, we can picture them to ourselves as distributed over concentric spheres (figure 1), the radius of each sphere diminishing as the complexity increases. Thus there emerges the pattern of a *centred universe* – elements of equal complexity (and hence of equal centricity) being spread out over what we may call isospheres of consciousness – and

---

1. By *atomic complexity* I mean here the number of atoms contained in the particle in question. That particles of low atomic complexity should appear 'inanimate' to us is completely in line with the analogies we find in science. A number of fundamental properties of matter (variation of mass, the curvature of space, etc.) become perceptible to us only in the infinitely large or the infinitely small. From this point of view, we might say that biology is simply the 'physics of very large complexes' – the physics of the third infinite (that of complexity, in which life appears).

the whole family of isospheres defining, at the heart of the system, the presence, position and nature of a certain pole or focus-point of universal synthesis, Omega point (cf. sections 18–25).

4. Such an arrangement, it is only too evident, cannot be the manifestation of a static equilibrium. Just as unmistakably as the distribution of differently coloured stars in the sky, it points to the existence of a movement. Once the universe is ordered along its axis of increasing centro-complexity, it is seen to be not only centred in its totality but, what is more, traversed and moved by a stream of centration. In the organo-psychic field of centro-complexity, the world is *convergent*; and the isospheres are simply a system of waves which as time goes on (and it is they which measure time) close up around Omega point.[2]

5. From the above we may draw our first general conclusion: that if the universe is observed in its true and essential movement through time, it represents a system which is in process of internal 'centro-complexification'. Evolution does not exactly correspond, as Spencer maintained, to a transition from the homogeneous to the heterogeneous – but to a transition from a dispersed heterogeneous (lacking unity) to an organic (unified) heterogeneous – or, to put it still more clearly, *to a transition from a lower to a higher state of centro-complexity*.

We must now try to analyse in more detail the functioning of this cosmogenesis through centrogenesis, in the course of which the universe becomes interiorized and spiritualized by dint of, and, we might say, under the impact of, complexification upon itself.

2. It is said that no theory of evolution could be extended to the totality of the universe, because all evolution requires an 'environment' and, by definition, the universe is without any containing envelope. This objection has no weight against a cosmic transformation of the type put forward here, in which evolution is defined by a movement of the world *in relation to itself*.

2. Centrogenesis

I. INTER-CENTRIC LINKS: EXISTENCE AND SPECIES

6. The phenomenon of man forces us to see the universe as made up of psychic nuclei, each one of which acts as a partial centre in relation to the world and is therefore potentially co-extensive with the universe: to take this view is obviously to go back to Leibniz's monads. While, however, in the static universe of monadology, the cosmic particles 'have neither doors nor windows', from the evolutionary standpoint adopted by centrology, they are seen to be in threefold solidarity one with another, within the centrogenesis in which they are born.

a. In the first place, there is *tangential* solidarity, inasmuch as they hold together and are linked one to another on the surface of the isosphere n, on which they are disposed in virtue of the degree of centro-complexity they have attained.

b. Secondly, *radial* solidarity, inasmuch as they share, through the nuclei of lower centro-complexity which their unity embraces and organizes, in the sum total of all the tangential links proper to the isospheres (n^1, n^2, etc.) to which those subordinate nuclei belong.

c. Finally, *radial* solidarity again, inasmuch as they tend to move all together (and this includes all their roots) towards Omega, arriving themselves at, or giving birth to, an isosphere of a higher order $(n+1)$.

7. If we are incontestably to vindicate the existence of this threefold type of inter-connexions, we are obliged to admit that (contrary to Leibniz's view) the elementary cosmic centres can be partially themselves and partially one same thing upon which they impinge. This 'same thing', however, cannot be a vague initial unit starting from which the centres separate from

one another as they become individualized; for experience proves that their mutual solidarity increases with the *n*-order of the isospheres. We must, therefore, accept that they hold together from ahead, and through what lies ahead, cantilevered upon the total centre, Omega.

II. THE STAGES OF CENTROGENESIS: FRAGMENTARY CENTRICITY, PHYLETIC CENTRICITY, EU-CENTRISM

Matter, life, thought: three zones which are immediately perceptible in the world, even to common experience; and three zones, accordingly, the distinction between which must reappear, and must be accounted for, in any explanation, however learned, of the universe. From the point of view of centrology, which is at once pluralist and monist, how is this threefold form of being introduced into the stuff of the cosmos in the course of centrogenesis?

a. Fragmentary centricity

8. In the case of 'inanimate' matter (the most difficult section of the world for our minds to understand, since it is, evolutively, the furthest removed from us) we can figuratively picture to ourselves the cosmic nuclei (molecules, atoms, electrons) as *incompletely closed-in* on themselves: the elements already possess, it is true, a sort of psychic 'curvature' (otherwise they would not exist), but as fragments open at each end, as you would find with broken-off segments of a sphere or circle (figure 2). At this degree of disjunction there is as yet no true 'within' to things, but only the *'disposition'* to cause one to appear once the segments come together and fit in with one another – not, indeed, by deliberate intention (since they are still, by definition, only *fragments of immanence*) but through the play of chance (cf. section 31). It is at this preliminary phase of centrogenesis that practically the whole of time and space is *quantitatively* employed: the reason for this being precisely, perhaps, that in order to bring about the appearance of the

'first improbable' the play of large numbers needs a more extensive laboratory for its experiments.

It is thus that, through the fitting together of progressively more complicated atomic chains, an initial series of more or less loose-knit and confused isospheres must have taken shape: through the gradual fusing together of partial interiorities, these mark the progressive stages not of the a-centric but of the pre-centric towards centricity.

9. So far as we can judge, it is somewhere at (or a little below) the level of cellular structure that the segments of pre-con-sciousness at last joined up along a closed curve, and so the first closed nuclei (the first centred particles) appeared in the world, disposed on a particular isosphere which is none other than the oldest and outermost of the biospheres. Each one of them must have emerged upon this biosphere on its own account, as a result of the repeated play of large numbers; each one, more-over, in order to pass from pre-life into life, had to cross a certain *critical point of centration* (the *closing-up* on itself of a chain of segments), a replica of which in a higher form we shall meet again later in the case of *reflection* (cf. section 13).

And it is here that a new phase of centrogenesis opens.

b. Phyletic centricity

10. A characteristic that is proper to nearly all the fragmentary centres (or segments of centres) which make up pre-living matter, is stability. So long as the lower complex centres remain at the stage of an open chain, they seem unable to advance further, once they *have* closed up, except through the enriching effect of new accidental encounters with new seg-ments; and, except in the comparatively rare cases of spon-taneous disintegration, their duration would appear, by our human scale, to be indefinite.

The behaviour of closed particles – specific elements of the biosphere – is quite different. Hardly is such a particle centred upon itself, before it displays a remarkable power of self-complexification (and therefore of auto-centration). It is not that it is already emancipated, to its advantage or detriment, from the laws of chance (for such emancipation occurs only in the neighbourhood of Omega); but, though still immersed in chance, it behaves there as though it were in a nutritive medium, choosing, seizing hold of and actively incorporating, at the whim of chance,[3] the elements of a higher centro-complexity. In other words, animated by a sort of elevating force, it seeks to rise up radially, like a rocket, from the mono-cellular stage to polycellular stages, in the direction of Omega, *so marking out a phylum.*

11. *A priori* one might imagine that from the first and outer-most of the biospheres up to the outskirts of Omega, *one and the same* particle *itself* passes through the whole zone in between – in that case its ontogenesis would exactly coincide with a phylogenesis. In fact, a universal experience teaches us that this is not so. As a result of a sort of exhaustion or hardening of the centres which occurs in the course of their activity, each particle is found to be capable of producing only an infinitesimal advance along the phylum to which it belongs; after that it disappears, though not without having previously undergone multiplication.

Thus every phylum can be seen, in fact, as broken up into a multitude of elementary segments, each one of which serves as a starting point and an anchorage for a complex ramification.

12. From the point of view of centrogenesis, this phyletic segmentation and ramification have obvious advantages. As a result of them a maximum density of particles with a corre-sponding maximum of tentative gropings (cf. section 31) is produced on each isosphere; while at the same time the greatest possible richness and variety of inherited properties accumulates in the phylum under the repeated influence of

3. And at the same time (which appears paradoxical but is what man succeeds in doing in all his free creations) in conformity with the physical laws of energy (cf. section 30).

each generation's cross-fertilization. In short, the two factors combine as a direct encouragement to the operation of centro-complexity.[4] On the other hand, their mechanism gives rise to a difficulty. Seen from outside, cellular division, which is the fundamental operation of reproduction, seems simple enough, for matter is essentially divisible. From the internal or centro-logical aspect, however, how can we explain the psychic fission it entails? Since a centre of consciousness is essentially turned in, and closed in, on itself, how can we conceive the passage and communication of a 'within' from mother-cell to daughter-cell?

The only way out of this deadlock, I believe, is to imagine *two sorts of ego* in each phyletic centre; first *a nuclear ego* (more or less complete or rudimentary, according to each case), and secondly *a peripheral ego*; this latter is incompletely individualized, and is therefore *divisible* – after separation, it can develop by producing buds and isolate in itself a new nucleus of in-communicable ego (figure 3).[5]

This distinction, among living centres, between the peripheral and the nuclear, has more than the advantage of providing us with a verbal solution to a local deadlock. It will enable us to follow and analyze the process of centrogenesis even in the case of hominized life.

4. As a result, a living being has a twofold complexity: spatial, deriving from the number of sub-centres it embraces, and temporal, from the number of 'trials' of which, through its ancestors, it represents the total sum.

5. It is through this integument of the 'peripheral' (germinal) that biological continuity is maintained, that is to say, that the stem of the phylum holds together. Looked at from the 'nuclear' point of view, the phylum breaks down into a discontinuous string of (somatic) centres, into which it tends more and more to disintegrate as the centres increase in centricity. This phenomenon of 'phyletic granulation' which in its natural course reaches its maximum in man, is followed, biologically, by the phenomenon of 'collectivization'; in virtue of this, the centres (freed, sometimes more, sometimes less, from their subjection to the phylum) group together in the form of organic wholes (cf. section 16).

c. Eu-centrism

13. Precisely in virtue of the notion of centro-complexity, there are as many degrees of centricity in the cosmic nuclei as there are degrees of complexity. What we have so far, in the case of the lower zones of life, called 'centres', cannot therefore be compared to geometric points, but rather to limited circular surfaces which become progressively smaller but at the same time retain an appreciable 'centric diameter'.

It is the transition from this diffuse state to one that is strictly punctiform (figure 4), which defines the great phenomenon of hominization. Just as, at the origin of the phyletic, it was the closing-up on itself of a chain of segments (centration) that determined the first appearance of *living* centres, so here again it is in virtue of the arrival at zero of its centric diameter (reflection) that the living centre, in its turn, attains the condition and dignity of a 'grain of thought'. Thus, by passing through a new critical point, an isosphere of a fundamentally new type is produced: the isosphere of spirit, the noosphere.

14. It is true, of course, that in the human grain of thought, 'reflection' as yet affects only the *nuclear* portion of the being (cf. section 12) – and not the peripheral portion: the latter remains divisible, and still, accordingly, capable of reproduction (gametes). Nevertheless, however partial this transformation may be, it is still sufficient to cause the emergence within the individual of a eu-centred, 'point-like' focus: in other words of an *ego* that is personal in order. And this is enough to allow the appearance of a series of new phenomena in the later advances of centrogenesis.

15. First of all, in virtue of its new personal nature, the hominized cosmic centre finds that it possesses the sense of *irreversibility* and feels the demand for it. Being conscious both of its own oneness and of the existence of a future, it realizes that it is 'incompossible' with a destruction that would annihilate in it an *irreplaceable* fragment of the cosmic effort. Later

(sections 24 and 30), when we come to describe Omega point, we shall see how such an escape from total death is possible for a personalized being.

16. This, however, is not all. A new way of being linked together, unknown on the other isospheres, is set up between the 'reflective' units now spread out over the noosphere. Henceforth, an 'excentric' way of association – or one, at any rate, that is tenuous – is replaced, for the cosmic particles, by the possibility of 'centre-to-centre' contacts between perfect centres. At the same time, too, it is their united totality that lends itself to being animated by a sort of common personality. Welded together in this way, the noosphere, *taken as a whole*, begins to behave tangentially (cf. section 6), like a single megacentre; while, radially, it bestirs itself in forward motion, animated in its entirety by a phyletism or, more correctly, by an ontogenesis that is proper to it: phyletism, ontogenesis of collective consciousness and human memory, which through tradition and upbringing has continually grown more profound as it increases, ever since the first moment of hominization – and always in conformity with the fundamental biological law of centro-complexity.

17. Such, at this very moment, is the situation of the cosmos that surrounds us. Mankind, the leading wave of a universe which becomes luminous as (under the influence of complication) it contracts upon itself, encloses within its moving circle the still formless future of things, the secret of the final syntheses. What will emerge from this still fluid nucleus of the world? If our law of recurrence is correct, what can be distinguished on the horizon is nothing but, and nothing less than, a continual increase of organization and of centricity – and this time on the scale not of the particle but of the sphere: the accelerated impetus of an earth in which preoccupation with production for the sake of well-being will have given way to the passion for the discovery for the sake of fuller being – the super-personalization of a super-humanity that has

become super-conscious of itself in the increasing light of Omega.

III. OMEGA POINT

18. If the law of centro-complexity is extended indefinitely backwards along the axis of past aeons, it affords us a glimpse of progressively more diffuse zones, in which more and more fragmentary elements of consciousness float in a state of more and more unorganized heterogeneity. In this direction there is no lower limit to 'recurrence' (figure 1). There is an indefinitely continued widening of the lower surface of the cone. On the other hand, if it is carried in the opposite direction, that is, into the future, the extrapolation of the series defines a *peak*. The existence of a cosmic Omega point became apparent to us (cf. section 3) from the moment when our minds had to accept the evidence that the universe was psychically convergent. We must now be at pains to determine the properties of this supreme focus point of evolution.

19. Genetically speaking (that is, when observed from the position we occupy in space-time), Omega appears to us fundamentally as the centre which is defined by the final concentration upon itself of the noosphere – and indirectly, therefore, of all the isospheres that precede it. In Omega, then, a maximum complexity, cosmic in extent, coincides with a maximum cosmic centricity.

20. In itself, the idea that the universe is moving towards some form of final unity has haunted the minds of all the philosophers; and there is nothing new in the idea. What gives the notion of centro-complexity its originality and fruitfulness is that it imposes on the term of cosmic synthesis, in virtue of its very structure, a series of positive determinants; the effect of these is to bring home to us its existence in terms not only of intellectual apprehension but also of action. Indeed, if Omega, as revealed to us by our law of recurrence, is to satisfy the

conditions attached to its position and function, we can readily appreciate that it must present itself to us when we examine it, as at the same time: personal – individual – already partially actual – and also partially transcendent.

21. That, first, it is personal goes without saying; since it is centricity that makes beings personal and Omega is supremely centred.

22. Secondly, individual: in other words distinct from (which does not mean cut off from) the lower personal centres which it super-centres (a very different thing from confusing together) as it associates them in its unity (cf. section 28). Omega possesses an ego proper to itself and distinct from ours. This results from the mechanism of a centrogenesis which, at every degree, allows the higher centres to emerge only if they respect, and even complete, the centric plurality of the elements on which their complexity is built (cf. sections 27 and 28).

23. It is partially actual, too – that is to say, it is already capable of acting upon us as an object that is *present*. Omega, in the form that the evolutionary structure of the world demands for it, is much more than the 'real' image which is destined to take shape in the future at the focus point of the convergent universe. It is as a *source* of light that it acts. Is it not Omega that causes to spring up and maintains *here and now* the fascicle of radial ties (cf. sections 6 and 30)? And is it not Omega again, as we shall see later, whose love, felt at this moment (for there is no love except *in the present*), is the only agent that can polarize the collectivity of man without mechanizing it?

24. Finally, it is partially transcendent, which means that it is partially independent of the evolution that culminates in it. If Omega were not in some way emancipated from the conditions of time and space, it could neither be present for us – nor (since it would itself be completely subject to inexorable entropy) could it be the basis for the hopes of irreversibility without which centrogenesis, from man onwards, would

cease to function (cf. sections 15 and 30). Thus it is through one aspect of itself, different from that in which we see it take shape, that it has been emerging since all time above a world from which, seen from another angle, it is nevertheless in process of emerging. And it is precisely in the meeting of these two halves of itself (the emerged and the emergent) that universal unification, in the form of a 'bi-polar' union, moves towards its completion.

25. So defined in its nature and properties, Omega in very truth stands radiant in the heaven of the future as that which provides the momentum for centrogenesis and serves to make it completely total. Drawn by its magnetism and formed in its image, the elementary cosmic centres are constituted and grow deeper in the matrix of their complexity. Moreover, gathered up by Omega, these same centres enter into immortality from the very moment when they become eu-centric (that is, personal) and so structurally capable of entering into contact, centre to centre, with its supreme consistence (cf. section 30).

26. *Note on the 'formal effect' of complexity.* In developing the foregoing theses, I have taken as my basis the fact, clearly evident in man and 'traceable' throughout the whole living series, that the centricity (the consciousness) of a being increases with its complexity. Underlying this experiential, and undeniable, interdependence of the two variables (centricity and complexity) we can distinguish a fundamental ontological relation between *being and union*; it may be expressed in two converse and indubitably complementary forms:

1. The one passive: '*Plus esse est a* (or *ex*) *pluribus uniri*' (passive evolution).

2. The other active: '*Plus esse est plus plura unire*' (active evolution).

To examine more deeply these two *metaphysical* axioms would seem beside the point for my thesis, since whether they are more true or less true would make no difference to the *physical* law of recurrence on which I have relied. On the other hand it is, I think, worth emphasizing the fact that if the law of centro-complexity is studied in its phenomenal operation, it appears and functions with a number of different modifications; and these it is important to distinguish.

a. In the domain of pre-life, the centres are built up additively, through the fitting together and gradual fusing of 'segments' of centres: *'Centrum ex elementis centri'*.

b. In the domain of the phylum, the individual metazoon, born from an egg (*centrum a centro*) complexifies upon itself by cellular multiplication.[6] It is just as though each new centre increased its own depth by itself weaving its own internal complexity.

c. Finally, in the eu-centric domain, the noospheric centre, Omega, is not born from the confluence of human 'egos', but emerges from their organic totality, like a spark that leaps the gap between the transcendent side of Omega (section 24) and the 'point' of a perfectly centred universe: *centrum super centra*.[7]

Accordingly, it is not strictly accurate (however suggestive and useful the analogy) to compare the progress of the human social consciousness to the formation of a collective brain. In the brain the thousands of millions of ordered particles (nervous fibres) act, it would appear, only through their peripheral *ego*, as assembled mechanisms much more than as a number of small 'withins' added together. In nascent super-humanity, on the other hand, the thousands of millions of single-minded

6. Initially, the metazoon seems to be formed not by the coming together and fusion of independent cells, but by non-separation of elements that have successively emerged by division from one and the same mother-cell. Cf. the case of insect colonies, which derive not from a group of associated adults but from a family that increases its own size without breaking up.

7. Or, to put it still more precisely, from the Christian point of view, Omega enters into centrogenesis in the form of a *leader-element* (the Christic centre), appearing phyletically in the noosphere and gradually subordinating all the other centres.

individuals function in a nuclear way, by a direct tuning and resonance of their consciousness. In both cases it is indeed the complexity that conditions the super-centration: but at different depths of being, on either side, in the elements employed.[8]

3. Corollaries and conclusions

Now that the main lines of the process of centrogenesis have been determined, we may, by way of conclusion, examine a number of fundamental points in which we meet again, from various angles, the properties of a world that is dominated by the law of centro-complexity.

27. *The laws of union.* From one extreme to the other of evolution, as we have defined it, everything in the universe moves in the direction of unification: but this it does with a train of concrete modifications which correct or give particular accuracy to the theoretical ideas of union we might entertain.

    a. In the first place, union (true, *physical* union) creates.

8. This brings out what truth there is in the allegedly 'definitive' criticisms levelled by Durkheim, Cournot, Tarde and others against any 'assimilation' of sociology to biology: but what it does very much more is to emphasize the injustice of those criticisms. It would obviously be absurd to *identify* a society with a group of cells (particularly if they are defined – wrongly – as without any psychic content). But it would be still more mistaken and unproductive not to recognize in social groupings the 'hominized' extension of the same mechanism as that which produced the metazoa from isolated cells. In virtue of the structural unity of the cosmos, and if man is not, to his eternal cost, to remain an 'epiphenomenon', he can be understood and his measure taken only in the light of a *generalized biology*: this simultaneously respects two things: on the one hand, the continuity, throughout all the degrees of life, of one and the same fundamental evolutionary process; and on the other hand, the essential differences that distinguish the various forms assumed by this process, according to whether they are considered in fields of higher or lower centro-complexity. There can be no sociological science except as an *extension* of physics and biology.

Where there is complete disunity in the stuff of the cosmos (at an infinite distance from Omega), there is *nothing*. And when consciousness takes a step or a leap ahead (the appearance of life through association of fragments of centres, deepening of phyletic centres, emergence of reflective centres, birth of mankind, dawn of Omega) this progress is invariably linked with an increase of union. It is not, of course, that the coming together and ordered arrangement of the centres are *by themselves* sufficient to increase the world's being; there can be no doubt, however, that they succeed in doing so under the influence of the radiation of Omega.

b. Secondly, *union differentiates*. By that I mean that by reason of their association under the influence of a centre higher in order $(n+1)$, the centres of the order n do not tend to become blurred and confused together: on the contrary, their own nature is reinforced: just like the working parts of a mechanism which can be adjusted to one another only if they are constructed in a large number of exactly determined shapes. Such are the multiple cells that make up a metazoon, and such again the nervous fibres of a brain, and the various members of an insect colony. Organization not only presupposes but also produces the complexity upon which its unity flowers. This is a fact of universal experience.

c. In consequence, *union*, when operating in the eu-centric domain of the reflective, *personalizes*. Since personalization is a *creative differentiation* (*is* creative differentiation), this third law of union does no more than sum up, link together and clarify the other two. It does this not only in the sense that the grain of thought emerges from the perfect centration on itself of complexity, but in the further sense that through centre-to-centre (that is, personal) aggregation with other grains of thought, it is super-personalized. Such again, as experience shows, is indeed the result on our human consciousness of unanimity. Whether it is a matter of a team, or of a pair of lovers, or, even more, of a mystic absorbed in divine contemplation, the psychological result is invariably the same. Far from tending to be confused together, the reflective centres intensify their *ego* the more, the more they concentrate together. They become progressively more super-centred as they come closer to one another in their convergence on Omega.[9] This, I insist, is a fact of experience: and at the same time a simple re-affirmation of the law of centro-complexity.

28. *The evolution of the personal.* 'Union personalizes.' Expressed in this new form, the principle of centrogenesis enables us to formulate, in its most intimate essence, the nature of cosmic evolution. Earlier (cf. section 5), we started by defining it as the 'transition from a lower to a higher state of centro-complexity'. We can now put it in words that are both clearer and more profound and simply call it 'a cosmic process of personalization'.

Indeed, whether we consider the initial appearance of living centres from their disconnected segments, or follow, within the phyletic centres, the gradual isolation of the nuclear within the peripheral, or observe the reflective transition of the nucleus to personal eu-centrism – or whether, finally, we extrapolate the effects on man of hominization – the direction and significance of the movement we note remain identically the same. Throughout time (of which, just like centro-complexity, it can

---

9. Hence the necessity and importance of not confusing the two notions, which are to some degree independent of one another, of *personal* and *individual*. What makes a centre 'individual' is that it is distinct from the other centres that surround it. What makes it 'personal' is being profoundly itself. We would instinctively be inclined to add to our *ego* by an increased separatism and isolation – which is an impoverishment to us. The laws of union show us that true and legitimate 'egoism' consists, on the contrary, in being united to others (provided the union be centre-to-centre, that is through love – cf. section 29); for it is only in that case that we succeed in realizing ourselves fully, without losing anything (but rather attaining the true maximum) of what makes us incommunicable. If individuality is understood in a restricted sense, as defining not the *distinction* between beings, but their *separateness*, it decreases with centrogenesis and ceases to exist (in Omega), when personality reaches its maximum.

serve to provide an absolute measure) *the personal* – considered *quantitatively no less than qualitatively* – *is continually on the upgrade in the universe.*

When we feel the circle of the noosphere inexorably closing in on us (economically, politically, socially) we should not be afraid that we shall see our own petty personality, treasured by us, founder in a blind collectivism. Submerged in this flood, or caught up in this mechanism, we are terrified of sinking back into unconsciousness. This, however, is because we have failed to understand that, like the fragments of centres that seek for one another in the pre-living zones of matter, we are still, at our level of evolution, no more than rough drafts, than pieces, of persons calling out for one another. We may, perhaps, fancy that personality is a specific property of the isolated element, of the grain of consciousness. Centrogenesis intervenes to teach us that on the contrary only the whole is finally and fully personal (provided that we position it in the only place and in the only form in which it really exists – which means Omega point). Thus we can be completely ourselves only when we give totality to one another under Omega, in the universal.

In a centro-complex universe there is no opposition but rather a coincidence between the personal and the universal.

From this point of view there is nothing disturbing in the irresistible concentration that forces us, more and more, mutually to penetrate one another on the closed surface of our planet. It is no more than a manifestation, vaster than the others, of the cosmic forces that have always been at work to unify and give profundity to the world by making it more complex.

29. *The function of love.* It is clear that the forces of love occupy a dominant position in a world whose formula is 'towards personalization through union' – since love is precisely the bond that brings persons together and unites them.

This, indeed, is confirmed by observation.

Strictly speaking, love does not as yet exist in the zones of the pre-living and the non-reflective, since the centres are either not yet linked together or are only imperfectly centred. Nevertheless there can be no doubt that it is something in the way of love that is adumbrated and grows as a result of the mutual affinity which causes the particles to adhere to one another and maintains their unity during their convergent advance. In any case, the least one can say is that, through the critical threshold of reflection, the transformation undergone by this vague inter-sympathy between the first atoms or the first living beings, as it becomes hominized, is a transformation into love. In the case of sexuality, of the family, and of the race, the transition is apparent. For a careful observer, however, the phenomenon extends much further. For the last two thousand years there has been much talk (though it often raises a smile) about a love of human kind. Is it not finally such a love that, logically and in fact, is now rising and taking distinct shape on our horizon? As soon as men have woken to explicit conscious-ness of the evolution that carries them along, and begin as one man to fix their eyes on one and the same thing ahead of them, are they not, by that very fact, beginning to love one another?

In truth, the rise in warmth on the surface of the contracting noosphere is not confined to a small group of specially favoured associations, but extends to the whole of inter-human relation-ships. And, with that, we find love emerging into the fullness of its cosmic function. To the psychologist and the moralist love is simply a 'passion'. To those who, following Plato, look in the very structure of beings for the explanation of its ubiquity, its intensity, and its mobility, love appears as the higher and purified form of a universal interior attractive power.

In a universe whose structure is centro-complex, love is essentially nothing other than the energy proper to cosmo-genesis.

That is why, alone of all the world's energies, love displays the power of carrying cosmic personalization, the fruit of cosmogenesis, right to its term. Union, we were saying, personalizes. We must never forget, however, that this is on one condition: that the centres it associates must come together not in some indeterminate way (whether by compulsion or indirectly) but spontaneously, centre-to-centre: in other words, *by mutual love.*

In short, only love, by virtue of its specific and unique power of 'personalizing complexes', can achieve the miracle of super-personalizing man through and by means of the forces of collectivization; and, in a still more decisive phase, only love can open for man the door to Omega.

30. *Physical energy and psychic energy.* From all we have so far said, it follows that, taken in its totality, the universe concentrates, as it complexifies, under the influence of an attractive force that derives from Omega. Starting with the human isosphere (the noosphere) this force takes the form of love. And it is ultimately because the presence of the common term to which all men are advancing can be distinguished deep within every man, that it is possible for them to become all of one mind. From the point of view of centrogenesis, in short, everything floats on a tide of convergent psychic energy which rises both qualitatively and quantitatively from isosphere to isosphere, in step with personalization.

This being so, what is the relationship between this interior energy, always increasing and always more 'amorized', and the goddess of energy worshipped by physicists – an energy that is always constant and at the same time (by dissipation) always more 'calorized'?

The behaviour of these two energies (physical and psychic) is so completely different, and their phenomenal manifestations are so completely irreducible, that we might believe they derive from two entirely independent ways of explaining the world. Nevertheless, since they both carry through their evolution in the same universe, in the same temporal dimension, there must surely be some hidden relationship which links them together in their development.

In order to solve that difficult problem, let us go back to the distinction we made earlier (section 8) between pre-centred (pre-living) cosmic elements and centred elements.

Omega cannot act *internally* (nor, in consequence, by attraction *ahead*) on elements of the first type, since their centres are not yet individualized. It must, therefore, set them in motion *a retro* and by some sort of external impulse.[10] Everything, *in fact*, behaves as if this setting in motion bore the characteristic of a single impulse, productive of a definite 'quantum' of actions; this is precisely the energy, subject to conservation and dissipation, with which physics is concerned.

By contrast, when we come to elements of the second type, the very fact that they are centred now allows the centric influence of Omega to get a direct purchase on them. Starting with the first of the living isospheres, a new form of 'motive power' comes into operation: this is now continually maintained (and, in consequence, continually grows greater as it proceeds from a less centro-complex sphere to a more centro-complex) as a result of the centrifying action received from above. Thus, by a sort of reversal, we find we have entered the domain of psychic energy. Even then, however, the initial centricity of the centres that are simply living is still based on the play of physico-chemical activities (the agents of the first centration – cf. section 9); in consequence, those centres are still

10. This is one explanation; but is there not another, which is simpler and fits in more smoothly? Let us admit that the attraction of Omega can make itself felt internally, even in the fragmentary (pre-living) centres (psychic energy, cf. above). In that case could not physical energy (and its over-all conservation) be interpreted as the statistical 'by-product' of a great number of elementary psychic energies (energies of atoms) which combine tangentially (section 6) and peripherally (cf. section 12), with practically no variation in number – just as the regularity of physical laws (the determinism of matter) is explained by the statistical play of a great number of infinitesimal, inorganic, free impulses (section 32, b)? From this point of view, one would have to say that everything in the universe (back to the most distant isospheres) moves in one and the same internal stream, emanating from Omega: *physical energy* being no more than *materialized psychic energy*.

radically subject, in their internal structure and interactions, to the laws of thermodynamics and statistics. They are still reversible and *perishable*.

It is only with the critical threshold of reflection that the human particles become capable, through their spiritualized peak (their 'soul') not only of being distinctly subject to the action of Omega but also of *sharing* in Omega's essentially personal consistence. They then (as does a body which crosses the dividing line between the gravitational fields of two planets) experience a reversal of equilibrium. *To the extent that* the grain of consciousness is personalized, it becomes released from its material support in the phylum. When detached from its matrix of complexity, which falls back towards the multiple, the reflective centre can at last, finally unified upon itself, meet the ultimate pole of all convergence.

Thus it is that all around us the universe, reduced to its eu-centric portion (to its essence) is continually re-shaping itself, 'omegalized' grain by grain, through death – until such time as the same phenomenon is one day produced globally and simultaneously for the whole of the noosphere – that noosphere having reached the critical limit of its organization and centration.

31. *Unity and large numbers.* One of the most interesting consequences of the notion of centro-complexity is that it brings out an intimate and direct relationship between quality and quantity within the universe. Since the cosmic centres grow deeper as a function of organic-complication, it follows directly that the perfection of Omega (the term of the transformation) defines a certain strictly determined *number*, N, of elements involved in centrogenesis – this number corresponding, moreover, to the sum of two other numbers, N_1 and N_2.

N_1: the number of grains of thought finally incorporated in the Omega centro-complex.

N_2: the number of non-reflective particles required to

obtain NI, in conformity with the laws of chance and of life.[11]

Again, this shows us a first way of envisaging the cosmic relationship between unity and large numbers. There is, however, another way, as follows: not only can the tremendous mass of particles operating in the universe be explained by the richness of the unity in which they are associated, but, what is more, it is vindicated by the support provided for the very process of centrogenesis itself by the play of large numbers.

The nature of psychic energy is such that it struggles against the forces of chance which are supreme in the domain of physical energy, and it gradually eliminates them. In so doing, however, it is obliged to come to terms with them. Then, instead of running directly counter to them it makes them, one might say, serve its own ends, making use of the twofold property chance possesses of either developing constant determinisms (physico-chemical laws) through the imposition of statistical uniformity, or, on the contrary, creating improbable combinations through repeated attempts over a long period.

This explains, in the first place, the remarkable structure of living beings, whose liberty is displayed only through and by means of a closed circle of physico-chemical and physiological determinisms, a superficial study of which might well detect no more than a bewilderingly complicated mechanism – the mechanical side of centro-complexity.

Secondly, this explains why *forces of divergence* occupy so important a place in evolution. The universe, as we have continually been emphasizing, converges upon itself. How then is it, one might ask, that all around us we can see life developing plurality and ramifying – each phylum splitting up into a continually more densely packed fascicle of individuals, races and species? The first answer I would give is that this is no

11. Thus the relationship NI-N2 would measure the 'yield' of centrogenesis for a certain quantity of work (the psychic portion, cf. section 30), itself also representing a determined cosmic constant: the world's effort, its 'travail'.

more than the manifestation of a centrogenesis that must necessarily renew its complexity at every level (cf. section 12); but I can now add that it is no more than the manifestation also of a method of *groping* in which there is a happy combination of the play of chance (which is physical) and that of finality (which is psychic).

In working on large unorganized numbers, the personalizing action of Omega can operate (particularly in the first stages) only by being on the look-out for favourable opportunities produced sporadically by chance and seizing them as they go by. The probabilities of such a chance must therefore be multiplied. In this can be seen the function of life's innumerable *try-outs*. Not, it is true, like atoms that move restlessly in every direction indifferently, but like a swarm that is attracted towards the light, the 'centred' cosmic particles exert pressure in every way and from every angle – *always, however, with a positive radial effect* – on the containing wall of their isosphere. This they continue to do until a crack is found, through which they crowd, to spread out over the next isosphere. Thus the movement extends decidedly in an upward direction, over psychic surfaces that are progressively more restricted and closed. Nevertheless, for all the control exercised by the polarizing action of Omega, convergence is effected only by means of divergencies that allow life to *try everything*.

32. *Matter and spirit*. From the sum of the above considerations there clearly emerges a particular way of envisaging the nature and the relationship of matter and spirit. This view may be summarized in a number of propositions, as follows.

a. If matter and spirit are regarded as synonyms, the former of multiplicity and the latter of unity, then they are not two heterogeneous or antagonistic things, coupled together by accident or force. In virtue of the genetic relationship (centrogenesis) which causes centricity (unity) to depend on complexity (the multiple), the two aspects, spiritual and material, of the real necessarily and complementarily call for one another, like two sides of one and the same object – or, rather, like the two terms '*a quo*' and '*ad quem*' of one and the same movement. In the field of cosmic evolution, the one chronologically presupposes, and structurally integrates, the multiple – and this, nevertheless, under the primordial influx of the transcendent nucleus, Omega (section 24), itself presupposed at the first appearance of the multiple.

b. Strictly speaking, if matter is defined as 'something with no vestige of consciousness or spontaneity', it does not exist. Even in pre-living particles, we saw, we must conceive some sort of curvature which prefigures and initiates the appearance of a freedom and a 'within'. *In fact, physical determinisms* ('laws') *are simply the effects of large numbers, in other words, of materialized freedom. This statistical materialization of the 'Weltstoff'* is, of course, most marked in the zone of 'fragmentary centres' (infinite in number and infinitely spontaneous); but it is still perceptible among centres that are higher in order, and even in the noosphere, where cases of mechanization, in the very core of human energy, are still distressingly frequent. From this point of view there is nothing in the universe except spirit, in different states or degrees of organization or plurality.

c. Nevertheless, this should not be understood as though spirit were gradually formed simply as an effect of polarization or mathematical summation, with *the totality* of the centres initially involved in centrogenesis remaining intact (and with no additions) at the term of the unifying transformation. During the process, *centres that are truly new* emerge from successive syntheses or segmentations (cf. section 26) under the influence of centro–complexity.[12] And finally, only the reflective nuclei (because they alone are capable of adhering to Omega) represent the irreversible portion of the spiritualized universe (cf. sections 30 and 31).

d. The two critical surfaces of centration and reflection (cf. figure 1), which mark out the stages of this evolution, allow us to distinguish an 'inanimate' zone, a simply 'living' zone, and

12. This is the phenomenon of *the multiplication of centres*.

a 'thinking' zone in the stuff of the world. For all that, these zones are only secondary, since they do no more than divide up a continuous psychic medium which is subject to one and the same general transformation (centrogenesis) and depends entirely, from above, on Omega.

33. *Are there other spheres?* At the psychological root of all the difficulties that men of science still raise against a spiritual interpretation of the world, there certainly lies an acute sense of the cruel lack of proportion between physical energy and psychic energy within the universe. Whether we consider the infinitesimal quantities of cosmic matter, motion and heat involved in the whole body of biological operations – or whether we concentrate our attention on the haphazard way in which the solar system (and, in consequence, organic matter) seems to have been formed – a sort of conviction seems to overwhelm the mind: the conviction of man's insignificance in the presence of the rest of nature. How can one have the courage to look in the direction of life for an explanation of things, when everything proclaims so unmistakably that life is no more than a local, momentary, accident – an unforeseeable by-product of evolution?

The considerations outlined in this essay will, I hope, have helped the reader to break the spell of this false evidence. The notion of centro-complexity provides us with a sure criterion by which to judge, in their 'absolute magnitude', the cosmic value of beings, and in consequence objectively to establish the primacy of spirit: but it does even more – *it explains to us* (through the links it discloses both between quality and quantity, and between finality and chance, cf. section 31) *why* consciousness, this unique essence of things, can appear in the history of the world only in the form of a *rarity* and an *accident*, without thereby being an *accessory* or an *incident*.

To complete our rescue from the vertigo induced by our own insignificance, and at the same time in order to drive right home the explanatory power of centrology, I cannot do better than to conclude by recalling this fact: in spite of the extraordinary coincidence of chances (two stars in collision) which the birth of planets presupposes, there is no proof that the same chance has not been at work, or may not still occur on more than one occasion in the immensities of time and space: there is no proof, in consequence, that in conformity still with some law of large numbers many obscure stars, many earths besides our own, may not already be scattered, or may not still be expected, among the galaxies.

In this hypothesis, which has positive likelihood on its side, the phenomenon of life and more particularly the phenomenon of man lose something of their disturbing loneness. And at the same time it is the vistas of centrogenesis that are fantastically magnified, without distortion, to a further order. Indeed, if there have been, if there are, if there are going to be, n earths in the universe, then what we have earlier called 'spheres', 'isospheres', and 'noospheres' no longer embraces the whole but applies only to an isolated element (a mega-particle) of the total phenomenon. With centro-complexity dealing not simply, now, with grains of thought upon a single planet but with as many noospheres as there will be thinking planets in the firmament, the process of personalization takes on a decisively cosmic aspect. It is almost more than our minds can dare to face.

The law of recurrence, however, remains the same. And there can still be only one single Omega.

Unpublished, Peking
13 December 1944

The Analysis of Life

I. THE PROBLEM

NOTHING in the world around us is more obvious than the existence – indeed, the *fact* – of life: and nevertheless nothing is more elusive, more difficult to pin down, than this same life when we try to handle it by the general methods of science. As experienced in ourselves, and as it seems to develop in the course of time, the living being is consciousness, freedom, and finality. As soon, however, as we try to look at it under the microscope, or to submit it to instruments of measurement, all that we can distinguish even in the very depths of this same living being is a pyramid of associated chances and interwoven mechanisms, without apparently a single crevice in which to accommodate the intervention of the conscious and guiding action of the least free factor. In the eyes of the modern biologist, the orthogenesis of living groups tends to be reduced to a random interaction of chromosomic encounters, and the most spontaneous animal seems to be no more than a 'sum-total of assembled reflexes'. Thus the whole phenomenon of consciousness, when submitted to scientific investigation, gives the impression of dissolving and melting away, like an illusion, in the uniform flood of a universal determinism: as well might one try to grasp a rainbow.

II. A GENERAL ANSWER

Many biologists, baffled by this singular capacity that life displays of dissolving into non-life, believe that they are now forced to jettison it, as a pseudo-reality and a mirage. Surely, however, this is simply because their eyes are still closed to the fundamental and mutually opposed operation of synthesis and analysis in the general structure of the universe. In every field, the mere organic combination of a number of elements inevitably brings about the *emergence* in nature of something completely new (something 'higher'). Conversely, the suppression of a combination, no matter what it be, causes something to disappear. Seen under too great a magnification, the finest of paintings is reduced to shapeless blotches, the purest curve to divergent strokes, the most regular of phenomena to disordered turbulence, the most continuous movement to jerks. Bearing that in mind we can hardly wonder that under the solvent, 'occulting', influence of analysis the living being, in turn, is reabsorbed into unconsciousness, chance and determinisms, while all the rest – all, I mean, that is specifically living – slips through the mesh of the filter. The analogy between the two cases is too obvious to allow any doubt. In both the 'trick'[1] is certainly the same.

It would be naïve, therefore, to believe that if we are to solve the matter-life antinomy each of the two must be sacrificed to the other. All we have to do, in fact, is to establish an acceptable structural relationship between the two opposed terms, which will explain how there can, by synthesis, be an ascent from one to the other and, *reciprocally, a descent by analysis*.

There we have the whole problem.

III. THE EMERGENCE OF LIFE

Reduced to its essence, the scientific problem of life may be expressed as follows.

Having admitted the two major laws of the conservation and dissipation of energy (to which physics may be reduced), the problem we have is to superimpose upon them, without contradiction, a third universal law (in which the whole of biology is summed up), that of the *organization of energy*. In the language of the atom, science tells us, cosmic evolution represents, for the indestructible grains of energy which make up the universe, the transition from an initial heterogeneous distribution (im-

1. Père Teilhard uses the English word. (Tr.)

probable, but nevertheless without order) to a final homogeneous (that is to say the more probable) distribution. How are we
to conceive that in the course of this process, at once conservative and entropic, a portion of the grains of energy is gradually
withdrawn, in such a way as, for a time, to build up the
organic associations, *progressively more improbable*, which living
beings constitute? and this in such a way, again, that beneath
the biological arrangement so produced the physico-chemical
arrangement be respected, so that at any moment it may again
be revealed by analysis?

Let us see what we can do to solve this problem.

In order to do so, it is not, I believe, necessary to modify the
starting point accepted by modern atomic science, which is the
initial existence of a mass of granular energy, distributed in a
way which is at once without order and improbable; all we
have to do is slightly (but even so decisively) re-touch the
picture which is normally drawn of the primordial grain of
energy itself. Hitherto this elementary grain has always been
regarded as without any vestige either of consciousness or of
freedom. Supposing, however, we define it as possessing the
three following properties:

1. A rudimentary 'within' (or immanence).

2. A radius and effective angle (both as narrow as you please)
of self-determination.

3. A psychic polarization, producing a fundamental tendency
to associate with other particles in such a way as to form with
them progressively more complex units: the effect of this
complexity being (in virtue of a primordial and essential
property of cosmic being) to increase simultaneously the
degree of immanence in the particle which develops it, and its
possibilities of choice.

It will be noted that, initially at least, this threefold correction
in no way alters the universe of the physicists.

What happens is that on the one hand, *in virtue of the play of*

large numbers, the orderless multitude of elementary consciousnesses, taken as one mass, behaves exactly as though it were
devoid of any 'within'; in other words it develops exactly the
same over-all determinisms as those produced by the primordial
granular energy of the physicists.

On the other hand, *the radius of choice* allowed to each
elementary particle can be drawn short enough to remain
within the sphere of indeterminacy recognized by the most
extreme determinist science as a specific attribute of the
infinitesimal. To put it in another way, the 'creation' of
energy involved in the choice (what we may call in this
context 'choice-energy' or 'choice-quantum') can be conceived as being of an order of magnitude so small that it has no
appreciable effect on the sum total of universal energy.

At the starting point, then, there is no measurable change in
the conditions of the universe. With time, however, the
effects produced by the three corrections we have applied will
gradually make themselves felt. Initially, the play of chance
which shuffles the grains of energy continues unaltered; but
once two particles of appropriate psychic affinity happen to
brush against one another within their 'radius of choice' (and
in its effective angle), then, exercising choice, they will fasten
on to one another. And so a movement is triggered off which
nothing can then halt. Gradually, step by step, an organic
heterogeneity develops around this first nucleus of improbability; it extends itself – always, it is true, at the whim of
chance, but constantly in a definite direction: the direction of a
continually increasing complication and unification. It is a
phenomenon that would be inconceivable if the particles were
completely 'inanimate', but is perfectly intelligible if they are
both rudimentarily free and polarized.[2]

2. At our own level, indeed, we find an echo, or even an exact extension, of
this process of organization in the way in which, in daily life, any business
or research or religious association is set up. It starts by two or three individuals who are inspired by the same plan meeting by chance. After that,
as chance circumstances and the grasping of opportunities determine, the

Now let us consider a little more closely how the double play of determinisms and of chance is respected around and within the growing nuclei of complexity and consciousness, and how it adapts itself to them. In this context, three observations are called for, and they must be carefully understood.

First observation

During the building up of organic complexes, there is no necessity for the quantity of 'choice-energy' to increase with the degree of consciousness. A greater variety and a wider radius of indeterminacy become apparent as one rises higher up the scale of beings: but neither the one nor the other is ever obtained except through the amplifying action of mechanisms which (just as industrial servo-motors do) make it possible to produce, from an extremely small initial impulse, effects as exact as they are powerful. There is nothing therefore to forbid the notion that 'choice-energy' represents an invariable cosmic quantum – the same in the atom and the human brain.[3] This, when the whole question has been weighed up, would explain the paradoxical fact that freedom can grow indefinitely in the universe without producing any appreciable increase in the output of universal energy. In short, the development of life does not interfere with the release of the material energy of the cosmos, because it can ultimately be reduced to a series of

---

nucleus grows and the ramifications reach out further. Finally, by the mere association of pre-existing units and relationships, with no breaks and no alien intrusion into the system, a new organism is found to have been born into the milieu of man.

3. This is perhaps too loosely expressed. It would be better, in the case of complex centres, to say that the 'choice-quantum' makes itself felt in a control (organic and centred) exercised by each complex centre on the *sum total* of all the elementary 'choice-quanta' which that complex centre integrates in its complexity. From that point of view, the human 'choice-quantum' would be co-extensive with the global totality of the human body – the control levers being, moreover, collected and distributed in the system of nervous determinisms (mechanisms).

infinitesimal arrangements, each one of which calls for only an infinitesimal impulse – and all this *within a fringe of indeterminacy* which molecular physics itself recognizes in material reactions.[4]

Second observation

As, under the influence of a growing complexity, the 'radius of choice' increases and opens up to a wider angle, so the cosmic organic centres exercise a continually more effective control over the chance in which they are adrift; but it is always only with *the chances they make use of* that they gradually build up the fabric of their finality. This explains two things: first, the localization of the phenomenon of life in the narrow confines of time and space; and secondly, the enormous part played in biological evolution by *tentative probing*. Traces of this can be seen everywhere in nature (think of all the trial and error, all the oddities, all the uselessness, all the setbacks, in the zoological world), and in the mechanism that is still at work at the very core of our spirituality (recognizable even in the birth and maturing of our loftiest concepts). In truth, if we study it care-

---

4. We may in consequence say that the physicists' principle of indeterminacy does not prove the existence of a measure of freedom, but *makes allowance* for it in the world of atom.

Editorial note: Louis de Broglie writes as follows on the principle of indeterminacy: '. . . no process of measurement can give us the exact position of a corpuscle in space and its momentum, or the energy of a corpuscle at a well-defined moment of the interval. Interpreting these conclusions in a quantitative form, Heisenberg has expressed them by inequalities connecting uncertainties . . .' (*Physics and Microphysics*, Hutchinson, London, 1955).

'The ultimate question, which Einstein has often stressed, is whether the current interpretation with its exclusive use of a purely statistical ψ wave is a *complete* description of reality, in which case indeterminism would be a physical fact and we could never hope to give accurate descriptions of atomic events within the framework of space and time, or whether, on the contrary, the interpretation is incomplete' (Louis de Broglie, *New Perspectives in Physics*, Oliver & Boyd, Edinburgh, 1962).

fully, all life, and all thought, is simply the seizing and organizing of chance.

Third observation

If, then, we take an over-all view of the cosmic process of vitalization on the earth, we must distinguish absolutely two principal phases in the phenomenon.

During a *first phase*, the grains of consciousness arrange themselves spontaneously *in mechanisms*, in such a way as to construct the selector-switches and amplifiers (the 'servo-motors') required to widen the 'angle and radius of choice' around psychic centres: the consciousness of these latter, moreover, increasing in direct ratio with their field of action. At this stage, since the elementary consciousness is still too imperfectly centred, one can join up with another only super-ficially, in some external common function; thus their association can as yet result in producing no more than a *syn-ergy* (the most finished example of which is the human brain).[5]

During *a later phase*, on the other hand, which starts with man, the psychic nuclei are sufficiently centred to be able to come into direct contact and communication, that is to say from one consciousness to another; in consequence a new sphere of complexity and a new form of energy are introduced into nature:

– the sphere of *syn-psychic* arrangements and associations (which are not simply a grouping together of activities, but one of souls); of these, so far as we can see at present, a planetized mankind would appear to be the highest term.

– and then, to control this immanent network of 'inter-centric' operations, *spiritual energy*: the energy of sympathy and attractive power in which, to some degree, there is a con-tinuation of the play of chance and the materializing effects of large numbers. It is an energy, however, whose law is no

5. An intermediate example between 'syn-ergy' and 'syn-psyche' is to be found in insect colonies, which are lower and rudimentary forms of human society.

longer conservation in dissipation but an intensification that increases until the complete organization of the 'centrified' portion of the world in the unity of the 'focus-point Omega': this latter is the ultimate source of the impulse that drives the initial dust of the cosmos in the upward, improbable, direction of higher complexes.

It is conceivable that at the term of this evolution (at the death, that is, of each individual man, and at the death of mankind) the hominized essence of man may be released from, and continue to subsist outside of, the machinery of physical energies within which it developed – for those energies, far from representing the fibres from which consciousness is born, are on the contrary no more than a veil which provides a statistical integument for the interplay of conscious centres. We should note, moreover, that this escape of spirit or its volatilization outside matter can ultimately be reduced to no more than the disappearance of a group of 'points or quanta of indeterminacy' in the cosmos;[6] it cannot therefore produce any perceptible repercussion on the general behaviour of universal determinism.

CONCLUSION

A world such as we have just been envisaging satisfactorily meets the conditions of the problem of life and matter in the form we expressed it in. While such a world possesses immanence, the power of choice, and finality, both in its totality and in its most elementary terms, nevertheless it displays these properties only in virtue of an infinite number of chances and mechanisms which are *imperceptibly* selected and associated: thus scientific analysis can break it down completely without meeting the least measurable vestige or intervention of consciousness, freedom, or finality.

This answers our original question.

6. Or, more exactly, 'of *an arrangement* between points or quanta of indeterminacy in the cosmos' (cf. p. 135, n. 3).

Here we should note (and this is well worth while) the close kinship that links together two intellectual attitudes to the problem of life that are considered to be irreconcilable. In spite of the apparent paradox, the man who believes in the creation of fixed species and denies the evolution of life on the ground that if it is examined in detail over very short periods of time it can be reduced to stable segments, falls into exactly the same sort of mistake as the materialist evolutionist who denies consciousness and freedom on the ground that the living being can be broken down into a system of elementary mechanisms. In both cases we can detect the effects of the same 'analytical illusion' – in one it materializes spirit, in the other it immobilizes movement. For all the difference in the consequences, the principle behind the mistake is the same. If we restore 'the effect of synthesis', then the two contradictory points of view immediately combine in the perspective of a vitalist evolutionism – the only evolutionism that embraces the whole of the phenomenon of life considered at all its levels simultaneously.

Unpublished, Peking
10 June 1945

Outline of a Dialectic of Spirit

In the course of its attempts to give clarity and coherence to the universe around it, the human mind does not work only through repeated tentative probings. It advances, too, in a succession of oscillations between the more known and the less known: each higher step taken in penetrating the less known allowing it the better to see (by stepping down again) the more known, and then to rebound towards a more advanced understanding of the less known. So the process continues in successive reflections. There is no continuous upsurge, but a spark that leaps to and fro: such is the mechanism of our vision.

It is from not having sufficiently noted this law of alternation (clearly indicated though it is in my writings, particularly in *How I Believe*[1]) that some readers have thought that they could detect 'pantheism' or 'naturalism' in the various essays in which I have tried to define the line followed by modern man in his quest for God.

In order that there may be no possibility of misunderstanding in the future, I think it will be well to put forward here the successive stages, clearly marked-out, of my apologetics – or, if you prefer the term, of my dialectic.

I. FIRST STAGE: THE PHENOMENON OF MAN, AND THE EXISTENCE OF A TRANSCENDENT GOD

Let us start by placing ourselves at the heart of the cosmic phenomenon: let us, that is, look at the universe around us in the linked totality of its psychic, temporal, and spatial dimensions. Within this limitless inter-dependent immensity, a rising current of complexification accompanied by consciousness can

1. Collins, London, 1969.

be distinguished, running counter to a general trend towards loss of tension and disintegration.

We must grasp this law of recurrence and try to follow it in all its implications. It is, I believe, the original thread which, through successive reinforcements, may well become the axis of a true and complete faith.

So far as our experience extends, it is in the individual human organism that the law of complexity and consciousness culminates at this moment in the world. Now, even if (through the appearance of the phenomenon of reflection) it does momentarily so culminate, everything goes to show that it has not reached its term at this point. Is there not in fact, beyond the isolated brain, a still higher *possible complex*: by that I mean a sort of 'brain' of associated brains? And, if we look at the problem carefully, is it not in this direction that the continually more unified mass of mankind is evolving organically, under the irresistible influence of a cluster of geographic, ethnic, economic and spiritual factors? From this point of view, the natural evolution of the biosphere is not only continued in what I have called the noosphere, but assumes in it a strictly *convergent* form which, towards its peak, produces *a point of maturation* (or of collective reflection).

If we now turn to this apex of the cone of terrestrial evolution and examine it, we shall see in it two groups of remarkable and contradictory properties.

In the first place, it is unique, and therefore final. Unless we are to imagine (a thing that is supremely improbable) that our noosphere may one day come into contact with other sidereal noospheres, collectively reflective mankind confronts nothing but itself. In these circumstances, it is impossible to conceive a further complexification which would determine a higher consciousness. Our law of recurrence automatically ceases to operate.

At the same time, however, this apex can be seen to bear within it a fundamental demand for irreversibility. In the case of an isolated human consciousness, really close introspection will already detect the radical incompatibility of 'total death' and 'reflective action'; this grows more pronounced and becomes glaringly obvious in the case of a collective, disinterested, human effort – and in consequence it tends to attain its maximum in a mankind that has become fully conscious both of the vast burden of its toil and of the value of its achievements.

It follows from this that, precisely in virtue of the process that draws him along, man sees himself drifting towards a final position in which:

a. organically, he cannot go further (even collectively) in complexity, nor therefore in consciousness;

b. psychically, he cannot accept the possibility of retreat;

c. and cosmically, he cannot even remain where he is,[2] since in our 'entropic' universe, to cease to advance is to fall back.

This can mean only one thing, that when the curve of the phenomenon of man reaches this ultra-critical point of maturation, it breaks through the phenomenal system of the cosmos, and asserts the existence, ahead and beyond, of some 'extra-cosmic' pole: in this is integrally gathered into one and definitely consolidated all the reflective incommunicability that has successively been formed in the universe (and more particularly on earth) during the course of evolution.

Seen as we ascend, from our side of things, the peak of the evolutionary cone (Omega point) stands out at first on the horizon as a centre of purely immanent convergence: mankind totally reflected on itself. On closer examination it is evident that if this centre is to hold together it presupposes behind it, and deeper than it, a transcendent – a divine – nucleus.

2. A hypothesis, moreover, that is psychologically untenable. When mankind has arrived at maturity, it must be conceived as having attained a maximum not only of its demand for irreversibility, but also of its acceleration (of its vital force) towards a continually increased consciousness. Far from conceiving it as at rest, we must picture it as in a state, looking forward, of supreme imbalance. To halt mankind would be to kill it.

Thus we reach a point in our dialectic where we have to reverse the direction of our reflection.

II. SECOND STAGE: EVOLUTIONARY CREATION AND THE EXPECTATION OF A REVELATION

God (the transcendent aspect of Omega), in the first rough picture we form of him when we follow the road on which we set out, is seen to be, in short, not simply a *hyper*-centre but at the same time necessarily an *auto*-centre. Since through at least one, and that the most central, part of himself, he is transcendent (that is, independent of evolution), it means that in virtue of this centre of himself he subsists in himself, independently of time and space. This is as much as to say that, as experienced by us, he behaves as an ultra-centre of convergence which is not simply potential but eminently *actual*.

In consequence, it is the humano-cosmic phenomenon which, by reaction, is profoundly modified in our eyes. Initially, we could only see in it (or we could not but see in it) an autonomous spontaneous movement producing a rise of consciousness. We now find that this flux is a tide produced by the action of a supreme star. If the multiple is unified, it is ultimately because it is *subject to a pull*.

If, proceeding from that, we fully analyse this new relation between what is more known and what is less known in our experience, we shall become aware of an unexpected aspect in it. Between God who draws and the elements of the world that are drawn, it is clear that the lines of force are, by nature, in proportion to the psychic quality of the elements: God draws them to the full extent that they are capable of being drawn. This is as much as to say that in the case of man (a centred, that is, a personal being) the descending influx of the divine hyper-centre can and must bear the evident character of being centric, that is to say personal.

Once again, then, as for a second time we ascend the thread of the universe (henceforth seen as *impelled* forward) we are

introduced to God at the summit – this time more profoundly:
a. not simply, in the first place, as pole of consistence, but as prime mover ahead;
b. not simply, secondly, as physical or biological prime mover, but as psychic prime mover, addressing himself, in us men, to what is most human in us – to our intelligence, that is, to our heart and to our power of free choice.

And this ultimately means that we are now faced by the question of determining whether, still overlooked by us in our examination, there may not be a hidden *message* in the complex flux of evolutionary energies which pour into us.

III. THIRD STAGE: THE CHRISTIAN PHENOMENON AND FAITH IN THE INCARNATION

And it is at this point, at the heart of the phenomenon of man, that the problem of Christianity makes itself felt and demands our attention. Historically, starting with the Man-Christ, a phylum of religious thought appeared in the human mass, and its presence has never ceased to have an ever wider and deeper influence on the development of the noosphere. Nowhere, outside this remarkable current of consciousness, has the idea of God and the deliberate act of worship attained such clarity, such richness, such coherence and such flexibility. And all this has been sustained and fostered by the conviction of responding to an inspiration, a revelation, from on high. At the source of this mystical 'vortex' which possesses such remarkable vitality, should we not recognize the creative flux at its maximum intensity – the spark leaping the gap between God and the universe *through a personal milieu*? The word, in fact, that we were justified in expecting.

It is, in very truth, a crucial choice, and one upon which everything else depends. Just, indeed, as our refusal to appreciate the organic value of the fact of society would (in the first stage of this dialectic) remove any reason for our believing in an ultra-human continuation of evolution, so here again our refusal to recognize the fact of Christianity would mean our seeing the vault of the universe, which for a moment opened up overhead, once again hermetically sealed against us.

If, on the other hand, we take the step, if, that is, in conformity with reasonable probability, we are ready to see in the living thought of the Church the reflection, adapted to our evolutionary state, of the thought of God – then the forward movement of our spirit can again be resumed. And if for a third time we ascend to the peak of things we see him not simply as a centre of consistence, nor simply as a psychic prime mover, nor even simply as a being who speaks, but as a Word who makes himself incarnate. If the universe is rising progressively higher towards unity, it is therefore not only under the influence of some external force, but because in that unity the transcendent has made itself to some degree immanent. This is the lesson of revelation.

Before we continue we must stop for a moment at this point in order to see what the step we have just taken entails, and what new contribution at the same time it makes to the nature of our adherence. Hitherto, in our anticipations of fuller-being we had proceeded entirely by the way of reason, our successive intuitions remaining within the scientific framework of 'hypothesis'. As soon, however, as we admit the reality of a *reply* coming from on high, we in some way enter the order of certainty. This, however, comes about only through a mechanism not of mere subject-to-object confrontation but of contact between two centres of consciousness: it is an act no longer of *cognition* but of *recognition*: the whole complex inter-action of two beings who freely open themselves to one another and give themselves – the emergence, under the influence of grace, of theological faith.

IV. FOURTH PHASE: THE LIVING CHURCH AND CHRIST-OMEGA

Once we have recognized the fact of the Incarnation (not, I

repeat, by the way of pure inference but by acceptance of an affirmation received from on high), then we are in a position again to return to what is more known and so see more deeply into the nature of the Christian phenomenon: not just the teaching Church, now, but the living Church: the seed of super-vitalization planted at the heart of the noosphere by the appearance in history of Jesus Christ: not a parasitic organism, duplicating or distorting the evolutionary cone of man, but an even more interior cone, impregnating, taking possession of, and gradually uplifting the rising mass of the world, and converging concentrically towards the same apex.

This takes us in conclusion, by a final ascent to the less known, to a last and supreme definition of Omega point: the centre, at once one and complex, in which, bound together by the person of Christ, may be seen *enclosed one within the other* (one might say) *three* progressively deeper *centres*: on the outside, the immanent ('natural') apex of the humano-cosmic cone; further in, at the middle, the immanent ('supernatural') apex of the 'ecclesial' or Christic cone; and finally, at the innermost heart, the transcendent, triune, and divine centre: The complete Pleroma coming together under the mediating action of Christ-Omega.

Humano-cosmic apex

Christic apex (humano- Christic)

Divine centre

= *Structure of Omega point*

Humano-cosmic cone

Christic cone (humano-Christic)

Note. In this combination it is arguable whether the humano-cosmic apex 'demands' a Christic apex. It is clear, however, that the Christic apex could not come into being without the existence of a humano-cosmic apex.

To sum up, the complete series of these ascending and descending reflections may be tabulated as follows:

	MORE KNOWN	LESS KNOWN
Phase 1.	(1) The Phenomenon of man	Transcendent Omega Ingathering centre, irreversible (2)
Phase 2.	(3) Evolutionary creation	God, mover and revealer (4)
Phase 3.	(5) The Christian phenomenon	God incarnate (6)
Phase 4.	(7) The living Church	Christ-Omega (8)

An examination of this table calls for the following comments:

1. That a number of my essays may have caused some bewilderment is generally due to the fact that, since I was writing for non-believers, my argument did not go beyond phase 1. If in other writings again, I may have given the impression of jumping directly from (1) to (8), it is either because, presuming my readers to be sufficiently informed, I did not think it necessary to distinguish the intermediate stages (to set out the intermediate operations) – or because there is a real difficulty, for a mind that is *already Christian*, in thinking of Omega (even at its elementary stage 2) without realizing that its function of gathering up and uniting necessarily implies that it is, in one way or another, to some degree involved in the world (cf. Duns Scotus's views on the necessity of *some* form of Incarnation).

2. In any case, the great advantage of the dialectic suggested here is that from the initial steps (phase 1) it shows that we must admit not only the mere existence of God but a *qualified* existence – this, acting as a *unitive* rather than an efficient cause, is from the outset seen by us to be clothed in the actual powers

and dimensions of the world. This stuff of the cosmos then enters into all the later determinations of Omega, up to and including Christ, so that nothing is left of the conflict that seemed as though it could not but introduce an ever more dangerous opposition between the majesty of the universe and the primacy of God.

Unpublished, Paris
25 November 1946

The Place of Technology
in a General Biology of Mankind

MAN has entered the age of industry, and this brings with it socialization. Let us examine the significance of this great fact which is inaugurating a new era.

Should we see in it a sort of dead weight bearing down on the shoulders of mankind, crushing it beneath the mass of processes it has discovered, something that calls to mind the gigantic phenomena of animal forms, the infinitely prolonged tusks of the great elephants, the huge shells which the molluscs build around themselves, to name only a couple?

Or, so far from being a parasitic adjunct, a meaningless step, may not the fact of industrial development have a profound significance; may there not be beneath it a biological reality which can serve as a signpost to our minds?

It is this reality that I hope to bring out by showing that the progress of industry is not accidental but constitutes an event that can entail the most far-reaching spiritual consequences.

For our starting point, let us go a long way back. If we are to understand the place of technical skills in human society, we must begin with the general progress of the world's evolution. We may look on this evolution as a development of life that includes a progressive rise of consciousness; consciousness for which, before it became reflective, the way was paved by the 'interiority' of things: things have a small-scale 'within'.

The rise of consciousness can be explained by a very simple and very clear law which I call the law of complexity and consciousness. It is necessary to emphasize the relationship between organic complexity and consciousness. For a long time there seemed to be an irreconcilable opposition between life and matter. It used to seem impossible to build a bridge between physics and biology, but a deeper appreciation of their relationship is now tending to eliminate that impossibility.

Physical science has made us familiar with the idea that certain magnitudes amount to universal properties that are perceptible only in certain conditions. We know that the mass of a body varies with its speed, but the change is perceptible only when great speeds are attained. Similarly, metals do not appear to us to give off radiation at all temperatures; but a piece of iron heated to 500° C gives off red radiations. Nevertheless, this does not prove that there was no radiation earlier.

Why should we not apply the same idea to life, as follows: supposing we divide the world into two parts – on one side, matter which has no roots in mass consciousness, and on the other side the living being. Would we not be justified then in saying, 'But – interiority, the rudiment of consciousness, exists everywhere; it is only that if the particle is extremely simple, the consciousness is so small that we cannot perceive it; if there is an increase in complexity, this consciousness comes out into the open and we have the world of life'?

Thus, when we reach an order of combined atoms whose number amounts to approximately a million, we meet these remarkable bodies, the viruses, which, without yet being living, display certain properties of life. And if we move up to still greater complexities, we find particulate elements in which consciousness can be seen unmistakably as a manifestation of life.

Seen from this angle, life, 'the within', is a universal property of things, perceptible only at certain extreme degrees of the complexity of matter; consciousness properly so-called is the property specific to very large complexes; it is a result of them. (To estimate the complexity of a living being, one would have to know all the degrees of inter-arrangement of the atoms.)

This can all be represented geometrically in the form of an ellipse of which one focus is complexity and the other consciousness. Without going into the question of the metaphysical relation between these two foci, I may say that it is just as though being were progressively propagated between them. The most general experience of evolution may be described as the appearance of consciousness as a function of its degree of complexity.

Along the line of evolution or of the rise of consciousness, the most advanced term is man. It is in his brain that the two foci attain their obvious maximum of complexity, in that organ where thousands of millions of cells are grouped in such a way as to constitute a transmitting and receiving and co-ordinating centre of which we can form only a very imperfect idea. Can nature show us, outside the human brain, a quantity of organic matter contained in a smaller volume? Hardly! But can there possibly be anything more complex outside the individual man?

We are confronted by the phenomenon of society, of which there are at this moment two conflicting interpretations.

The first is superficial and simply says that there is nothing very special in the phenomenon of society. Men live in association because there are so many of them; there is no particular value in the whole body; the economic and juridical links we notice have no resemblance to the structures of nature.

The second interpretation has suggested itself to philosophers for many years; we meet it again in the world of Islam, and among the Florentine Platonists. But it is most of all in our time that, based on a positive knowledge of the facts, it has come into its own. Following Cournot, Durkheim, and Lévy-Bruhl, the idea of a possible extension of the organic has again been entertained. Just as man appeared as the result of a process which complexified the cells, so, in virtue of the law of complexity, might he not seek to produce a complex of a particular type involving a higher 'within', a higher psychism?

For my own part, I incline to the second view. It rests upon a large number of observed facts. Let us, then, review the points that support the belief that the social phenomenon is more akin to a biological than to a secondary phenomenon.

From the sociological point of view, mankind is not an aggregation, but forms a structural whole. The more closely science studies the problem of man, the more he seems to have appeared in the same way as the other species, in the form of a cluster of types all extremely close to one another. While, however, in the case of the other species, the different modalities of the form that has just come into being tend to diverge, man's behaviour, by reason of his high degree of psychism, is quite different. What happens is that at the level of man, the cluster folds in on itself around the planet, so that mankind forms a bulb-shaped fascicle in which individual leaves are recognizable. Numbers of potential species appear within this mass, continually forming a whole whose closing-in on itself produces a completely determined structure. The fact that man represents the system produced by the closing-up of all the leaves, would bring about another cluster. This is one reason for recognizing the natural element in the social phenomenon.

However, this is not all: if we try to form a picture of the anatomy of mankind we recognize certain characteristics that point to a special order.

Man is a being characterized by hands and a brain: he is a cerebro-manual – and cannot we recognize this character of cerebrality and manuality in global mankind?

With hands, we are in the domain of the machine; machines are discovered by the individual; the tool is handed on from the individual to the group. Then there appears this machine-entity whose joint developments are so fully integrated that moral behaviour and the machine cannot progress divorced from one another.

What is true of the hand is even more true of the brain. Is not something, itself analogous to a brain, being produced within the totality of human brains? When we think about means of communication, we notice most of all their commercial side; but the psychological side is much more important, and brings with it far-reaching effects.

This cerebroid system, discussed by Julian Huxley, presents enormous differences in comparison with an individual brain, inasmuch as the latter is governed by a thinking ego; but it is nevertheless true that we would be mistaken in regarding the totality of human brains as forming no more than an added sum. There is something more: these united brains build up a sort of dome, from which each brain can see, with the assistance of the others, what would escape it if it had to rely solely on its own field of vision. The view so obtained goes beyond anything the individual can compass, nor can he exhaust it.

Take, for example, the concept of the atom: at the present moment the brain of no single physicist can embrace the whole of it, and yet each one has a view of it that he alone can have.

In the general organism constituted by the human whole we meet a reality which can be regarded as an extension of the law of complexity. The whole of mankind may equally well be compared to an ellipse in which a focus of technical organization is allied to a focus of psychic knowledge. And from the fact that mankind is accepted as a reality with its two foci, this conclusion follows automatically – general technology is not merely a sum of commercial enterprises, a mechanical dead-weight on our shoulders, but rather the sum of processes combined reflectively in such a way as to preserve in men the state of consciousness which corresponds to our state of aggregation and conjunction.

Technology has a role that is biological in the strict sense of the word: it has every right to be included in the scheme of nature. From this point of view, which agrees with that of Bergson, there ceases to be any distinction between the artificial and the natural, between technology and life, since all organisms are the result of invention; if there is any difference, the advantage is on the side of the artificial.

In recognizing what technology is in relation to mankind, have we really touched on the essence of its value? or have we still to face the important problem of deciding whether technology stimulates human consciousness? Have the two foci attained the limit of their influence? Has man reached his ceiling? What about the future? It is here that we meet the vast phenomenon of the almost unlimited power of disposition over matter that man is beginning to acquire in his environment.

In spite of its rudimentary forms of organization and its extremely simple techniques (the collar for draught animals, the discovery of the wheel), the beginning of socialization produced important technical results and improvements in methods of transport. When, however, we turn to our own case, we observe the enormous power over the elements that man has acquired: after obtaining new organic substances and after resistors, capacitors, the electronic eye, etc.) he is still not content with manipulating the stuff of the universe, but moves on to reconstructing its very fabric; this we see in the prodigy of physicists working on the nucleus of atomic structure. Similarly, biologists are making us envisage the possibility of working on chromosomes and of modifying the powers of the organism through hormones. Psychoanalysis, too, is trying to get down to the underlying forces which control what seemed to us the most intimate core of our being.

This power means that mankind holds in its hands the means of varying the complexity of the focus on which its whole future depends. In that case, however, the other focus will come into play with equal force in order to increase its concentration. There will be an upward leap in the consciousness of man. If we look around us, can we not see that psychic energy is even now rising in quantity, in intensity, and in quality?

In quantity – and I am thinking of the phenomenon of unemployment which causes such anxiety to economists but which, to a biologist, is the most natural thing in the world: it heralds the release of spiritual energy – every pair of hands freed means a brain freed for thought. I realize that this phenomenon is still not sufficiently advanced in maturity, but from the biological point of view it shows that, granted the increase in technical resources, the available energy will rise and be directed towards the focus of consciousness.

In quantity and intensity, I said: is it beyond the bounds of possibility that we should one day succeed in constructing certain instruments capable of recording the rays emitted by thinking brains, and channelling the whole of the energy of these highly charged brains in a given direction? From the psychic point of view the earth would seem to be becoming progressively hotter, continually even more incandescent. If we consider not its harmony but its general intensity, the earth has never been through a phase to equal the present.

We can appreciate, too, that this human energy is rising in quality. I am thinking of the phenomenon of the generalization of research among men. A century ago it was a practically unknown avocation. Today a large number of men have been enthralled by the daemon of discovery, and 'observation domes' – incomplete as yet – are being built which work together and develop common views. Here we have energy properly qualified as spiritual.

From this emerges a very simple idea: through man evolution is making a fresh bound. At this moment it is like those devices in which a first rocket is launched and then a second fires and continues the movement. That, when we look at the whole body of evolutionary phenomena, is how nature acts. It reached the point of producing man, while at the same time providing, through other launching pads, for the use of other energies. And now the phenomenon seems to be starting again towards a new rise of spirit.

If, through technology, evolution is making a fresh bound, at the same time it is becoming reflective. Huxley has said that man is evolution become conscious of itself. Evolution has now to make its own choice. So long as true freedom did not exist life seemed to grope its way forward; now that man has become conscious, reflective, and responsible for the dispositions on which the rest of the process is based, a direction must be found: life can no longer proceed at random – technology brings with it the inescapable necessity of an ideology.

Two ideologies now confront one another: a materialist

ideology which defines its meaning as follows: organization is everything; in other words only the first of our two foci is truly important and real; the focus of consciousness is secondary. This view, which would appear basically to be that of marxism, seems to me completely inadequate as a solution of the problem. It does not determine the direction to be followed: maximum organization is not a direction, it is not necessarily the road towards the optimum. If everything is put into organization, the individual feels that he is jeopardizing something that is essential. To confide the whole problem of man to organization is to lead us to a total, inevitable, death, for the more complex the arrangement the more unstable and reversible it becomes. The individual man can advance only in an irreversible direction, for otherwise he loses his zest for action; and that is the supreme criterion by which technology must be judged.

The other, the ideology of the spirit, asserts: of the two foci, it is the spiritual which is the more important and controls the other. From this point of view there is a complete change: we now have a means of judging the goodness or badness of arrangements. The individual is protected in the midst of technology because his focus of consciousness is still clearly recognized; life is safe, because while it is true that the focus of complexity is unstable, the other focus centres upon itself and acquires irreversibility.

This spiritual view must be pushed to its extreme limit. It is here that Christianity intervenes with a contribution of extreme value. It is, in fact, a spiritual ideology which offers a divine centre at once emerged and immersed; by its immersion this centre is in continuous contact with energy. The more one reflects on the deep harmony which the idea of incarnation displays with the relationships disclosed by the other phenomena, the more one becomes convinced that Christianity meets all the conditions necessary for it to become the religion of progress.

These conclusions are a complete confirmation of the

relationship between technology and consciousness, the impact of technology being such as to make us develop powers of a grander order – of a spiritual order – and to force us to make up our minds on the question of a religion.

Unpublished, 16 January 1947
Written after an address given on that
date in Paris, at the *Salle d'horticulture*,
rue de Grenelle

On the Nature of the Phenomenon
of Human Society, and its Hidden
Relationship with Gravity

1. The most comprehensive way in which we can express the life-factor is to picture it to ourselves as a movement of involution on itself of the stuff of the cosmos – a movement that draws matter (obeying an exponential law) towards states that are progressively more complex and more fully centred; the degree of complexity and centration (or involution) being measured by the increase in psychic charge ('temperature'), i.e. consciousness.

2. From this point of view, psychology and sociology are tending to make it clear that man is still incompletely centred upon himself (either as an individual element or collectively); for a correlated supercentration of the individual and of the human whole may readily be anticipated (and is even already noticeable), in the direction of a super-involution of mankind on itself and under its influence: collective unification (totalization) accompanied by an increase in psychic charge.

3. That being so, if we look for the origin of the force that acts on mankind to super-involute and super-centre it on itself, we find that it lies in the pressure exercised by our planet on a human mass that has reached the limit of its expansion, and is henceforth continually more compressed on the globe on which it came into being. This pressure increases exponentially, and the stuff of man tries to escape from it; just as a body which crystallizes under pressure, its reaction takes the form of a geometrically increasing organization (with, in consequence, a similar rise in psychic charge): this corresponds exactly to the laws of life.

4. Again, if we note that the (relative) compression exercised

on mankind by the earth, is ultimately an effect of the 'astro-genetic' compression exercised by gravity on diffuse sidereal matter,[1] we are obliged to conclude that anthropogenesis (just as the whole of biogenesis which preceded it) is, when we get to the bottom of it – seen 'from below' – *a phenomenon of gravity*; this does not, however, prevent the consciousness released by vital involution from gradually developing a *specific* ascending and unitive force (a pull towards unity) which is added to, and gradually takes the place of, the original, external, force of 'compression *a tergo*'.

Looked at as a whole, the process of cosmic vitalization could be expressed in this way:

Expansion→compression (gravitational)→organization or complexification (biological)→centration and emergence (both psychic).

Unpublished, 23 April 1948

---

1. It is the pressure of gravity that produces the stars.

The Psychological Conditions of
the Unification of Man

IF there is one event that is insidiously and irresistibly engrossing our thoughts, adding every day a further complication, it is undoubtedly that of the unification of man. All around us the tide of the world's economic, political and psychic socialization is continually invading, and even submerging, the life of even the humblest.

What exactly does this strange and disturbing phenomenon represent and what is its purpose?

For a long time we could believe (we preferred to believe) that in mankind's increasing aggregation upon itself nothing was going on except a superficial adjustment of the thinking units in relation to one another, a process that would have no difficulty in finding its correct equilibrium.

Today, however, as a result of a more accurate survey of time and space, another idea is forming in our minds: that beneath the veil of the phenomenon of society, a fundamental drift of the universe towards ever more organized states may well be making itself felt: it is no longer the mere spatial movement of the earth (Galileo's) but the continuation, overhead, of an involution of the universe upon itself, an involution that first produced each one of us individually and is now collectively carrying on in the direction of the future its advance towards complexity and interiorization.

In that case, three comments should be made about our historical and biological position as men of the twentieth century.

a. First of all, by the very fact that it is the expression of a drift which is cosmic in its embrace, the movement of organico-social unification which is drawing us along indicates the most reliable direction to which we can commit ourselves, if we wish not simply to survive but to super-live. Is it not, indeed, by following the 'clew' of the world that we can hope most surely to attain the beatifying plenitude whose expectation is the mainspring of life?

b. Next, to the extent that it claims our allegiance and urges itself upon us, this movement contains in itself, again, an element of irresistibility: the combined action of the two curvatures, planetary and intellectual; compression producing (through the medium of a technical arrangement or organization) a coming together and articulation of conscious minds and thoughts. There is no way by which we can withdraw ourselves from the mould, by which we can reject the form, in which we are being cast.

c. Nevertheless (this is our third comment), it is theoretically possible for us, through a faulty use of our freedom, to succeed in escaping (to our loss) from this enforced closer relationship. In order to meet the cosmic pressure of unification man has to develop his own self-organization. He must therefore have a *deep-seated, vital, zest for self-unification.* The preparation of the world's finest food calls for an oven – heated to a certain temperature. Similarly, all the pressure of the universe on the substance of man will be powerless to make his scattered dust cohere unless his ardour for super-humanization grows keener. And this we can see clearly at this very moment when – by a curious effect of 'inertial resistance to unification' – the first reaction of individuals and nations to the sharply increasing forces of planetization is a self-withdrawal and a desperate attempt to 'keep one's own distance'.

In short, mankind's bio-economic position at the present time may be seen as follows:

The problem – the spectre, I might say – of the earth's reserves of energy and food is widely, and rightly, canvassed. There is just one thing, however, which is forgotten: it is a point which I have been emphasizing for years. Mark my word: though man stands on great stacks of wheat, on mountains of uranium and coal, on oceans of oil, he will cease to develop his unity, and he will perish, if he does not watch over and foster in the first place the source of psychic energy which maintains in him the passion for action and knowledge – which means for growing greater and evolving – from which comes unity of mind. Man will never lend himself to the forces of unification that summon him – he will never devote himself to them – for the cosmic work now going on calls for nothing short of 'devotion' – unless he *believes in them*: and when I use that word it must be understood with all the force and all the (initial) indefinite range of meaning that it has in everyday speech.

We must try, therefore, to determine

1. what sort of thing the world around must be

2. what the soul that dwells in the heart of our being must be

if they are both – like an engaged couple, we might say – to come together and harmonize with one another in the mainstream of a mutual and ever more powerful attraction.

In other words, we must try to discover the conditions – objective in the first place, and then subjective – that are necessary for the maintenance and development in mankind of the ardour that is essential to the completion of its biological growth.

I. OBJECTIVE CONDITIONS

I can distinguish two principal conditions, and to these I shall confine myself.

If man is to have the zest for self-unification – if he is to believe passionately in the value and importance of the social phenomenon in which he is involved – it is absolutely essential, it seems to me, that the universe in movement (in course of cosmogenesis) be seen by him as both open and centred *ahead*. Let me explain what I mean.

a. First, what is meant by *open*?

Imagine a party of miners, cut off when their roof collapses, and trying to regain the surface through a rescue tunnel. It is obvious that they will not continue to make their way towards the top unless they have reason to believe from some indication (a glimmer of light, a draught of air from above) that the passage is not blocked ahead of them. Similarly (though not sufficient attention is given to this) man would have no heart, no reason, to exert himself in causing mankind to advance beyond itself through unification, if the only effect of this fine effort were one day to bring it up sharp, with added force and impetus, against an impassable wall. Both astronomically and biologically, one might well believe at first, we are irrevocably dependent on, and the prisoners of, the necessarily limited physico-chemical evolution of the earth. Such a dependence and limitation would be incompatible with a *reflective* evolutionary impulse, which must necessarily be irreversible. Unless life is, in becoming capable of foreseeing the future, to halt in its own tracks, it must not feel that there is any barrier or ceiling above itself. In one way or another it must be able to divine the existence ahead of some way out by which it may, when mature, escape a total death – and this not by hook or by crook, like a shipwrecked mariner, but retaining the essential plenitude of all that has enriched it and all that it has won: and that presupposes as an incidental condition (which is my second 'natural' condition) a universe that is not only 'open' but can also be seen to be:

b. *centred* (or, which comes to the same thing, personalizing) in the direction of the future.

This, too, though often forgotten, seems to me evident. If in fact a crystalline molecule could feel and speak, it would, surely, refuse to enter into a network that did not correspond to its own system. To be so incorporated would 'kill' it. Similarly, the human particle, with its high degree of psychic self-centration, can tolerate aggregation to, or unification with, all the other particles, only if this operation respects, and increases, its incommunicable power of thinking and feeling (in its own infinitesimal way) everything – of infinitesimally centring, that is, the universe around it. However compressed upon itself by the tightening grip of the planet the human particle may be, man would rebel (he will inevitably rebel) against the progress of socialization so long as this latter does not take for him the form of a force not, assuredly, of more or less anarchical individualization but of personalization – of a force, that is, that leads not to a blind, unfeeling, collectivity, but to an association that reflects upon itself and shares a common mind: in other words a convergent and definitively centred system.

Subject to these two structural conditions of the universe of being both open and centred, let me repeat, the unification of man assumes a form that seems acceptable and possible when presented to our consciousness. The individual man has no longer any reason to reject such a transformation. What, even so, has he still to do, and what is still lacking to him, if he is to be positively and forcibly aware of its attractive power? How is this marriage of the head to be converted into a marriage of the heart?

It is here that we meet the second side, the specifically psychological (or even psycho-analytical) side of the problem.

II. SUBJECTIVE CONDITIONS

If we are to appreciate a colour or a scent, we must have good sight and a good sense of smell. Similarly, if we are fully to experience the 'zest' for super-humanization to which the nature of things calls us with such urgency, there are, I am convinced, a certain number of 'senses', to which we have so far not given sufficient attention, which must make themselves felt, must be more fully developed in us and sharpened.

At this point a comparison may help to clarify the position. As every human being emerges from childhood, there is an awakening of what we call 'the sense of sex'. Vague at first, and ill-understood by the person who experiences it, the attraction gradually takes on form and consistence, until it becomes one of the key aspects of the psychology of the grown man.

If mankind, then, is taken as a whole, would it not appear from a number of indications that – in the same way as individual human beings – it can and must go through certain 'crises of puberty', and is now, in fact, doing so?

I spoke earlier of an 'open world'. Confronted by his own increased powers and duties (which helps to bring back the centre of gravity of our most essential cares from individuals to the species), does not man at this moment feel an increase in his anxiety for the permanence of his works – in other words, is he not aware of the emergence in himself of an increased demand for irreversibility?

I spoke also of a 'centred' world. Man has always, intermittently, been attracted by – intoxicated by – the feeling of union with the whole in which he shares. Recently, however, the immensities of the universe around us and its organicity have become better understood, with the result that this elementary sense of the whole is tending to become generalized in the consciousness of men – but with this essential modification that the totality which is divined and desired no longer appears so much as a shapeless ocean in which we are to be dissolved, but rather as a powerful focus in which we are to meet as one, to fulfil and concentrate ourselves.

A clarified sense of the irreversible, a corrected sense of the universal and the cosmic: is it not true, maybe, that these new faculties or 'feelers', hitherto more or less dormant, are now in the course of a stealthy development in us – precisely at the moment when, following the rhythm of cosmogenesis, we are reaching the time, or the phase, when if life is to advance further, it must give birth to a new burst (a new supply) of impassioned and reflective enthusiasm for further progress?

And it is here that, addressing myself to those who have a professional knowledge of psycho-analysis, I would say:

'Hitherto, and for excellent reasons, your science has been primarily concerned to make the individual recognize, deep within himself, certain forgotten impressions, certain hidden complexities, with the idea (confirmed by experiment) that once these suppressions and complexes have been brought into the open and accepted, then they will vanish in the light of day.

'So far, so good. But once this work of clearing up and liquidation has been done, surely a further task of clarification – one that is more constructive and therefore more important – still needs to be done. By this I mean helping the subject to decipher, in the as yet ill-explored and imperfectly cleared-up areas of himself, the great aspirations of which I was just speaking (the sense of the irreversible, the sense of the cosmos, the sense of the earth, the sense of man). It is the converse operation to the earlier one. I mean psycho-analysing not in order to bring something out but to put something in: to make man read what is to be found in himself, not in order to get rid of phantasms but in order to give consistence and direction to, and to satisfy, certain great needs or essential demands which, for lack of being understood and voiced, are smothered inside us (and which are smothering us). It is a complex and delicate work of discovery, indeed, since both teacher and pupil, guide and follower, have equally to grope their way in this field; but it is an eminently fruitful work, for it is directed to disclosing not restrictions and defects, but the most hidden and most comprehensive motive forces in the psychic dynamism which animates us.'

In short, psycho-analysis has hitherto been primarily interested in treating forces and individual cases from the *medical* point of view. At the most, it has been concerned to open up the subject and to centre him on himself, in relation to limited groups, in particular the family, in such a way as to make him capable of the first degree of socialization. If what has been said in this contribution is correct, surely the time has come when psycho-analysis must study each man's trans-individual aspirations and so occupy itself (as a problem not of healing but of engineering) with the working out of an energetics of man (a psych-energetics), on the scale of, and for application by, a zoological group which is in process of planetary totalization.

*

To turn back now to the two instances mentioned earlier, of the sense of the irreversible and the sense of the cosmos: even if we take into account only those who are most directly committed to research and the things of the mind, how small a proportion of us have become explicitly aware either of the fact that their activity imposes a radical requirement of refusing to undertake any work that will not be *immortal* – or of the vital need rooted in their minds of finding, and instilling, ever more unity, not only in the intellectual representation of a particular domain of things but also in the ontological structure of the whole universe? What task, then, can be more urgent than that of decisively bringing out into the open these two essential ardours, and systematically fostering them in the heart of every man?

It is not without amazement and anxiety that we are witnessing the mysterious cleavage which at this very moment is tending to divide the world from east to west into two hostile blocs. Well, then: if we want to know the true reason, a reason much more profound than any power-conflict, for this, the greatest schism history has ever known, surely we must look for it in the as yet inarticulate, mutually contradictory, statements of a nascent human faith, still unable to decide, in order to express itself either in words or deeds, between totalization and freedom. If this diagnosis is correct, what is the agonized, divided, earth waiting for if not the prophet who will make plain to it the mystery of what it is *nebulously* seeking and expecting?

Let me insist again on what I was saying earlier: the future of the world, as we now see it, is tied up with some sort of social unification of man – which itself ultimately depends on the free play in our hearts of certain forces that draw us towards fuller being – forces without which all science and all technology would lose their impetus. The world, our terrestrial world, is more and more irresistibly assuming before our eyes the form of a gigantic and gigantically complicated engine, ready for every sort of operation and every sort of conquest; but it will be able to function as such on only one condition: this is that if we are to get its mechanism under way, we must find and burn exactly the type and quality of fuel that suits it. In other words, if man's earth is still undecided today in its movement – if there is a danger that tomorrow it may come to a halt – this is simply for lack of a vision of sufficient width, a vision commensurate with the vastness and variety of the effort that has to be produced.

In these circumstances, mankind must in future devote an increasing part, the major part, of its attention – without, of course, neglecting material technology, but in an effort that goes hand in hand with its progress – to the maintenance and development of its psychic energies (the indispensable animating forces behind physical energy in a universe that has become a thinking universe); it must concentrate on the exploration and exploitation of its true, and truly noble, cosmic 'libido'.

That is why, in conclusion, I urge you to the quest for a faith that will truly serve as a driving force for the world, to pave the way for that faith and to distil its essence: nor must I forget to remind you that nowhere can the elements, the seed, or even the initial realization of that faith be found more distinctly (quite apart from any consideration of dogma, and simply from the point of view of psychology) than in a properly understood Christianity: Christianity, let me emphasize, which, more vigorously and realistically than any other spiritual current in sight, never ceases to persist – practically alone in the world – in preserving and sharpening its ardent vision of a universe that is not impersonal and closed, but opens out, beyond the future, upon a divine centre.

Paris, 6 January 1949. *Psyché*
December 1948 (published in February 1949)

A Phenomenon of Counter-Evolution in Human Biology

or the existential fear

B Y this phrase 'existential fear' I do not mean simply the fear that is accidentally experienced by this or that particularly timid individual man when he is confronted by material or social dangers which his life holds in store for him. Taking the words in a much wider and deeper sense, I use them here to designate the anguish not so much 'metaphysical' (as the expression goes) as 'cosmic' and biological, that may possess every man who is sensible enough – or rash enough – to try to locate and sound the abysses of the world around him.

This is a point which cannot be emphasized too repeatedly and forcibly. Within a universe that is in a state of genesis, what is being initiated by the intellectual phenomenon of reflection is not only a revolutionary change in the very mechanism of evolution (the appearance of foresight and invention); it is also a dangerous twofold moral crisis. In the first place it is undoubtedly a crisis of emancipation, stemming from the birth of freedom; but at the same time it is a crisis of panic, akin to the psychological shock of being suddenly woken in the middle of the night.

It is, then, precisely and exclusively this second form (the apprehensive form) assumed in the consciousness of man by what one might call 'the evil, or at least the pain, of evolution', which is my present concern; and my examination of it may be summarized under the two following headings.

1. Far from dying down with the passage of time, the existential fear (as defined above) is at the present time climbing in the world towards a certain paroxysm – and that for reasons that can be clearly defined.

2. To remedy this situation – an anomaly from the point of view of evolution, and critical from the point of view of

society – the only course open to the scientific mind is to make the universe psychologically 'reassuring' by recognizing in it – what is an objective condition of survival for the species – a structure that is ontologically convergent ahead.

Let us elaborate each of these points in turn.

I. THE RISE OF FEAR

In virtue of its very definition, there is something primordial in the cosmic *Angst* by which consciousness that has become 'conscious of itself' is possessed when confronted by the world: of its nature, it is born with man himself. This does not mean, however, that it attains its most advanced states immediately. However well marked – 'critical', we might say – we should assume it to be when it first appears, reflection (and, in consequence, we must add, the phenomena of apprehension which accompany it) develops only slowly both in the group and in the thinking individual. It is this that explains the gradual intensification of the 'existential fear' at a time such as our own, when the human-individual feels that he is losing his footing in the world – a feeling (as I shall show) that, by a contrast as dramatic as it is psychologically inevitable, is more vivid, and more reasoned, than ever before at the very moment when he thought that his basic self had finally won through.

In relation to this second point, I shall assume that everyone is agreed about the general progress of history. While ethnologists note the persistence of a sort of primitive co-consciousness in communities that are socially under-developed, we have no difficulty, on the other hand, in seeing a persistent advance towards individuation in more civilized nations. Their citizens enjoy an increasing measure of autonomy (sometimes even approaching anarchy), which as recently as yesterday was distinguished by the rise of the 'democracies'. After some hundred thousand years of existence and of groping his way forward, man had never been more sharply and proudly conscious of the value and rights of each human element, as he was in the nineteenth century in the West. And yet, let me repeat, it is at the exact moment when he was thinking that he had at last found himself (and in the light, moreover, of the same illumination as that which enabled him to do so) that he has begun permanently to feel alone and lost in the world.

Let us try to analyse this feeling of terror, as aroused in us by the confrontation of our own insignificant elementary ego, never before so highly prized, whether with the universe of matter or with the universe of man – the magnitude and menace of both of which have never before been so fully realized.

a. Fear in confrontation with matter

It is, rightly enough, through the staggering vastness of its dimensions that the universe deals us the first and most violent shock that tends to overwhelm us. Of old, when the earth was still believed to be stationed at the centre of a small number of spheres revolving in a perfectly stable and well-ordered fashion around it, the starry heavens could still be contemplated with serene admiration. But since the whole of this fine system was robbed of its centre in our eyes, was expanded and flung explosively into space – since we began to reckon in thousands of light-years and in galaxies – since, too, at the other extreme from astronomical magnitudes, the immense has reappeared, for our better equipped vision, in the incomprehensible swarming of the infinitesimal – since all this opening of our eyes, the feeling of our absolute insignificance and the dismay that accompanies it are continually becoming more pronounced. Pascal's two abysses, now more accurately sounded, and complicated by two others which that great seer could not, in the seventeenth century, as yet distinguish: the abyss of number, a terrifying flood-tide all around us of bodies and particles; and the abyss of time, an endless axis around which are carried out the coilings and uncoilings of space . . . Is there anything left of ourselves – or, rather, how can we fail to feel that we are simply annihilated, wiped out – in the midst of these enormous magnitudes and this vast multitude? It is without any doubt, as each one of us knows by experience, by the shadow of its ever growing *immensity* that the cosmos first introduces anxiety into the modern soul. Soon, however, this initial cause for spiritual unease is reinforced by another, even more subtle and dangerous: and this one derives from the way in which the cosmos presents itself to our experience as 'a sealed system'.

Sealed, I repeat. That the world should be so large and so 'multitudinous' that we can have the distressing feeling of vanishing in it, is already serious enough. But it would be much worse if we could feel not only that, because of our insignificance, we were lost in this ocean for a first time, but that we were lost again for a second time because we were hermetically sealed inside it. And is not that exactly what is now happening? Until the dawn of the present era, one could say that man still had the illusion of living 'in the open air' in a universe that was penetrable and transparent. At that time there was no hard and fast boundary, and all sorts of exchanges were possible between the here below and the beyond, between heaven and earth, between relative and absolute. Might one not expect to meet a genie or a god on the high peaks, in the bowels of the earth or at the antipodes? Then, with the rise of science, we saw the gradual spreading over everything of a sort of membrane that our knowledge could not penetrate. We met the radical impossibility, as a dimensional fact, for our experience, of emerging from time and space: the impossibility, as a historic fact (whether in biology or in physics), of finding in any direction the end of a fibre of reality – except, perhaps, by getting back to a natural zero at which the universe vanishes in its entirety, instantaneously, without leaving a single trace. The impossibility, as a psychic fact, for our mind (an impossibility which repeated setbacks daily make more likely) of entering *phenomenally* into direct contact with any person or thing whatsoever of the trans-human or super-human order. The truth is, we must yield to the evidence. Just as, after many fruitless attempts, the physicists have had in the end to give up all hope of determining an absolute movement of bodies in space, so we too, in a wider and more heart-rending field, have to resign ourselves to the inevitable. In every direction we are, in a very true sense, enveloped as though in a veil with neither rent nor seam, and there is no point at which we can effect a direct breakthrough and emerge experientially from the phenomenon.[1] Thus, for all its gigantic size, the universe is our prison; and holds us in such a way that it seems that we are never to escape alive from its curvature, both geometric and psychic.

This feeling of confinement and asphyxiation is finally aggravated by the additional fact that, as a third way of destroying us, it would appear at every moment to be about to invade us from within and so bring about our disintegration.

It is immense, it is sealed – and finally, it is *hostile*.

This has been noted (Freud) for a long time. Starting with the Copernican revolution, man has continually, as the centuries unfold, felt more and more 'de-centred': de-centred first of all in the universe, by astronomy; then de-centred in the living world, by biology; and now de-centred in the innermost core of his own self, by psychology. I shall show later by what revolutionary change of perspective this impression of vanishing into nothingness is to be not only corrected but positively reversed. It remains a fact that the most agonizing experience of modern man, when he has the courage or the time to look around himself at the world of his discoveries, is that it is insinuating itself, through the countless tentacles of its determinisms and inherited properties, into the very core of what each one had become accustomed to calling by the familiar name of *his* soul. At that peak of our selves, we used to believe that we belonged entirely to ourselves, or that at least it was there that we had the full solidity of being. And now analysis, after ruthlessly dissecting the substance of our bodies, is

---

1. In so far as they are authentic, cases of mystical contact with the divine operate not through the sensorial surface of individual consciousness but through its core (and along what we shall later call the axis of convergence).

beginning to disclose a complex and delicate fabric in what had been thought our most spiritual substance. In our intelligence and in our will, we thought that we were extremely simple and very much masters of ourselves. Now, instead of that, we find with horror that we are made up of all sorts of fibres – even in those hallowed heights we are caught up in that monstrous knot – fibres that come from every quarter and from very far afield, each with its own history and life – fibres that are always ready to escape from our control and unravel.

Thus, not content with being impenetrable and without limits in its outer layers, the other (the non-human, the in-human) wells up again, through every pore, as though to dislodge and expel us, in the most intimate depths of ourselves.

When we see this, our instinctive gesture is to turn our eyes from this faceless matter, to hasten back towards 'others' and to take shelter in the human, safe and snug among men: but with only this result, that we then realize to our distress that even there – where we might have thought we were at home – exactly the same spectres were lying in wait for us, and now rise up to confront us, as those which seemed ready to devour us in the great outside world.

b. Fear in confrontation with the human

We may well believe that, just as the contemplation of the heavens, so the sight of the inhabited earth had, for our fathers, something harmless or even comforting in it. Some thousands of years of history – some millions of living beings – no cause, surely, for feeling so hopelessly lost. But now, in the merci-lessly increasing light of reflection, we find that a profound change is distorting for us the face of the social world, even when we approach it from its most civilized side. Among men at least, we used to think, it would be possible to keep things in proportion, even within a universe of such disproportionate dimensions. Clarity and individuality would be ours, in this refuge built by our own efforts. Instead of this, we now find – certain horrifying aspects imperceptibly creeping in beneath the features that seemed to us the most familiar – that the human mass, in its turn, is beginning to take on a strange and disturbing aspect. In its turn, too, we can see it becoming disfigured. And in the end we can again recognize in it the three cosmic characteristics that our minds find so terrifying, of immensity, opacity and aggressive impersonality.

First, *immensity*: we seldom have occasion to find ourselves confronted by an extremely large crowd or to feel that we are lost in one. But what our senses still perceive only in exceptional circumstances, or with difficulty, inexorable statistics are making us see ever more clearly. Soon, the figures tell us, the volume of the human river will amount to three thousand million individuals living cheek by jowl on this planet; and if we reckon the total output, in the course of the nineteenth century alone, we may estimate the number of men flowing onto the surface of the earth in that period at a hundred thousand million. On that basis, supposing we amuse ourselves by roughly extrapolating those figures not only in the direction of the past (where we would find they decrease comparatively rapidly, in spite of the great depth of time), but also in the direction of the future (where it is to be anticipated that mankind will function for hundreds of thousands of years in full flood):[2] and then, supposing we take a good look at those hundreds of thousands of millions which that adds up to, and try to understand them. Must we not admit that, confronted with such numbers, which can be compared only to those so far met by physics in its study of stars and atoms, we feel an utter collapse of our individual value and reality?

Secondly, *opacity*: the world of sensation, I pointed out earlier, causes us consternation by reason of the impenetrable membrane which the phenomenon stretches between us and all that lies above the human mind. But further, even inside the thinking bubble in which we, we men living here and now,

2. So far as the possible future of the species is concerned. Of the acceleration observable in mankind's psychic and dynamic progress, the author admitted that it could rapidly attain a critical point. (Ed.)

feel that we are irrevocably imprisoned – even there again we find the same watertight integrity (in a less marked degree, it is true, but in a still exasperating form) – for we find it in the foreignness, not to say the repulsion, which ruthlessly cuts us off from one another. Years ago Leibniz spoke of the monad: our modern existentialists echo him when they speak of the 'closed being'. Since all time, it is true, man has been suffering in a more or less nebulous way – but never, we may be certain, has he developed so vivid and widely-felt a consciousness of his interior isolation as in this age – our age – of extreme individualization and extreme introspection. To be cosmically shut up, all together, in the universe; to be shut up, as individual atoms, each on his own, each inside himself: must we accept that such is the tragedy of man's condition?

Finally, *impersonality*: and by that I do not mean a mere anonymous toughening in attitude and manners, to be found in a mankind that has grown too large for its elements – I mean a virulent force of depersonalizing intrusion which emanates from it. It is not simply the abyss in which we feel we are disappearing, but the gigantic, devouring, organism by which we feel we are sucked up, absorbed, and, one might say, digested alive: the universe in process of totalization, the universe that mechanizes and concentrates, the universe all of whose human influences, working as one, seem to be transforming themselves into one single massive force of dehumanization.

In truth, as I said at the beginning, does not it appear that the thinking individual, as yet hardly emerged psychically from animal instinct and primitive co-consciousness, can now see opening up in front of him another tunnel, much darker and more final than the earlier, while he is powerless to escape from the cosmic current that is carrying him into it? Have we come out into the light of day only to feel ourselves inexorably recaptured by night? There, surely, we get to the bottom of the modern existential anguish. But on the other hand, to have succeeded in locating and expressing this fear, which is at once physical, metaphysical and moral (for moral it undoubtedly is, inasmuch as it is shot through with an inexplicable feeling of guilt) – to have done that, is it not also, and primarily, to have found an indication, a sign, that there is something false and unjustified in such anxiety? and is that not so true that it *must* be possible, by one expedient or another, to neutralize it?

II. THE REVERSAL OF FEAR, OR EXISTENTIAL ASSURANCE

Apart from a few anti-intellectual fanatics, whose very extravagance rules them out, nobody has any serious doubt but that if the world is *to be*, it must *be thinkable*. From this it follows that its existence is in itself a positive guarantee for our reason that it does in fact possess all the properties without which it could not be fully an object of thought. This is the foundation on which every true metaphysics rests. May we not, then, in a general way and with equal force (if not precision) make use of the same argument, applying it this time to physics, simply by substituting the word 'livable' for 'thinkable'? In other words, are we not entitled legitimately to conclude, from the fact that a thing exists, and holds its own and grows *in natura rerum*, that this thing finds in and around itself everything without which, on no matter what grounds (air, food, light etc.), it would be completely impossible for it to subsist? Biological coherence thus being the complement or extension of logical coherence.

The more one considers this general economy of being and life, the more one is convinced that if, in the case of the human element which has newly arrived at the extreme limit of its individual requirements, we can recognize that there is one means, and one only, of making the cosmos breathable, then we may be sure that such a means exists – that is, that it corresponds to a real and objective structure of the world that contains us.

This is exactly what I would like to show, by giving a brief description (a specific antidote to the existential fear) of the reassuring, emancipating, properties of a *convergent universe*.

In the course of our preceding analyses, we have made no special assumption concerning the form of the multiple (animate or inanimate) in which the consciousness of man, once its eyes are opened, finds that it is immersed. A vast orderless plurality, or, at the most a plurality that is mechanically or statistically arranged – that is all we have considered (and, in fact, all that is at first apparent) in the blind dance of the elements of the world around us. That being so, may not our bewilderment and terror when confronted by time and space and number derive, perhaps, from precisely this very failure to assume any orientation in the restless motion of the cosmos?

Let us, then, construct a plausible hypothesis; and, in agreement with a great number of indications, all equally on our side, let us suppose that the universe has not come organically to rest upon itself in the course of its expansion in space – but that, in virtue of a segregation that affects the whole of its substance, it is drifting, from within, towards states of progressively more complex synthesis: the organic complexity of its stuff entailing as a specific effect an increase in its psychic innerness. In other words, and for all sorts of convergent reasons that I cannot detail here and now, let us lay it down in principle that the universe is not diverging explosively at random. Far from it: because it carries an interior 'ballast' of complexity-consciousness, it is falling and progressively concentrating, through a sort of essence of itself, upon an ultimate centre of unification and reflection. In that case, if I am not mistaken, whether in the domain of matter or in that of man, the spectres that are the objects of our terror fade away in turn under this shaft of illumination; and it is fear that is banished.

Let us see how this happens.

The universe, I said, crushes us in the first place (to a first degree) by the impact of its blind immensity; this is because, as in a forest or in a big city, we feel that we count for nothing in it; we can only trail along like lost souls. On the other hand, however, the forest and the big city – and nature herself – lose their horror and arouse love the moment we recognize around us a *radiating* system of paths, or roads, or lines of evolution, and so feel certain that, however thick the undergrowth may be, however inhospitable the district, however dark the life we are passing through, warmth and friendship and shelter are waiting for us at the centre of the star – and that we can no longer lose our way to them.

The universe, again, causes us anguish (and this time to a second degree) because of its impenetrability and opacity. Under its sealed vault, as among its echoless crowds, we feel that we are as isolated and lost as the miner in a narrow gallery, blocked perhaps, with the full weight of the rock threatening to fall on him. But supposing, in fact, the miner sees a ray of light high up above his head, supposing he feels a current of fresh air blowing on him from ahead – supposing, I mean, we ourselves, human beings busied in our work, can take hope again *because the world is converging*, can again be certain that one day the double breakthrough we are awaiting will be made simultaneously in the iron curtain – a breakthrough into the beyond through a rent in the phenomenon, and a breakthrough into other men through mutual interiorizing of souls – if that should happen, then have we not, the miner and we human beings, good reason once again to rejoice?

Finally, the universe terrifies us (at a third degree), I said, by the insidious and inexorable way in which its various determinisms (physical, biological, psychic, social) seem to be getting ready at every moment sometimes to capture and absorb us and sometimes, on the contrary, to forget us and cause us to disintegrate. Here again, however, our terror disappears of itself when, for reasons that are inherent in the very texture of the stuff of the cosmos, we recognize two things: on the one hand, that the reflective peak of our consciousness, for all its apparent fragility and instability, is in a state not of equilibrium or even retreat, but on the contrary of continual consolidation; and on the other hand, that, through the ordeal of the totalization of society, it is towards a completion of our personality that we are being driven, along the road of un-animization. What have we to fear in a universe all of whose forces, when the *whole story* is told, are working together to fulfil us?[3]

In short, while it is inevitable that the appearance of reflection shall immediately produce a wind of fear and anguish at the heart of an orderless or divergent plurality – within that same plurality, once it is recognized as convergent, it is equally inevitable that with the awakening of thought a breath of peace shall pass over the world. This is for the simple and profound reason that in a universe which 'gathers itself together', *the other*, however terrifying it may be in the ever more pene-trating eyes of our consciousness, ceases to frighten us – and rightly so – since from being alien and hostile, it becomes *patient of union*. With the retreat in the other of exteriority and distance, it ceases, I repeat, to terrify us. But, what is much more welcome, its very vastness tends to make it eminently attractive and lovable. For ultimately, the more immense the layers of the multiple, the more inevitable and all-embracing the flood that brings us together is seen to be – and the deeper promises to be the central intensity into which the irresistible whirlpool of things is sucking us. The universe was dark, icy and blind; now it lights up, becomes warm, and is animated. As though by magic, our terror of matter and man is transformed, is reversed, *into peace and assurance* – and even (for the man who knows the bliss of realizing that if a centre of cosmic attraction is to be personalizing, it must itself possess its own super-personality) *into existential love*. At last we have emerged from the labyrinth.

3. If the convergent structure of the world is thoroughly analysed in its specific properties, it entails (as can be demonstrated) the conservation and consummation in the centre-peak of all that is both incommunicable and irreversible in the universe: that is to say, all the reflective consciousness that has appeared at any moment in history.

We have escaped from our agony. We are made free. *And all this because the world has a heart.*

It is, then, with this metamorphosis, this interior reversal, before me, that I shall turn back to the line of reasoning I was putting forward a moment ago, and conclude as follows:

Given the two theoretically possible ways of looking at the reality that surrounds us – one leading most assuredly to asphyxiation and paralysis through fear – the other, on the contrary, spontaneously engendering the zest for living and the impetus for action – then, I maintain, no hesitation can be allowed between two such interpretations of the universe. And this does not apply simply to the moralist or the philosopher, but to the biologist, too, and the physicist. The organo-psychic convergence of the world is not possible or desirable only by reason of the peace of mind it brings us. Just as much as the oxygen that tangibly fills our lungs, it must be regarded as objectively and scientifically *true*: true, because it alone is capable of producing a *livable* atmosphere for our conscious-ness; and because it alone is, in a word, livable (as we should have noticed earlier) by reason of the homogeneity in the structure of the cosmos. For, if (as is proved by the phenomenon of man) our universe tends unmistakably, through each and all of its elements, to find its equilibrium at a higher level in the 'centric', there is no way in which the process could continue and culminate except within a system that is completely centred, in its totality, upon itself.

Unpublished, Paris
26 January 1949

The Sense of the Species in Man

I. THE SENSE OF THE SPECIES BEFORE MAN

AMONG animals, the life of the individual is clearly controlled, dominated even, by what one might call 'the sense of the species'. Under the complex action of automatic mechanisms and instinctive reflexes, the animal, untiringly and without understanding, never ceases working to ensure the integrity and survival of the zoological group to which it belongs: not, it is true, that one cannot already distinguish in it (at least in the case of the highest forms) a self-centred tendency in the individual to 'save his own skin'. This, however, occurs only as an exceptional or secondary manifestation. On the whole, and predominantly, the animal behaves as a link in evolution. The soma *for* the germen. Hence the sharply defined character, the impatience of adulteration, and the remarkable length (broken only, here and there, by some explosive mutation) of the phyletic lines of descent in palaeontology. All this makes itself apparent to us, to use anthropomorphic language, in the presumed existence, in the depths of every pre-human living being, of a double psychic polarization – a polarization simultaneously towards what lies ahead and towards the other: towards what lies ahead, in the form of a drive in the direction of what appears to be a greater organic complexity, which itself entails a greater degree of consciousness; and towards the other, in the form of a 'sympathetic' cohesion with the other members of the same phylum. In all cases, this double polarization is obeyed blindly. This explains the amazement we experience simply by watching ants scurrying to and fro at their work.

II. THE INDIVIDUALISM OF THE CIVILIZED

Starting with man, and as a consequence of the transition from instinct to *reflection*, a profound twofold change affects the course of action followed until then by evolution.

On the one hand, the individual (because he has become conscious of his *ego* 'to the second degree') finds that he attains a richness of life which, increasing almost without limit his own incommunicable values, makes him stand alone among his own kind, gives him an 'absolute' quality and makes him autonomous.

On the other hand, the phylum, as a result of its newly acquired ability to retain and synthesize with itself the branches that are constantly produced on its stem (instead of allowing them to diverge), tends to spread out uncontrollably in the form of an organically knit membrane or tissue, until it attains dimensions that are strictly planetary. By itself, the human 'species' constitutes nothing less than a new envelope of the globe: a 'noosphere' (or sphere of thought) above the biosphere.

There is an extraordinary accentuation of the *soma* – and (at first sight, at least) an extreme diffusion of the *germen*: two factors that operate in the same direction to upset (at least for the moment) the balance of biological values: a progressive and general granulation of the human mass: a gradual emancipation of the elements, which now, rejecting all control, set themselves up, each for himself, as the organic peak of the social structure. In other words, we have the loss of the sense of the species. Is not this, succeeding the residual co-consciousness found in primitive peoples,[1] the new orientation, the new 'orthogenesis', recorded by history for the human group, throughout the whole of the process we call civilization?

III. FORCED RE-GROUPING UNDER PLANETARY PRESSURE

It is here that a cardinal fact comes into operation, one which it is strange that we can so easily overlook: by this I mean the

1. Cf. Gerald Heard, *The Ascent of Humanity*, London, 1929.

enforced involution of the noosphere upon itself which is at the moment being initiated. From its origins until our own day, mankind (however close-knit its substance) has developed principally (or so at least it would appear) under the old aegis of multiplication and divergence. Its first concern was to occupy the earth. Now, with that first objective attained – that is, with the *expansive* phase of population reaching its term – it is becoming clear that hominization is coming under the combined and irresistible influence of two planetary curves of progress, the one spatial, and the other psychic: as a result of this we can now see it entering a *compressive* phase from which it cannot emerge. For on the closed surface of the globe a continually increasing mass of elements (each one of which has a radius of action and cohesion which grows wider as socialization grows more marked) cannot fail to extend its co-penetration and totalization more and more.

The meaning, I know, if not the reality, of this totalizing process is still a subject of argument. Does the phenomenon represent simply a materializing mechanism, a sort of retrogression or senescence – a disease of the species that must be suffered as stoically as possible? Or on the contrary has it not, rather, a biological value, inasmuch as it corresponds to the direct continuation, on a supra-individual scale, above our level, of that very mechanism of 'complexification' to which the vitalization of matter can experimentally be reduced? We have only, I believe, to note to what a degree human consciousness becomes more highly charged[2] in step with planetary socialization, to realize that of the two conflicting ways of answering the question, it is the second that corresponds to the direction indicated by the facts.

This can only mean, in that case, that now that modern man has been sharply brought back to a sense of reality by the sudden pressure around him of the forces of totalization, he

2. This rise makes itself felt today in the vigorous expansion of a scientific outlook – while tomorrow we may anticipate other more profound effects which will reach the mind's esthetic and mystical levels.

must reject as an illusion the idea that he can reach the peak of his own fundamental being in isolation, egoistically, 'individualistically'. No: there is no end waiting for each one of us, within a universe undergoing the involution that engenders spirit, other than the end of mankind itself. There is no way out, therefore, open to our individual drive towards survival and super-life, other than resolutely to plunge back into the general current from which we thought, for a moment, we could escape. And if we are to carry out that deliberate act, there is (from psychological necessity) no possible way of doing so other than to re-animate and renew in ourselves, to the measure of the new age, the sense of the species.

IV. THE NEW SENSE OF THE SPECIES

In animals, I recalled when I began, the sense of the species is essentially a blind urge toward reproduction and multiplication, within the phylum.

In man, by virtue of the two allied phenomena of reflection and social totalization, the equivalent of this inner dynamism in a different context can only be a reasoned urge towards fulfilment (both individual and collective, each being produced through the other), followed in the direction of the best arrangement of all the hominized substance which makes up what I earlier called the noosphere.

The best arrangement with a view to a maximum hominization of the noosphere.

From this there follows, as a first priority, a fundamental concern to ensure (by correct nutrition, by education, and by selection) an ever more advanced *eugenics* of the human zoological type on the surface of the earth.

At the same time, however, and even more markedly, there must be an ever more intense effort directed towards discovery and *vision*, animated by the hope of our gradually, as one man, putting our hands on the deep-seated forces (physico-chemical, biological and psychic) which provide the impetus of evolution.

Finally, and at the same time, inasmuch as evolution is tending, quite rightly, to be identified (at least so far as our field of vision extends) with hominization,[3] there must be a never-failing concern to stimulate, within the personalized living mass, the development of the *affective* energies which are the ultimate generators of union: a sublimated sense of sex, and a generalized sense of man.

In short, there must be a collective faith (active and productive of unanimity) in some maturing of mankind still to come: such, if we wish not to be crushed but to be fulfilled by the totalizing involution of the noosphere, is the attitude of mind which that process forces upon us: it calls for the new sense of the species.

Precisely, however, for such a faith to be possible, something further is necessary. The universe must show itself to be capable of kindling and maintaining in us a sufficiently powerful illumination of hope and a sufficient warmth of love. No end awaits man, I said earlier, other than the end of mankind itself; but if this end of mankind is to be worthy of attainment, if it is to be tempting to us, it is essential that it present itself to us (both to our minds and to our hearts) in the form of some issue that opens on to indefinite freedom: an issue that widens out into full consciousness, through all the forces of death and materialization.

There is no future for man, I repeat, without the neo-sense of the species.

But there can be no neo-sense of the species, we must be at pains to note, outside a universe which, by its nature, converges irresistibly upon some centre of ultra-personalization.

Unpublished, St-Germain-en-Laye
31 May 1949

3. In this sense, that in our more informed view man is no longer simply the artisan but also the object of an auto-evolution, which is seen to coincide, at its term, with a concerted reflection of all the elementary human reflections, now mutually inter-reflective.

The Evolution of Responsibility in
the World

In the *juridically* social form in which we habitually consider it, the responsibility of a being may be defined, in rough and ready terms, as the moral compulsion that makes it impossible for the being to develop without having to some extent to make allowance for the development of the other beings around him.

A *moral* compulsion, I say advisedly: by that I mean that if we are prepared fully to analyse its nature and value, it raises the problem, to which philosophers have always devoted so much discussion, of the objective foundation of *obligation*.

Speaking here as a biologist, I would like briefly to make one point clear – that, if we leave aside any metaphysical considerations and if we accept at the outset a certain concept (every day more surely attested) of the experiential structure of the universe, then we must realize the presence, deep within us, of a 'sense of responsibility'; not only is its existence immediately vindicated but the forms it takes can readily be determined with accuracy, and this inasmuch as this 'sense' does no more than express in each one of us, at the reflective state, a primary and therefore 'categorical' property of the universal datum.

I. THE CONVERGENCE OF THE UNIVERSE AND THE RISE OF COSMIC SOLIDARITY

Physicists and astronomers are gradually making us familiar with the notion of modalities (dynamic or tensorial) that structurally affect the totality of space and time. There is much talk nowadays of a curved universe, or of an explosive universe. But why not rather of a *self-arranging* universe – and one that arranges itself, I mean, not simply in the geometric and indefinite way in which a crystal does so, but in the organic and centred ('synergic') way proper to the chemical, cellular and zoological particles of which we ourselves form a part? As yet, it is true, there is only one point in the universe – our earth – at which we can appreciate such a drift of the stuff of the cosmos towards states that are continually more complicated physically and more interiorized psychically. Nevertheless, however restricted that field may be, how can we fail to recognize that the phenomenon is developing within it with a deep-rootedness, a regularity, and a power which is evidence of a general – not to say a *dominating* – propensity of the universe around us? If matter is left to itself, in a sufficient mass and for a sufficient length of time, and in suitable conditions of temperature and pressure, it always in the end, through the effect of chance and large numbers, becomes vitalized: as though by statistical necessity it found in this supremely improbable direction the only higher form of equilibrium that could satisfy it. This can only mean that, to judge by our own planetary mesh, the universe may legitimately be regarded, in its totality, as an immense system which is organico-psychically converging upon itself.

Let us accept that proposition; and with it we find, for a start, all around us a tri-zonal structure that since all time has been noted by the wise men of all nations, but one whose genetical significance and operational value emerge only as a function of a very well-defined and advanced theory of evolution.

At the very bottom, we find the region (which is by far the largest) in which the cosmic elements, still insufficiently concentrated together, show us no trace of spontaneity or sensibility. Higher, there is the more effectively grouped domain (already very restricted) of substances that are not yet reflective but are already 'living'. Finally, higher still and clearly as yet incomplete, we have the thinking peak of the human: a peak that is still rising, I must emphasize, because it is still in process of ultra-hominization.

There are, then, three major zones in the arrangement of the elements of the world, and therefore in their degree of consciousness. But there are in consequence three zones, too, in the possible non-arrangement or derangement of the same elements, that is to say in the individuation and aggravation of cosmic evil: the zone of purely material disintegration – the zone of suffering – the zone of wrong-doing. And, most important of all, there are, finally, three zones in the solidarity produced by the stream of universal convergence: the lower zone of physico-chemical interdependence between inanimate bodies; the zones of 'symbiotic' relationships between living beings; and finally the higher zone of the reflective interaction of free agents.

This simultaneously takes us to the heart of our problem and provides us with a general solution.

This is because it is immediately apparent – and this calls for no subtlety of discursive reasoning but comes simply through intuition and logical coherence – that the altruism of the moralists is no more than the form assumed, as it becomes hominized, by the fundamental inter-connexion of the particles which at all levels make up the stuff of a world which, as time moves on, not only condenses but *concentrates*. This amounts to saying that if responsibility is considered in conjunction with its roots it is found to have a common origin with, and to be co-extensive in its genesis with, the totality of time and space.

From this point of view, and as a rough initial description, we may say that the evolution of responsibility is simply one particular aspect of cosmogenesis. Or to put it more exactly, it is cosmogenesis *itself* observed and measured not (as we customarily do) by the degree of organic complexity or psychic charge, but by the degree of constantly increasing inter-influence within a multitude which is progressively concentrated upon itself in a convergent medium.

Now that we have seen and accepted that this is so, let us analyse rather more closely the present state of the phenomenon and its probable future. By that I mean, instead of following it through the main, rather indistinct, lines of the universe, let us do so within the well-defined field constituted by the human group; and there let us try to discover under the influence of what mechanisms and at what speed there continues to increase (as we had to anticipate), in step with the advance of anthropogenesis, the solidarity of a reflective mass that is seized and sucked up ever more tightly, as though in a whirlwind, by the forces of socialization.

II. PLANETARY COMPRESSION AND THE RISE OF HUMAN RESPONSIBILITY

To an attentive observer, the most remarkable aspect to be found at the moment in the thinking layer of the earth (the noosphere) is its state of extreme and continually rising compression – deriving, without doubt, and in the first place, from an almost vertical rise in the population of the globe – but also, and even more, from the rapidly increasing influence of a more specifically human factor, and one that must be sharply realized if we wish to understand what is going on: by that I mean the variation in *the radius of individual action*.

It calls for no great learning to appreciate that, in nature, the more a being becomes 'living', the more it enlarges its living space. The process is already evident throughout the history of the vertebrates. The scale is fantastically enlarged with the human threshold of reflection; but we may say that it is only now, with the entry of civilization into its modern phase not only of differentiation and expansion, but also of concentration and totalization, that it is developing its full vigour, whether in extension, in depth or (if one may put it so) in volume.

First, *in extension*. Formerly, countless bulkheads (slowness and difficulties of communication, racial, political and economic barriers) divided the human mass into compartments, to the point of almost immediately damping down the waves that appeared at any place on its surface. This produced a lifeless, sealed, environment, in which the average radius of each man's influence did not normally exceed a few kilometres; but today, with the astonishing increase in the speed of transport (particularly in the air), with radio and television, each one of us can already be physically present, in practically a few hours, to any person whatsoever, anywhere at all on the surface of the earth, and enjoy verbal or visual contact with him in a few fractions of a second.

Secondly, *in depth*: and here I am thinking primarily of the latest advances achieved by science, in all its forms, in the direction of a general control (atomic, chemical, biological and psychic) of the actual driving forces behind our organic and mental structure. Man is no longer at the elementary stage where all he could do was to persuade his adversary by reason, or win him by charm, or conquer him by force. Nowadays, there are surgical processes, narcotics or hormones can be given as injections, individual or collective psychoses can be systematically induced; and so by one means or another man finds that he possesses nothing less than the staggering power artificially to break himself down and reassemble himself from within. It is a possibility that may well make us shudder, but it would be puerile to imagine that if it can in fact be realized we shall ever be able to escape it.

Finally, *in volume*: in that phrase I am trying to express the situation towards which each one of us is rapidly being drawn (as a result of the progressive totalization of the noosphere), of being able, by *one single act*, to carry with us – to salvation or to ruin – progressively larger 'batches' of other human beings. We have only to call to mind (not to mention the thinker who uses the press to launch inflammatory ideas) the captain of a big modern vessel or the pilot of a huge aircraft – or the act of dropping an atomic bomb.

The truth, I repeat, is that the principal and specific event of our biological era is, initially, nothing more nor less than the compression, compenetration and consolidation upon itself of the human mass, reaching a paroxysmal climax in the vice-like grip of the planet.

It is, without doubt, a dangerous and distressing situation, inasmuch as it presents us with a whole world of vital problems: food supplies, health, the easing of the nervous strain suffered by a vast number of human beings brought into such close proximity and so involved with one another as hardly to have room to breathe.

On the other hand, however, there is also something else that is too often forgotten: an impressive dynamic power which can produce, together with a great deal of suffering and many mistakes, an intense spiritual energy, the first symptoms of which can already be seen.

It is in any case (and this brings us back to the particular subject of this article) the obvious source of an increasing responsibility; since, as we said, besides consciousness and evil, there is also *solidarity*, and these are the three magnitudes that cannot escape the necessity of increasing (in intensity even if not, in the case of evil, in quantity) simultaneously with an increase in the organic arrangement, both particulate and global, of a convergent system.

We cannot, therefore, fail to recognize that this one fact can by itself serve as the basis for a new ethics of the earth.

There was, perhaps, a time before our own when individuals could still try to better themselves and fulfil themselves, each on his own, in isolation. That time has gone for ever. We now have to make up our minds to recognize that at no moment of history has man been so completely involved (both actively and passively), through the very foundations of his being, in the value and betterment of all those around him, as he is today. And all the evidence indicates that this regime of interdependence can only become more pronounced in the course of the coming centuries.

A sort of generalized ultra-responsibility, affecting and heightening the whole range of virtues and vices – such, then, to conclude, would appear to be the most pronounced moral characteristic of the ultra-human towards which, by cosmic necessity, we are, even now, willy-nilly, drifting.

CONCLUSION. JURIDICAL RESPONSIBILITY AND BIOLOGICAL RESPONSIBILITY

If the foregoing considerations have some weight, we can see that when responsibility is restored to the setting of a world that is recognized and accepted once and for all as being by nature convergent, then it is automatically and immediately *universalized* and *intensified*, to the very dimensions of cosmic evolution and in exact step with it. And I need hardly point out that by that very fact it becomes *organic*.

Within the static Nature of Aristotle or Plato, a certain ontological exclusiveness which was inevitably retained between matter and spirit, had the continual effect of encouraging the use of abstract or juridical terms to express the relations between beings that existed in the field of the psyche. One world for bodies, and another world for souls. There are still any number of people to whom it comes as a shock if we speak of the physical reality of a mental phenomenon, or of the essentially biological nature of social or moral laws. It is precisely here that the newly opened up vision of a world in a state of evolution intervenes irresistibly, to release us from this sort of flat, hard and fast, dividing of things intellectually into compartments. Within what is now seen to be not merely a cosmos, but a cosmogenesis – crossing the successive thresholds of materialization, vitalization, and reflection – one and the same energy circulates, one and the same solidarity is built up. Without becoming materialized (in the pejorative and philosophical meaning of the world), but by following the opposite road of spiritualization, everything throughout the entire universe passes into the ultra-physical. Everything, mark you – and, in consequence, this applies as much to the effects of solidarity as it does to all the rest.

Here, indeed, if I am not mistaken, lies the radical transformation (not an objective but a subjective transformation) which is at this moment being effected in the way in which we have hitherto been able to become conscious of our responsibilities as men. It is not simply that the radius of our influence over others is suddenly increasing so rapidly that even the most superficial and self-centred of us are beginning to have to take it really seriously; what is more, mankind's social ordering of itself has acquired an evolutionary value, and in consequence the very stuff of this peripheral activity exercised by our being – to judge from the inexorably determined character of the effects it produces – is assuming for us an impressive consistence.

So long as we thought that all we were confronted with was a set of rules (to be respected or disregarded) more or less arbitrarily decreed by man for the use of other men, we could believe that some escape from them or some violation of them was still possible. As soon, however, as we realize with excitement that socialization is gradually enclosing us in a network not of conventions but of organic bonds, we begin mentally to appreciate the true greatness and gravity of man's condition.

One can always, you see, reach a compromise with the juridical and so rub along together; but thwart the organic, and there can be no pardon.

Paris, 5 June 1950
Psyché, July–August 1951

A Clarification: Reflections on
Two Converse Forms of Spirit

MODERN science has made us familiar with the notion of *isotopes*: bodies that are of the same 'atomic number' and therefore impossible for the chemist to distinguish, and are at the same time so different in their nuclear make-up as to give evidence of histories and display physical properties that are strangely different. Uranium 234-238, lead 204-214, carbon 12 and carbon 14, etc.

What happens in the realm of atoms has surely a remarkable equivalent in the field of psychic energies. Selfishness, detachment, love, intelligence – are all dispositions of the soul which appear identical to a naïve observer; and yet, according to the subject or the 'race' under consideration, do they not, in reality, include activities that are profoundly different? At first sight, nothing appears so homogeneous as the current of Christianity. And yet, within the Church, under the shadow of the monasteries, do not *two distinct species* of the faithful gather together, impelled to the same religious act (towards the same Cross) by two diametrically opposed motives? In one case it is *through an excess*, in the other *through a lack*, of vitality: in one, it is in order to sublimate something with which they are filled to overflowing, in the other it is to make up for something they lack.

It is not yet possible, I believe, to judge where and how far we shall one day be carried by the identification and differentiation, deeply rooted in our hearts and our institutions, of such spiritual isotopes. All I wish to show here, by way of example, is the extreme degree of clarity introduced into the whole body of our interior religious experience, simply by the distinction which has at last been established between *two* forms of spirit, hitherto strangely confused by philosophers no less than by mystics: the spirit of identification, and the spirit of unification; or, if the terms are preferred, the spirit of fusion and the spirit of 'amorization'.

Let us try to make this plain by means of a few carefully linked propositions.

I. THE SIGNIFICANCE OF THE HUMAN INDIVIDUAL

From the 'existential' point of view, each reflective monad may be defined (in nature, value, and function) as a particular focus-point of vision and action which, from a single determined point in time and space, radiates over the totality (past, present, and future) of the world around it. This amounts to saying that, by construction and structure, each human *ego* is, as an element, but as one that cannot be replaced or transposed, co-extensive with the entire universe.

Initially, therefore, we can represent the universe symbolic-ally as a sphere, filled with a dust made up of infinitesimal and incommunicable centres – each one of which occupies, within the sphere, a point strictly determined by the play (whatever it may be) of evolution.

II. THE YEARNING FOR UNITY

That being so, one and the same fundamental and primary disposition can, in our experience (and without any prior ratiocination) be recognized at the heart of each elementary centre. By this I mean the dream of a different state of affairs, in which the present multiplicity of focus-points of conscious-ness would in some way or other disappear, and each *ego* would find that it coincided not simply infinitesimally but integrally with the plenitude of being.

In many men this *cosmic sense* of the one and the all is still obscured or dormant, but even so it seems to me to be at once the most primitive and the most progressive form of psychic energy into which the other energies of the world around us are gradually being transformed. This would lead one to believe that a psychological disposition hitherto regarded as an anomaly is in fact destined to become general, and then to become unassailably dormant on the ultra-humanized earth of tomorrow.

Without urging the point further, and confining ourselves to what is indisputable, we need do no more than note the following highly significant fact: throughout history, wherever man (either in isolated cases or collectively) has effected a sufficiently deep breakthrough into the domain of religious forces (whether among the Vedantists, the Taoists, the Sufis or the Christians) – in each case he has felt that he is drifting towards a mysticism of the monist or pantheist type.[1]

This amounts to saying that, reduced to its essence, the problem of 'holiness' has lain, ever since its origins and in all cases, in the search for the 'great secret' which will allow the isolated particle that each one of us feels himself to be, either (as some say) to establish or (as others say) to re-establish a contact of communion with the whole of the Other that surrounds us.

Here, then, both *a priori* and *a posteriori*, two possible solutions, and *only two*, have since all time suggested themselves to men, as they still continue to do in our own time; solutions that offer them both an intellectual and a practical answer. The one involves relaxation and expansion, the other tension and centration.

---

1. Père Teilhard often uses the words 'pantheism' and 'pantheist' in various senses. He rejects pantheism, when it is used in the strict sense it bears in ordinary speech and in philosophy, as being opposed to personalism. For convenience, he uses it in a very wide sense which includes, as it does here, all forms of the tendency towards unity. In an exact and personal sense, as on p. 223 where he relates it to the 'God who is all in all' of St Paul (1 Cor. 15: 28), he accepts pantheism. (Ed.)

III. UNITY THROUGH RELAXATION, OR THE SEARCH
FOR A COMMON FOUNDATION

Going back to our symbol of 'the polycentric sphere', let us note how, within this particular environment, the element (which is still ex-centric in relation to the principal centre in our picture) will be able to conduct itself in such a way as to succeed in forming one with the totality.

In the case of youthful mankind, just as in that of the young human individual, there can be no doubt about the reaction: to open out wide, to try immediately to embrace all – and, in order to do that, *to become all things and all persons*. Such, in its youthful form, buoyant and poetical, is the first gesture of every nascent pantheism. Since, however, this effort to achieve direct communion ultimately allows the whole of the multiplicity of the world to subsist, its impotence soon becomes apparent. In the end, accordingly, the consciousness of the sage develops the idea of a more subtle solution (even though it is still sought in the same direction of an expansion to the limits of the universe). In order to become 'spiritual' (that is, one with all beings), why exhaust oneself in pursuing a multitude that can never be caught – why not, instead, follow the road of suppression and negation and so try to wipe out everything that produces the 'difference' between us and all the objects in the world? This is an attempt, both intellectual and practical, to achieve de-determination; in it, starting from and below the superficial plurality, an effort is made to enter the undifferentiated zone of *prime Stuff*,[2] where, by the elimination of all opposition between things, everything is identified with everything in a foundation that is common to all things. Each infinitesimal centre expands, through release of its individual characteristics, to the dimensions of, and within, one and the same general substratum in which its dream is realized and in which it forms one with all the rest around it. And so, by entry

2. Cf. the Aristotelian 'prime matter'. (?!)

into unconsciousness, we find a complete solution, it would seem, to the problem of perfection and happiness.

IV. UNITY THROUGH TENSION, OR THE ROAD TO THE UNIVERSAL CENTRE

In order to become all, to be re-dissolved in something that lies *below* everything . . .

It is curious to note the great fascination that this first way of answering the call of the One has been able to exercise over the mind of man – so much so as completely to obscure (right until our own day, in fact) the existence of a second way of conducting the battle against the multiple: one that is theoretically just as effective as the first, even though of a diametrically opposed type.

Instead of allowing our interior gaze to be drawn towards the ill-defined circumference of the cosmic sphere, why not turn it, rather, towards its general centre?

Ordinary pantheism has always taken for granted that if we are to overcome the plural, we must eliminate it: if we are to hear the fundamental harmony, we must first create silence. There is, however, an experience whose general applicability, daily ever more evident, is perhaps the most important discovery ever made by the human mind: why not fall into line with that, and admit that, through the miraculous operation of a certain curvature proper to our universe, each particular being contains the hidden power of making one with all the others and achieving harmony with them – but by developing to the full limits of its own self? So true is this that we must conceive the single essence of all things, and seek it, not in the form of a common foundation with which we make one by de-centration, but rather in the form of a universal peak of concentration, which is arrived at through a super-centration of human consciousness.[3]

3. It is, I think, a misunderstanding of this effort to concentrate (rather than the 'eastern' reaction of denial of the multiple) that produces the manichean

'True union does not fuse: it differentiates and personalizes'. This is a perfectly simple principle – and yet, if it is properly understood, it can open our eyes to the springing into being of a new world.

V. EFFECTS OF SYMMETRY AND ASYMMETRY: THE TWO ISOTOPES OF SPIRIT

Unity through the base, by dissolution: or unity through the apex, by ultra-differentiation.

It cannot be denied that these two extreme poles enjoy a certain number of properties in common, which makes them extremely alike.

For example, in either case – whether it be 'spherically' or 'centrically' – the stuff of the world is reduced (by a collective effort of all the associated *egos*)[4] to a certain common state in which the dualism between matter and spirit is obliterated. In both cases, again, psychologically speaking, consciousness is assumed to arrive, at the term of the operation, at a state of *inexpressibility* in which all opposition between the me, the you, the other, ceases to have any meaning – as, in a more general way, the opposition disappears between all the terms whose distinction is the normal basis of our speech.

Nevertheless, it is equally undeniable that a radical contrast

---

or Catharistic tendency to conceive spirit as the result of a *separation* between two components of the universe, one pure and the other impure. This is an attitude that has subtly made its way into many manuals of Christian ascesis. To my mind, however, it is a misbegotten concept, in as much as it does not respect the fundamental mystical demand that, through the process of spiritualization, 'all shall become All'. This is quite apart from the fact that, from this point of view, there is no explanation of why or how the spiritual portion of the world is automatically and 'lovingly' unified simply as a result of being 'poured into' All.

4. Since, in order to reduce the cosmic sphere to a unified state, *all* the elementary centres have to disappear – whether by way of dissolution or by the contrary way of mono-centration.

can be distinguished beneath these resemblances which might lead us to believe in a basic identity: for in one of the two directions (that of the 'spherical') the elementary *egos* disappear, while in the other (that of the 'centric') they reinforce one another as they come together. In the latter case, a first type of the inexpressible is attained by intensification (by excess) – in the former, another type of the inexpressible is obtained by decrease (by lack) of centration and reflection.

Pantheism of identification, at the opposite pole from love: 'God is all'. And pantheism of unification, beyond love: 'God all in all'.

– Two isotopes of spirit.[5]

VI. THE VERDICT OF EXPERIENCE, OR THE CONVERGENT UNIVERSE

Thus, theoretically speaking, it is perfectly true that two converse methods (and only two) confront the mystic who wishes to effect in and around himself the great cosmic work of unification. He can either concentrate upon the centre, or he can embrace the sphere.

Are we, then, to believe that we may choose between these two symmetrical ways: as though the two roads, even though they followed two opposite slopes, led equally well to the same peak?

I am absolutely convinced that this is not so – and for two reasons. The first, as I said before, is that by structural necessity there is no conceivable common measure between the inexpressible of identification and the inexpressible of unification, nor can they be in any way complementary to one another.

---

5. In slightly different terms, one might say that the pantheist (or cosmic) line tends to be expressed in one or other of the three following formulas:

1. *To become all beings* (erroneous, and impossible to effect): para-pantheism.
2. *To become all* ('eastern' monism): pseudo-pantheism.
3. *To become one with all beings* ('western' monism): eu-pantheism (see below).

The second reason is even more categorical, and it derives from the fact that, concretely speaking, the universe in which we are involved displays indisputably a bias towards the spirit not of diffusion but of concentration. Throughout the thousands of millions of years in which we can follow its course, cosmogenesis has continually developed in the form of a *noogenesis*, in other words in the direction of an equilibrium that lies not this side, but the further side, of all organization and all thought.

In such a system there is no room for even a partial retrogression of the reflective towards the unconscious.

In planetary terms, the human forms but one. It is therefore as one body (that is, in a unanimous movement) that it must abandon the mirage of a mysticism of relaxation and conform to the particular type of spirit determined for it by the immutable axes of *a convergent universe*.

VII. COROLLARY: AN ATTEMPT AT AN ABSOLUTE CLASSIFICATION OF RELIGIONS

Once we have recognized the distinction between the two 'isotopes' of spirit and appreciated their relative cosmic value, it immediately becomes possible to characterize and accordingly to classify, in their absolute value, the principal religious currents which at this moment claim the allegiance of consciousness on earth.

In the eastern (or Hindu) *quarter*, there is no doubt but that, from the very beginning, the ideal of diffusion and identification has been dominant. The elementary *egos* are regarded as anomalies to be reduced (as holes to be filled up) in universal being; or, which comes to the same thing, the biological evolution of the world represents for the sage no more than an illusion or an insignificant eddy – in that we have, patched-up though it may be in minor ways, the unchangeable essence of the Vedantic mystiques of affinities, and (from the point of view of the implacable demands of noogenesis) their incurable weakness.

In the marxist quarter, I would not hesitate to say that it is very clearly the spirit of centration which is striving to emerge through the 'communist' effort, in order to super-differentiate man and super-organize the earth. 'Striving to emerge', I say advisedly; but it will never succeed in doing so until the party theoreticians make up their minds at last to accord to the superstructure of the world the final consistence which they still confine to the material infra-structure of things.

Finally, *in the Christian quarter*, two remarks are required to cover the situation, one affirmative and the other restrictive.

First and foremost, it is clear that since all time Christianity has, by virtue of its structure, fallen into equilibrium in the direction of the spirit of unification and synthesis: God finally becoming *all in all* within an atmosphere of pure charity ('*sola caritas*'). In that magnificent definition of the pantheism of differentiation is expressed in unmistakable terms the very essence of Christ's message.

Nevertheless, that is far from meaning that the centric and centrifying character of the movement can be considered as having yet been perfectly defined, either in its mystical expression or in its dogmatic formulation.

In the first place, mystically speaking, it is difficult not to be aware of considerable traces of fusionism in the appeals directed towards the inexpressible by an Eckhart or even a John of the Cross: as though, for those great contemplatives, the two isotopes of spirit were still appreciably confused.

Secondly, theologically speaking, I may be forgiven for pointing out that it is simply impossible for any true universalist vision to develop untrammelled within a certain Aristotelian concept of the universe.[6]

---

6. The 'certain' Aristotelianism referred to, and briefly described in the next paragraph, is a cut and dried Aristotelian concept of the elements of the world, carried over right into the twentieth century by certain philosophers and theologians, without taking into account (in particular) the transposition necessitated by the transition from a static universe (cosmos) to a dynamic universe (cosmogenesis). (Ed.)

Such a concept gives us a world so thoroughly divided up into immutable sectors and zones that it retains, even in its final state, a mixed stuff in which an incomprehensible 'matter' is still coupled to a concretely objectified 'spirit': and a Pleroma, whose cement ('sanctifying' grace) cannot logically be considered or classified except as a mere 'accident' (!) In short, something that would like to be a 'monism' of the centric type but which (from refusing to go beyond the cosmos and take its stand in cosmogenesis) is much more akin to a juridical association than a biologically organic system.

Is it not evident that Christianity will be able to breathe freely and spread its wings to their full span only in the prospect that has at last been opened up for its spiritual potentialities by a true philosophy, not simply of the whole, but of a convergent whole?

VIII. CONCLUSION: THE URGENT NEED FOR THE FORMULATION OF A MYSTICISM OF THE WEST

The more, as an irresistible effect of technical progress and reflection, mankind becomes conscious of the immensity, and even more the *organicity*, of the world around it, the more the necessity for *a soul* makes itself felt: for a soul that is capable of maintaining and directing the vast process of planetization in which we are involved. The more, too, it becomes clear that the only form of spirit capable of producing this soul is that which we defined earlier as sustaining and impelling the universe in the direction of progressively better forms of arrangement: isotope 2 (the most recently discovered!) – the spirit of greater love and greater consciousness.

And at this point we meet a paradoxical situation.

While the Hindu mysticism of fusion and the juridical type[7]

7. The expression 'juridical type of Christian mysticism' calls for more exact qualifications, which the author would probably have added if he had published this essay. Père Teilhard came into conflict with what he calls 'juridical' (on other occasions, 'artificial') in a number of fields. In the first

of Christian mysticism have for centuries been the object of countless descriptions and codifications, it is still impossible at the present moment to find a single printed work which affirms the existence and describes the specific properties of an interior attitude (the *centric* cosmic sense) which, through force of circumstances, is coming to be the hidden mainspring of the life of each one of us.

Every day the reality of an ultra-human becomes more insistent; and there is no possible way for our generation to enter into it except with the help of a new form of psychic energy in which the personalizing depth of love[8] is combined with the totalization of what is most essential and most universal in the heart of the stuff of the cosmos and the cosmic stream – and for this new energy we have as yet *no name*!

The time has certainly come when a new mysticism, at once fully human and fully Christian, must emerge at the opposite pole from an outworn orientalism: the road of the West, the road of tomorrow's world.

Unpublished, Paris
25 July 1950

place, in the 'social' field, where his concept of society, linked with that of noogenesis, was of something *organic* and not simply 'juridical': parallel with this, in the 'field of the mystical body of Christ' (cf. *Le Milieu Divin*) he controverted *one* theological concept which tends to reduce the union of the members of Christ to a 'moral' union, but was in no way opposed to the Thomist concept which sees in it a 'physical' union. (Cf. the related question of the 'physical' causality of the sacraments.) (Ed.)

8. A personalizing depth already vouched for in other contexts by patristic and theological tradition (for example, St Bernard). (Ed.)

The Zest for Living

By 'zest for living' or 'zest for life', I mean here, to put it very approximately, that spiritual disposition, at once intellectual and affective, in virtue of which life, the world, and action seem to us, on the whole, luminous – interesting – appetizing.

It is a disposition that is by nature gay and agreeable (as opposed to nausea or disgust), but we must take good care not to confuse it with a mere phenomenon of euphoria.

– In the first place because, when considered in its most fully developed forms, it displays the character of being essentially dynamic, constructive, and adventurous.

– and secondly, because, however readily it may envelop itself in an atmosphere of exultation and intoxicated delight, deep beneath it there lies hidden (as we shall show) a cold and primordial determination to survive and super-live: what Édouard Le Roy, carrying on from Blondel, has so well called 'the rock-bottom will'.

It is something utterly and entirely different from a mere emotional state.

At first sight, the presence in each one of us of this 'rock-bottom will' and its degree of intensity might seem to have importance and value only as affecting *individual* well-being; one would be inclined to say that it was a private health problem – something to be discussed in each case with one's spiritual director or one's doctor.

However, if we examine it more thoroughly, we shall find that the importance of the problem it raises is of a very different nature.

In the reflections that follow, I hope to make it clear that in the 'zest for life' there is

– nothing less than the *energy of universal evolution*, which, in the form of an innate pull towards being, wells up in what is most primitive, and therefore the least directly controllable, in each one of us;

– an energy, *the feeding and development* of which is to some degree *our responsibility*;

– and this we must do by a supremely vital *operation*, the nicest part of which is *entrusted* to the expert knowledge and skill of *religions*.

Three points, then, which will supply the matter of this discussion.

I. THE ZEST FOR LIFE: THE ULTIMATE MAINSPRING OF EVOLUTION

In the world all around us, an immense variety of fathomless currents spread wide and run together in a way that might at first seem impossible to understand.

Gradually, however, under long and intensive observation, an order and a hierarchy emerge in the end from this confused muddle. As our experience recognizes that bodies gradually fall into a natural distribution, so we note that the vast agglomerations of matter brought together by the combined play of gravitational and electro-magnetic forces tend to lose their importance: *their place is taken by the infinitesimal* but extraordinarily active nuclei of organic substance – of which we know, in fact, only one good example (our own bio-sphere) – but whose presence scattered throughout stellar space is coming to appear potentially more and more probable in the eyes of present-day scientists.

From this completely modern point of view, the most significant, and the truly specific, movement of the cosmic system in which we are caught up, is not the formation of galaxies and stars; it is much more (and through the medium, and as a function of, those bodies) the genesis of large mole-cules, followed by that of cells and then by that of the higher living beings. In other words, the most exact definition for our intelligence of the nature of the universe is (at the opposite pole from mass-phenomena) the process of 'auto-arrangement'. It is in virtue of this latter that, in the course of a drift which affects the totality of space and time, 'matter' passes, locally and partially (though at the same time in an over-all operation) from more simple and less conscious states to states that are both physico-chemically more complex and psychically more interiorized.

The problem is how to explain this arrangement itself, which is taken to be the principal effect of universal evolution. In other words, to the influence of what factor are we to attribute it?

To an effect of *selection*, is the unanimous answer today of the chorus of biologists and physicists. Among the countless combinations effected in the course of time by the vast turmoil of the cosmos, some (which are extremely improbable but for some reason 'advantageous') are picked out, retained and multiplied; they are then used again (still through the play of chance) to obtain a further increased state of complexity and consciousness. So it is that by dint of and under the impact of tentative gropings, by the operation of chances that are seized and added one to another, life automatically functions and increases around us.

However, this first answer, valid though it be, obviously does no more than introduce a new question.

To what type of energy known to us is it possible ultimately to attribute the sort of preference accorded by nature in her experimenting to the more complex (and in consequence more 'psychized') combinations that emerge from the cosmic play of large numbers – a preference she shows in spite of their extreme fragility?

Since Darwin there has been much talk (and with justification) of 'the survival of the fittest'. Yet surely it is obvious that if this Darwinian struggle is to be effective it inevitably *presupposes* in the competing elements a *tenacious sense of con-*

servation, of survival – in which we meet again in a concentrated form the very essence of the whole mystery.

Years ago, when Lucretius and Epicurus were looking for something that would explain the coming together and entangling of their rain of 'hooked' atoms, and start it off, they introduced an obliquity of motion into the drops as they fell: a *'clinamen'* they called it, or 'bias'.

In a more modern form we meet the same problem again when we are confronted by a universe that is clearly going through a process of complexification. If you have a cosmic stuff that is *perfectly indifferent*, then, however great the number of occasions envisaged, it is inconceivable that the play of chances may produce even the shortest linear progression in arrangement. Why is it, then, that right back to the furthest point at which matter concentrates and compresses upon itself – why is that, historically, it has persisted for tens of millions of years in introducing order into itself? In other words, how are we to justify this *priority* that has unswervingly been accorded, in a vast sector of things and throughout geological eras, to the improbable over the probable, to order over disorder, to life over death?

The more deeply one studies this problem, the more one is convinced (by reference to what happens in the depths of our reflective ego) that the *fundamental polarity* required to initiate and advance the cosmic phenomenon of vitalization is by nature, and in its dimensions, *psychic*. This means that it is this polarity, in the threefold form of 'a will to survive', turning into a 'will to live fully', itself then included in a 'will to super-live' – it is this, and nothing less than this, which rises up in each one of us, unmasking its features, one might say, *in the hominized state*.

If, then, we wish fully to explain the 'preferential field of arrangement' which alone can completely account for the formation within sidereal matter of nuclei of organic substance, there is only one way, it would appear, of doing so. It is to picture the cosmic mass as animated by a primacy that is accorded absolutely to being over non-being – the degrees of clarity with which that primacy is apparent varying from a zero of consciousness up to the reflective, and the modalities it assumes being as diverse as all the countless zoological types ever realized.

And that, briefly, amounts to saying that the world would remain stationary or continually turn back upon itself in a circle, without ever getting off the mark, if primordially it did not find in its very core an elevating factor: *expressed in terms of human experience*, this is precisely the 'will to live' defined earlier.

A zest for living, *the* zest for living – such, when we get to the bottom of the problem, would appear to be the fundamental driving force which impels and directs the universe along its main axis of complexity-consciousness.

This, then, is the basic situation with which we are confronted, and now we have to carry our line of thought a little further and see what we can build up on it.

II. THE ZEST FOR LIFE: A VARIABLE AND PRECARIOUS MAGNITUDE

If what I have just been saying about the fundamentally psychic nature of evolution is correct, it is immediately apparent that a new and hitherto strangely neglected element is unexpectedly introduced into the various calculations by which our science is at this moment trying to construct an energetics of the human mass.

While, that is – so long as we are dealing with 'inanimate' beings or even with simple forms of animal life – the 'tendency to survive' can be regarded *as an assured constant* (whether because of negligible psychism and the vast number of elements under consideration, or because of the unreflective docility of the instinct for preservation which animates them) – in the case of man the phenomenon begins to behave in an entirely different way.

On the one hand there is this, that at the level of man the controlling effect of large numbers is vastly reduced: the population is comparatively small – what are two thousand million compared with molecular or monocellular multitudes?

On the other hand, and still more important, there is this: in the cosmic *reflective* zone to which we belong, individual psychisms have attained extreme values of intensity, of sensibility, of variability, of contagious influence, and even more of *auto-criticism*; as a result of this, at this same level, all sorts of irregularities, all sorts of overtones, good or bad, may theoretically be anticipated in the 'yield' of the zest for life: a leap this way or that, positive or negative, and we have only to open our eyes to see all around us, at every moment, the advantage or threat they contain.

Let us confine ourselves to a single case, the clearest and most serious of all. Imagine (and in the eyes of our existentialists this is no chimera) that, by extending his power of vision, man has become capable of reaching the confines of his cosmic domain, and sees tomorrow that he is decisively caught in the trap of a blind universe, cold and hermetically sealed. Is it not obvious that in this case anthropogenesis – while it is true that it might for some time drag along from force of habit or inclination – would be struck to the heart as though by a canker, so that before long its actual leading shoot would wither away?

It is, in truth, a strange prospect and one which for a very long time now I have been unable to dismiss from my mind: that all over the earth the attention of thousands of engineers and economists is concentrated on the problem of world resources of coal, oil or uranium – and yet nobody, on the other hand, bothers to carry out a survey of the zest for life: to take its 'temperature', to feed it, to look after it, and (why not, indeed?) to increase it.

Like a sick man revolted by the sight of a banquet, so man, struck down by biological nausea, would certainly go on strike against life – even though he had reached the zenith of his power to discover and create. And this strike will certainly *come about* unless, keeping pace with his science and power, there is an upsurge in man of an ever more impassioned interest in the task entrusted to him. In us, evolution (in Julian Huxley's phrase) has become conscious, dangerously and critically so – conscious and perfected to the point of being able to control its own driving forces and to rebound upon itself. But what good would this great cosmic event be to us if we were *to lose the zest for evolution*?

We still treat this precious and primordial appetite just as healthy people do their health – as though it were a fixed, assured, capital: the world, we imagine, will always have plenty of it available for us.

A most dangerous sense of security, and a most grave error in dynamics!

In the end, the ultra-human cannot be built except with the human; and the human is, essentially, nothing but a will to subsist and grow greater, which can equally well be intensified or wither away.

It is, then, to the theoretical and practical study of this will (a will that radically conditions all our forms of power) that a new science – the most important, perhaps, of all sciences – must be devoted: and tomorrow it will inevitably be so devoted. Its problem will be, 'How to maintain deep in the heart of man the source of his vital impulse, and open it up ever more widely'.

A priori, we dispose of two very different, and at the same time allied, methods of tackling the problem so presented.

a. We may either, acting physico-chemically on the 'complexity' focus of our being, try, by the application of certain substances or certain methods, permanently to increase our organic vitality. And we all know, do we not, the passing moods of intense excitement (or on the other hand, of depression) which follow upon such treatments.

b. Or, acting psychically on the 'consciousness' focus, we may work intellectually and affectively to release and heighten in ourselves, and provide a solid basis for, ever more powerful rational motives and inducements for living.

By organic means, to give added vigour to our temperaments: or, on the contrary, by the presentation of some ideal, to kindle the ardent impulses of the soul.

Which of these two methods should we choose?

It is obviously impossible completely to separate the two, since once again we find in them the mysterious interaction of body and spirit. On the other hand, at the point in evolution at which the earth stands at this moment, it is difficult not to accord a large measure of priority (not only in dignity, but also in effectiveness and urgency) to the effort to cultivate in modern man an increasing reflective passion for the universe which envelops him – or, more precisely, for the cosmogenesis which is engendering him.

In a world which has become conscious of its own self and provides its own motive force, what is most vitally necessary to the thinking earth is a faith – and a great faith – and ever more faith.

To know that we are not prisoners.

To know that there is a way out, that there is air, and light, and love, somewhere, beyond the reach of all death.

To know this, to know that it is neither an illusion nor a fairy story.

– That, if we are not to perish smothered in the very stuff of our being, is what we must at all costs secure.

And it is there that we find what I may well be so bold as to call the *evolutionary role* of religions.

III. THE ZEST FOR LIVING: THE FRUIT WE MAY EXPECT FROM THE COMBINED EFFORT OF RELIGIONS

With the rise of modern technology and thought it was not difficult to believe (particularly in the nineteenth century) that we had left behind the age, or phase, of religions. It is quite certain, too, that in the light of science – re-cast in its crucible –

a profound refashioning and a dynamic sorting-out have been effected in the field of 'creeds' and 'beliefs'. Nevertheless we are beginning to realize that this is far from meaning that where mysticism is concerned the flames of experimental knowledge have been exclusively destructive. On the contrary (unless I have gone astray in the course of the foregoing reflections) the forces of religion are emerging from the ordeal they have just gone through as a more important auxiliary to human phylogenesis than ever before: this is because it is henceforth to them, as 'nursemaids of our faith', that we must look for the maintenance and development of the energy required for the newly recognized needs of a vigorously active anthropogenesis: to give it enthusiasm for growth – *the zest for the world*.

In our day, this is something that can never be emphasized too forcibly. Because, as we are coming to see for ourselves, the universe is organically resting on – cantilevered on, I might say – the future as its sole support – precisely in view of that, and because of that, the 'reserves of faith' (that is, the quantity and quality of the religious sense available) must continually increase in our world.

Moreover, in consequence of this, we must add that the era (I do not say of *religions*) but of *religion* has by no means been left behind: it is quite certainly only beginning.

IT IS STILL THE DUTY OF BELIEVERS TO GIVE BODY TO AND SAFEGUARD THE EARTH'S NEW RELIGIOUS NEEDS.

Hitherto the various forms of 'faith' have been essentially *ascensional*, following the line O Y. In future they must be *motive* (propulsive), following the new axis O X.[1] 'Unsatisfied theism'.

Let us, in conclusion, try to make this point unmistakably clear.

We are surrounded by a certain sort of pessimists who continually tell us that our world is foundering in atheism. But

1. Cf. diagram in 'The Heart of the Problem', *The Future of Man*, p. 269.

should we not rather say that what it is suffering from is *unsatisfied theism*? Men, you say, no longer want God; but are you quite sure that what they are rejecting is not simply the image of a God who is too insignificant to nourish in us this concern to survive and super-live to which the need to worship may ultimately be reduced?[2]

Hitherto the various creeds still commonly accepted have been primarily concerned to provide every man with an *individual* line of escape; this is because they were born and grew up in a time when problems of cosmic totalization and maturing *did not exist*. However universal their promises and visions of the beyond might be, they did not explicitly (and with good reason) allow any room to a global and controlled transformation of the whole of life and thought in their entirety. And yet, in the light of what we have already seen, is it not precisely an event of this order (an event that involves the expectation and the advent of some ultra-human) that we are asking them to include, to hallow, and to animate, now and for ever after?

No longer simply a religion of individuals and of heaven, but a religion of mankind and of the earth – that is what we are looking for at this moment, as the oxygen without which we cannot breathe.

In these circumstances, we are forced to recognize that nothing can subsist tomorrow – nothing has any chance of heading (as must be done) the general movement of planetary hominization – except those mystical currents which are able, through a synthesis of the traditional faith in the above and our generation's newborn faith in some issue towards the ahead, to make ready and provide a complete pabulum for our 'need to be'.

A SIFTING AND GENERAL CONVERGENCE OF RELIGIONS, GOVERNED BY AND BASED ON THEIR VALUE AS AN

---

2. Cf. St Irenaeus, who expressed this by saying, 'the glory of God is the life of man; and the life of man is the vision of God'. (Ed.)

EVOLUTIONARY STIMULUS – THAT, IN SHORT, IS THE
GREAT PHENOMENON OF WHICH WE WOULD APPEAR TO
BE AT THIS MOMENT BOTH THE AGENTS AND THE
WITNESSES.[3]

But, then, it will be said, if the great spiritual concern of our
times is indeed a re-alignment and readjustment of old beliefs
towards a new Godhead who has risen up at the anticipated
pole of cosmic evolution – then why not simply slough off the
old – why not, that is, regroup the whole of the earth's
religious power directly and *a novo* upon some 'evolutionary
sense' or 'sense of man' – and pay no attention to the ancient
creeds? If we wish to satisfy the planetary need for faith and
hope which is continually increasing with the world's technico-
social organization, why not have a completely fresh faith,
rather than a rejuvenation and confluence of 'old loves'?

Why not? – for two good reasons, is my answer: they have
both a solid foundation in nature, and they may be set out as
follows.

First of all, there can be no doubt that, in each of the great
religious branches that cover the world at this moment, a
certain spiritual attitude and vision which have been produced
by centuries of experience are preserved and continued; these
are as indispensable and irreplaceable for the integrity of a total
terrestrial religious consciousness as the various 'racial' components which have successively been produced by the phylogenesis of our living group may well be for the looked-for
perfecting of a final human zoological type. In the matter of
religion, just as in that of cerebration, the cosmic forces of
complexification, it would seem, proceed not through individuals but through complete branches.

This, however, is not all. What is carried along by the

3. I am, advisedly, adopting here a strictly neutral point of view. Were I
speaking as a 'Catholic', I should have to add that if the Church is not to be
false to herself, then (without any 'arrogance' but by structural necessity)
she *cannot but* regard herself as the *very axis* upon which the looked-for
movement of concentration and convergence can, and must, be effected.

various currents of faith that are still active on the earth, working in their incommunicable core, is no longer only the irreplaceable elements of a certain complete image of the universe. Very much more even than *fragments of vision*, it is *experiences of contact* with a supreme Inexpressible which they preserve and pass on. It is as though, from the final issue which evolution demands and towards which it hastens, a certain influx came down to illuminate and give warmth to our lives: a true 'trans-cosmic' radiation for which the organisms that have appeared in succession throughout the course of history would seem to be precisely the naturally provided receivers.

Beneath its apparent naïveté, this is an extraordinarily daring outlook; and, if it is justified, its effect is profoundly to re-cast the whole theory of the zest for life and its maintenance in the world.

To preserve and increase on earth the 'pressure of evolution' it is vitally important, I pointed out, that through the mutual buttressing provided by the reflection of religious ideas a progressively more real and more magnetic God be seen by us to stand out at the higher pole of hominization. We now find another condition of cosmic animation and another possibility in it. It is that sustained and guided by the tradition of the great human mystical systems, along the road of contemplation and prayer, we succeed in entering directly into receptive communication with the very source of all interior drive.

The vital charge of the world, maintained not simply by physiological artifices or by rational discovery of some objective or ideal, bringing with it – but poured directly into the depths of our being, in its higher, immediate, and most heightened form – love, as an effect of 'grace' and 'revelation'.

The zest for life: the central and favoured ligament, indeed, in which can be seen, within the economy of a supremely organic universe, a supremely intimate bond between mysticism, research, and biology.

The manuscript ends with the following notes added by Père Teilhard:

A different ending?

Religious 'contact'=Initiation of the 3rd *reflection* $(F^2/F^3)=$ *neo-zest made explicit*: *Love* (higher form of zest!!).

> Unpublished, Paris, November 1950
> Written on the occasion of a lecture given, for the *Congrès Universel des Croyants*, at the home of M. de Saint-Martin, Place des Vosges, 9 December 1950

The Spiritual Energy of Suffering

IF a perfectly keen-eyed observer were to watch the earth for a long time from a great height, our planet would first of all appear to him blue from the oxygen that envelops it; then green from the vegetation which covers it; then luminous – and ever more luminous – from the thought that grows in intensity on its surface; but at the same time it would appear dark – and ever more dark – from a suffering that, throughout the ages, grows in quantity and poignancy in step with the rise of consciousness.

Consider the total suffering of the whole earth at every moment. If only we were able to gather up this formidable magnitude, to gauge its volume, to weigh, count, analyse it – what an astronomic mass, what a terrifying total! And from physical torture to moral agonies, how subtle a range of shades of misery! And if only, too, through the medium of some conductivity suddenly established between bodies and souls, all the pain were mixed with all the joy of the world, who can say on which side the balance would settle, on that of pain or that of joy?

Yes, the more man becomes man, the more deeply engrained and the more serious – in his flesh, in his nerves, in his mind – becomes the problem of evil: evil that has to be understood, and evil that has to be borne.

A sounder view of the universe in which we are caught up, it is true, is now by way of providing us with the beginning of an answer to this problem. We are realizing that within the vast process of arrangement from which life emerges, every success is necessarily paid for by a large percentage of failures. One cannot progress in being without paying a mysterious tribute of tears, blood, and sin. It is hardly surprising, then, if all around us some shadows grow more dense at the same time as the light grows brighter: for, when we see it from this angle, suffering in all its forms and all its degrees is (at least to some extent) no more than a natural consequence of the movement by which we were brought into being.

Bowing to the evidence of a universal experience, we are beginning in an abstract way, in our minds, to admit this complementary mechanism of good and evil; but if our hearts are to conform without rebelling to this harsh law of creation, is it not psychologically necessary that we discover, in addition, some positive value in this painful wastage attaching to the operation which forms us, a value that will transfigure it and make it permanently acceptable?

Of that there can be no doubt. And it is here that there comes in, to play its irreplaceable part, the astounding Christian revelation of a suffering which (provided it be accepted *in the right spirit*) can be transformed into an expression of love and a principle of union: suffering that is first treated as an enemy who has to be defeated; then suffering vigorously fought against to the bitter end; and yet at the same time suffering rationally accepted and cordially welcomed inasmuch as by forcing us out of our egocentrism and compensating for our errors it can super-centre us upon God. Yes, indeed: suffering in obscurity, suffering with all its repulsiveness, elevated for the humblest of patients into a supremely active principle of universal humanization and divinization – such is seen to be at its peak the fantastic spiritual dynamic force, born of the Cross, of which the pages that follow are devoted to describing, among any number of similar cases, one concrete example.

In the woman whom Monique Givelet presents in this book, in the name of the Catholic Union of the Sick, there stand out with luminous clarity the inner features, the characteristics and the effects by which we can recognize an authentically *good* suffering: an unremitting refinement of the critical sense and a continually better balanced appreciation of human values; an heroic concern to meet to the end with a smile all the things that have to be passively borne by the sick; an increasing sensitivity of heart to the joy and sorrow of others; a clear realization of the way in which every reality finds added strength and simplicity within the embrace of the divine omnipresence. And all this combining into a singular power of peace-giving attraction, radiating like a halo.

An overplus of spirit born from a deficiency of matter.

Here, indeed, is the miracle, continually renewed for the last two thousand years, of a possible Christification of suffering.

O Marguerite, my sister, while I, given body and soul to the positive forces of the universe, was wandering over continents and oceans, my whole being passionately taken up in watching the rise of all the earth's tints and shades, you lay motionless, stretched out on your bed of sickness; silently, deep within yourself, you were transforming into light the world's most grievous shadows.

In the eyes of the Creator, which of us, tell me, which of us will have had the better part?

> Paris, 8 January 1950. Preface by Père
> Teilhard to Monique Givelet's life of
> his sister, Marguerite-Marie. (Ed.
> du Seuil, Paris, 1950)

A Mental Threshold Across Our Path:
From Cosmos to Cosmogenesis

1. The Intellectual Event:
a world which is getting under way

IT is only natural that we should be engrossed by our concern
to respond to the special factors and problems that are introduced into our field of vision and action by an almost explosive
development of science, technology and sociology; but it has
this consequence, that we are not trying hard enough to get
clear of the turmoil in which we are involved and so find out
whether we can distinguish and define the general shape and
the over-all direction and, most of all, the underlying generating
cause of, the remarkable cyclone that has suddenly blown up
and in less than a century secured its grip on mankind – and is
now carrying us along, powerless to resist.

What I hope to do here is to add my contribution to this
effort to extricate ourselves and see more clearly what is
happening, by pointing out the most unusual, and determining,
influence exerted on the behaviour of modern man by the
very recent (or at any rate as yet incomplete) awakening of our
minds to the perception of a world that is in a *state of operating
an organic shift upon itself.*

This involves a mental transition from cosmos to cosmogenesis.

Before we describe (see part 2) the consequences of this
psychic revolution for our fundamental rational and affective
attitude when confronted by matter and life; and before (in the
conclusion) taking up a definite line in relation to the true
nature of the phenomenon (whether its stuff is simply 'cognoscitive' or on the contrary 'entitative') – before we do either of

these, let us try briefly to determine the chief historical phases of the transformation and its present condition.

a. The Galilean 'lysis' (sixteenth–seventeenth centuries)

In a general way it is obviously to Copernican influences that we must attribute, in its origin, the intellectual movement from which our modern view of the universe ultimately emerged. However, if we look more closely, we shall realize that what the change in astronomical perspective which is so characteristic of the sixteenth century seems explicitly, in a first phase, to have served to do was much less to build up positively a particular physical system; it was primarily to clear the way for new constructions. In the first place, during this initial period, only the sidereal structure of the world was formally challenged. And further, in this particular field, it was apparently only *a change of axis* that was proposed, to be applied to, and be effective within, a universe in which space was still absolute, and time, too, was as completely homogeneous as before.

We can never over-exaggerate the decisive part played in the birth of the modern mind by the intuition of Galileo. On the other hand, neither can we emphasize too strongly the fact that the collapse of geocentrism during the Renaissance in no way had as its specific effect the bringing out of the features of a new cosmogony; all it did – and a tremendous achievement it was, for those days – was to break the spell that ever since the Greeks (and in spite of Epicurus) paralysed human thought and confined it to the contemplation of a cosmos whose mechanism was harmoniously and permanently stabilized. With the mere admission (for all the naïveté of the concept) of a revolution of the earth around the sun; simply, that is, by introducing a dissociation between a geometric and a psychic centre to things – the whole magic of the celestial spheres fade away, leaving man confronted with a plastic mass to be re-thought in its entirety.

It was like the caterpillar whose substance (apart from a few rare cerebral elements) dissolves, as its metamorphosis draws near, into a more or less amorphous product: the revived protoplasmic stuff from which the butterfly will emerge.

b. The appearance in human thought of the first evolutionary nuclei (eighteenth–nineteenth centuries)

While, as we have just seen, it was in the field of positional astronomy that there originated the psychic upheaval which, starting with Galileo, began to blow the notion of the cosmos into smithereens, we have to look back in a quite different direction – to that of the classification of living forms – if we are to see the idea of cosmogenesis make its permanent entry into science. For Newton, gravity was still no more than the way of explaining the working of a stationary system. We shall have to wait for Laplace and, after him, spectral analysis, before a mechanics of the heavens begins to be transformed into an embryology of heavenly bodies. On the other hand, towards the end of the eighteenth century, an active focus of 'genetic' thought makes itself felt in the world of the 'natural philosophers'. It was among the zoologists that this 'transformist' germ first appeared and increased in vigour, and it was as an effect of the contagious influence of that germ, we may say, that a rapidly increasing number of 'evolutionary' nuclei have since that time continued to appear in all the various departments of knowledge. This we find at the very highest level, in the domain of the sciences of man (the history of institutions, of ideas, and of religions) and also, by a remarkable and powerfully directed reversal, at the very lowest level, in the kingdom of pure matter (the genesis of atoms and stars).

Thus were produced multiple centres of mental reconstruction; we might well at first have thought that they radiated independently of one another, but we can now realize that their apparent plurality (just as that of the isolated groups of cells that are formed in a living tissue that is healing) soon joins up and fuses together when it is seen as part of the coherent and integral picture of a universe that is in full process of being made organic.

c. The emergence in our day of the idea of evolution

If we look around us (and more particularly in the conservative sections of the religious world) we are amazed to note how obstinately the truly infantile idea persists that the word 'evolution' does no more than disguise a mere 'local' dispute between biologists who are divided on the question of the origin of living species. We still hear the word 'Darwinism' used as a synonym for 'evolutionism'. As though what has happened in a mere half century goes for nothing: the rapid integration of the various individual trends recorded, more or less independently, by all groups of scientific researchers without exception, which is every day making it more evident that the ontogenesis of the microcosm (which each one of us represents) has no physically possible significance or context unless it is restored to its correct place not only in the phylogenesis of some zoological branch but in the very cosmogenesis of an entire universe; and that it is in the perception of this fundamental dynamic unity that we find the essence of the great modern advance represented by the idea of evolution.

This is something that we must fully understand once and for all: henceforth, for us and for our descendants, there is a complete change of psychological time-relationships and dimensions.

Well into the nineteenth century, man could still, on the whole, tell himself (without reacting to what was *physically* contradictory in this concept) that it was *only* the living being that was born, grew, died, within a matter that was always identical with itself – that only in connexion with the living could we speak of its *age*.

Now, however, we find that for every modern mind (and the more modern the mind, the truer this is) there has emerged, never to disappear, the consciousness – there has been born *the sense* – of a universal, absolutely specific movement, in virtue of which the totality of things is shifting, integrally and as one whole, from top to bottom, not simply within space and time, but in a (hyper-Einsteinian) space-time whose special bias is *to* introduce an ever higher degree of arrangement into that which moves within it.

It is what I have often called a movement of 'complexity-consciousness', or of 'corpusculization', or of 'centration', or 'interiorization'; inasmuch as the arrangement it produces rises up in the direction of groupings that are at once more astronomically complicated, more physically organic, and more psychologically free from determinism.

It is not a relative movement, we must note, but a true absolute movement, inasmuch as it advances towards a state that is definable *in relation to itself*.

Finally, it is not a movement of oscillation, nor is it simply an onward flow; it is a true genesis, inasmuch as in virtue of its structure – subject to a suitable working out of chances and free options – it grows additively in only one possible direction: that of an ultra-consciousness which, in the context of our planetary experience, can be expressed in terms of the *ultra-human*.

It is, I am convinced, in the ever more habitual and general perception of this global physico-psychic convergence (hitherto completely unsuspected) that there lies the essence of the modern notion (so often ill-defined) of evolution; but, what is even more, here we have the most sensational threshold crossed by man's consciousness in the million years for which it has been reflecting upon itself on the surface of the earth.

However, before I venture to pass such a judgment on the importance of the level at which we have just arrived, let us examine in rather more detail the situation that results, for our interior life, from a spiritual shock from which we emerge mentally changed to a degree of which, for the most part, we have as yet no conception.

2. The Situation: a cogitative transformation

I. A NEW TYPE OF UNIVERSE: THE ORGANICITY OF THE WHOLE

For our ancestors, time was both extrinsic in relation to themselves and isotropic in relation to itself. For us, it is becoming, more and more insistently, organic and convergent: the very stuff of things and the seat of their ontogenesis.

There is a whole series or family of questions that have hitherto always remained obscure or insoluble – the relationship between matter and spirit, the origin of evil, the place of the element in the whole, the terminal forms of the universe. If we look at them from our rectified point of view, it is surprising to note how simply they are cleared up and disentangled, when presented to a mind that disposes, in order to grasp the real, of *a further dimension*.

a. Relationship between matter and spirit

In the first place, under the cosmos-system, a fatal dualism was inevitably introduced into the structure of the universe. On one side lay spirit, and on the other matter: and between the two there was nothing but the affirmation of some unexplained and inexplicable coupling together – in other words there was ultimately no more than a verbal inter-dependence, which too often was akin to a subjection of one to the other. And all this was because the two terms of the couple were halted and fixed and had lost all genetic connexion with one another. On the other hand, consider what happens when there comes a breath of wind both to bring them to birth and set them in opposition to one another; when what, only yesterday, was regarded as two *things*, becomes no more than two aspects or phases of a single 'interiorizing arrangement'. Then the current can pass from one extreme to the other of the cosmic spectrum – from the infra-unconscious to the ultra-reflective – and an ontological coherence is established. We no longer have matter the junior partner, matter the handmaid, but matter the mother – *Materia matrix*. Phenomenally speaking, the stuff of things passing from the simplified, pulverized, state to the unified state – in other words, matter becoming charged with spirit: surely, that is indeed the most general, the most all-embracing, and the most fruitful, expression, for our experience, of the universal operation in which we are involved.

Let no one, I pray, intervene at this point to accuse me of materialism. In the idiom of cosmogenesis, what specifically brings the materialist into conflict with the spiritualist is *most certainly not* (as it is in fixist philosophy) the admission of a transition from the physical infra-structure of things to their psychic super-structure: it is *exclusively* the wrongful locating of the *final* point of balance of the cosmic movement on the side of the infra-structure (that is, the *de-composite*) and not on that of the super-structure (that is, the *super-composite*). That is quite another matter, and one that we shall meet again later when we speak of the 'termination' of the universe.

b. The origin of evil

Secondly, under the cosmos-system, it was always extremely difficult, if not impossible (except by the intervention of an *accident*, itself practically inexplicable) to justify to our reason the presence in the world of sufferings and wrong-doing. On the other hand (for how much longer shall we have to emphasize this, before we can shake 'public opinion' out of its rut and make it understand us?), when cosmogenesis is accepted, then, intellectually (I do not say *affectively*) speaking, not only is there a solution to the problem of evil, but the problem itself *ceases to arise*. This is because, for inexorable statistical reasons, it is physically impossible for some lack of arrangement, or some faulty arrangement, not to appear within a multitude which is *still undergoing the process of arrangement* – and that applies to every level of the universe, pre-living, living, and reflective. In such a system, which advances by tentative gropings, the laws of large numbers make it absolutely inevitable that every step towards order is paid for by failures, by disintegrations, by discordances: the proportion of these depends upon certain cosmic constants which it is impossible to determine, but to which it would certainly be useless to claim to fix *a priori* an upper limit beyond which one could say that the world was corrupted or evil.[1]

Like the powerful rockets that modern man so daringly launches in his attack on inter-stellar space, a cosmos in controlled movement cannot conceivably progress except by leaving behind it a more or less dense trail of smoke.

Evil[2] is thus a *secondary* effect, an inevitable *by*-product of the progress of a universe in evolution.

c. The place of the element in the whole

Thirdly, in the cosmos-system there would appear to be no structural reason for localizing and delimiting within the whole the sphere of existence and action of each individual centre considered on its own. In a world that is by nature convergent, on the other hand, we have only to reflect for a moment to realize that any element you please – already inaugurated however far back we go towards the origin of things – extends its influence in one way or another to the extreme end of the process in which it is involved; and this extension is accompanied for the element by an effect of continued unification

1. Thomist philosophy tries to solve the problem of evil (physical and moral) by insisting that it is purely negative (an absence or privation of being). In a fixist view of the cosmos evil appears as a *degradation* of being, a 'descent of being into the multiple, and so into the imperfect, from its starting point in the one and the supreme' (Sertillanges). In a view of the universe that sees it as a cosmogenesis, evil appears as an *incompleteness* of imperfect being advancing towards a higher state of organization under the influence of a transcendent pole of unity. Both types of explanation are based on the imperfection of the creature. (Ed.)

2. Not a *catastrophic* but an *evolutionary* evil.

and, provided it be psychologically reflective, by a constant heightening of its *personality*.

In other words, however dispersed and seriated they may be in their birth, both chronologically and spatially, as a result of the process of evolution, the particles in a cosmogenetic universe all possess the property of being infinitesimally *co-extensive* with the totality of time and space.[3] While they are all positioned, some more, some less, out of centre in the general system which is undergoing centration, each one plays, in relation to the whole, the part of a partial and incommunicable centre; and the convergence of the cosmos makes itself specifically apparent in the tendency which these countless elementary centres display to close up, to come together and, as we shall see, to reinforce one another in a universal super-centre of things.

d. The terminal form of the universe

Fourthly and finally, in the case of a static world, no specific configuration and no particular time could be assigned to the conclusion of the cosmic phenomenon. There was nothing, it would appear, to prevent the universe of Ptolemy or Aristotle from continuing indefinitely along its present course, or, on the other hand, from suddenly coming to a halt. Once again, in the cosmogenesis system, we find that the prospects for the future are vastly different and vastly more interesting.

In the first place, for objective reasons that derive from its very method of construction, a world of the convergent type cannot be conceived without some anticipated peak of maturing and consummation: a 'paroxysmal' peak.

3. This has the advantage of immediately dismissing from our intellectual horizon such monstrosities as the pseudo-ideas of 'separated souls',* or of metempsychosis.

* See E. Rideau, *Teilhard de Chardin, a guide to his thought*, pp. 157, 518–19, on Teilhard's view that the 'soul cannot be created *outside* a world.' 'The "separated" soul *continues to exist only in so far as it unifies the universe* – but in a new way (and one that will be fully realized only at the resurrection).' (Tr.)

Secondly, for equally cogent subjective reasons (the necessity inherent in a system that is in process of *reflective* evolution, of maintaining or even intensifying, right up to the imminence of a *foreseen* end, its psychic vital force, that is to say its zest for progress) – for these reasons, whatever external resemblance to a death that terminal paroxysm may possess, it can be envisaged only as a critical point of emergence and of the development of irreversibility.

As a result, therefore, of the ever more rapidly increasing influence of a collective reflection, what lies ahead of us, beyond a wide fringe of the ultra-human, is nothing less than entry into a final centre in which the human, through concentration, succeeds in forming one with some trans-human.

And here, in a new form, we are once again faced by the whole problem of God.

II. A NEW ASPECT OF GOD: THE UNIVERSAL CHRIST

Hitherto, a God of cosmos (that is, a creator of the 'efficient' type) was apparently all that was needed for our emotional and intellectual satisfaction. Henceforth (and it is here without any doubt that we should look for the underlying source of the modern religious uneasiness of mind) nothing but a God of cosmogenesis – that is a creator of the 'animating' type – can come up to the full measure of our capacity for worship.

We must, of course, in the first place and as a matter of cosmic necessity, at all costs retain the primordial transcendence of this new *evolutive God*, who rises up at the heart of the old maker-God; for, if he had not pre-emerged from the world, how could he be for the world an issue and a consummation lying ahead? It is, nevertheless, equally important to look more deeply into his immanent character, to appreciate it with wonder and delight – or even more important, since it is precisely in this immanence that the new vision of God we look for consists.

In a system of convergent cosmogenesis, to create is for God *to unite*. To unite, to form one with something, is to be immersed in it; but to be immersed (in the plural) is to become a particle within it. And to become a particle in a world whose arrangement statistically entails disorder (and mechanically calls for effort) is to plunge into error and suffering, in order to overcome them.

And thus it is that there gradually emerges a remarkable and fruitful connexion between theology and Christology.[4]

We may well say that, in spite of the spirit (or even the letter) of the writings of St Paul and St John, until recent times the figure of Christ as Saviour and his function as such retained, in current dogmatic formulation, something of the arbitrary, the juridical and the accidental. Why the Incarnation? Why the Cross? Affectively and from the pastoral point of view, the Christian economy was seen to be perfectly viable and efficient. Intellectually speaking, however, it was presented more as an arbitrary series of chance events than as an organically linked process. And this was a great loss to mysticism.

It is here, then, to make good this lack of ontological coherence (and, in consequence, of spiritual grip), that there intervenes the discovery of a type of universe in which, on the one hand, as we have just seen, God cannot appear as prime mover (ahead) without first becoming incarnate and without redeeming – in other words *without our seeing that he becomes Christified*;[5] and in which, by way of complement, Christ can

4. A fundamental humano-divine connexion that has the advantage of solving the twofold exasperating problem of divine ineffability and an absolutely gratuitous creation. For all the transcendence and self-sufficiency of the absolute being, something characteristic of him is inevitably impressed on nature since to some degree he informs it by causing it to emerge from 'non-being'. Moreover, some sort of complement is necessarily added to him by the creative act, once the latter is expressible in terms of *union* – creation becoming *a union* which engenders. We may note, incidentally, the religious importance of this new notion ('centripetal' as opposed to 'centrifugal') of the fatherhood of God.

5. From this point of view the 'triune' is now seen not as a higher continuation, but as the very heart of the 'Christic'.

no longer 'justify' man except by that same act super-creating the entire universe.

This is an important point and it must be emphasized.

I do not feel that I have either the capacity or the inclination to enter on a technical discussion of the problem of the super-natural; but what seems to me both vital to our mystical sense and evident to our reason is this: however ultra-gratuitous be the depth to which the heart of God opens up for us at this time, that God must, on the other hand, satisfy the condition of being (cf. below) *the one* peak of a universe which is henceforth recognized by us as structurally monocephalic and evolutively incomplete. In consequence, if Christ is (in the words of St Paul) to incorporate all things in himself and then to return to the bosom of the Father 'with the world gathered up in himself', it is not enough (as, maybe, we used to think it was) that he supernaturally sanctify a harvest of souls – he must do more, and in that same movement, he must creatively carry the noogenesis of the cosmos to the natural term of its maturity.

Thus we witness the gradual emergence of the astonishing notion and vision of a certain universal *Christic energy, at once supernaturalizing and ultra-humanizing*, in which is at the same time materialized and personalized the field of convergence that is necessary to explain and ensure the general and global involution of the cosmos on itself: an energy that has the power to embrace, in their full *extension* (if need be), the plurality of thinking planets engendered by the evolution of sidereal matter; or (if by some extraordinary chance no such extra-terrestrial reflective centres exist) at the very least an energy that is capable of *exhaustively* 'activating' (as I shall be showing) the totality of the psychic potential involved, on our earth, in the great venture of anthropogenesis.

III. A NEW FORM OF HUMAN ENERGY: LOVE OF EVOLUTION

As our science acquires a more distinct understanding of the bio-physical significance of the phenomenon of man – that is to say, of the role assigned to *reflective invention* of carrying further, by planned and combined effort, the psychogenic process of arrangement in which life consists – so, without our sufficiently realizing it, grows the need for some inner impulse which can provide fuel for the progress of evolution as it makes a fresh leap forward in its new form. In a first phase (that is under the governance of an imposed or at any rate irreflective evolution) the effects of planetary compression, combined with the instinct for survival, had been sufficient to ensure the progress of biogenesis. Starting, however, with man (that is, under the increasingly powerful governance of *auto-evolution*), a second and new type of driving force – by which I mean the reasoned passion for progress – emerges as ever more physically indispensable to ensure the continuation and the ultimate success of the cosmic movement of complexification.

Earlier, when considering the *negative* aspect of things, I have already referred to the intrinsic inviability of a universe which, by reason of its nature,[6] completely closed and subject to decay, would smother our power to seek and create. Turning now to the *positive* side of the problem, I shall emphasize once more the absolute necessity for mankind (if it is ever to effect a 'breakthrough') to be subject, in geometric progression with time, to the increasing magnetic pull of some object or objective that is more and more clearly distinguished ahead. At the level of, and starting from the reflective, there must not be simply an *absence* of revulsion; there must be the *constantly maintained influx* of an ever more rational, and ever more insatiable, zest for arriving at the end of the universe in movement, whatever that end may be: such, in brief, is seen to be in cosmogenesis the law or fundamental condition which governs the existence of a world around us.

Let us, then, in the light of this, turn back and again examine

6. And, we should add, by reason of a 'gratuitousness' so complete that it would become superfluous and dull. Nothing, not even evolution, can stand up to *boredom*.

the astounding Christic energy so recently born (as I was saying) in the subtle depths of human consciousness, through the coming together and cross-fertilization of the two psychic magnetisms – the one exerted upwards by an 'above' of revelation and the other propulsively forwards towards a cosmic 'ahead' of evolution.

We have no difficulty in seeing that in the field of this powerful discharge – inasmuch as it shows itself to be at once super-personal and super-personalizing – the universe (considered in the term of its total convergence) is completely *amorized*; since, for the reflective element immersed in a cosmogenesis whose pole is Christic, time and space (and that means every action and every event, everything that is done and everything that is undergone, every growth and every diminishment) are dynamically Christified in the very stuff of their fundamental reality.

Now, what is an *amorized* universe but a universe stimulated, *activated*, to the limit of its vital powers? We have known for a long time that, in virtue of its nature, love alone in the world was capable of indefinitely maintaining and realizing to their limit the potentialities of our action: but that this mysterious power could really operate (by which I mean, quite literally operate) no longer merely on the scale of the pair of lovers or of the family but on that of the whole of mankind or even of the entire universe – that was something that we could not seriously imagine or hope for, so long as in our eyes the cosmos was not transformed into cosmogenesis – and a cosmogenesis of union in which everything, by structure, became inflexibly lovable and loving.

Formerly we had no suspicion even that the world could move as one whole, in relation to itself. Now that we see that it is in motion, we realize that this movement cannot develop fully (that is, that it would lose its momentum) if we were not in the fortunate position of being able, and being obliged, to experience it, outside and beyond any anthropomorphism, as a supreme *Someone*.

Love of evolution: a phrase that was meaningless a mere fifty years ago: and yet an expression of the only psychic factor capable, it would seem,[7] of carrying to its term the effort of planetary self-arrangement[8] on which depends the cosmic success of mankind.

Conclusion. The perception of cosmogenesis: the particular and specific effect of cosmogenesis.

A new vision of the universe calls for a new form of worship and a new method of action.

Here we have the inner turning point, and a particularly sharp one it is, to which the general development of history has now brought us.

There are many who do not yet feel that this major psychological change of direction is a threat to the peaceful equilibrium in which they are quite content; or else they tend, if they are aware of it, to minimize it by attributing no more than a purely ideological or cognoscitive value to the phenomenon that is taking place. 'In fact,' they say, 'since the act of seeing the world more scientifically does no more than bring out a state of affairs that existed for a very long time already, without in any way modifying it, there is surely every reason to regard this act of which you make such a fuss, as superficial and secondary in relation to the underlying evolution (if indeed there be such a thing) of the universe.'

As a counter to this intellectual lack of commitment, I cannot, for my part, conclude the foregoing observations without re-affirming the specifically 'organic' nature of the mental transformation whose vicissitudes and effects on ourselves we can follow here and now in our own case. For if we admit (as we must indeed do if we are not to deny the very fact of cosmogenesis) that the initial step of reflection (from which

7. By reason of its unitive virtues, which, in a convergent universe, give it the quality of being ultimately the supremely effective and perfectly complete *evolutionary activity*.

8. Père Teilhard uses the English word. (Tr.)

the human zoological type emerged) represents an event whose substance is strictly *biological* – then how can we deny that same quality to the crossing of a characteristic *threshold*, in the course of time, by man's reflective power as it develops its system of mutual reinforcement? Particularly if the psychological crossing of this threshold is indeed accompanied by (– an infallible criterion of organicity –) a marked leap in the technico-social complexification of the noosphere?

A well-known tactical device employed by the fixists when they are driven into a corner, is to claim that even if life was formerly plastic and subject to transformation, since man this biogenesis has in any case been completely arrested. It is useless, too, in order to prove to them the contrary, to try to make them see that in the present manifest non-arrangement of the human mass can be seen, biologically, the potentiality and the imminence of some higher state of organization and consciousness.

In these circumstances, is it not interesting to note that by the recording deep within ourselves of an undeniable evolutionary shock, we are obliged to accept the direct evidence of an absolute drift of the universe in the direction of an increasing unity and interiority?

So we find the reality of a cosmogenesis established by the very self-perception[9] of this cosmogenesis.

It is, indeed, a remarkable and specially favoured phase of a movement whose crucial step, at a given moment, consists in becoming conscious of – and taking responsibility for – itself.

Unpublished, Paris
15 March 1951

9. Père Teilhard uses the English word. (Tr.)

Reflections on the Scientific Probability and the Religious Consequences of an Ultra-Human

In the course of the history of human thought certain general changes are periodically produced as the result of our suddenly acquiring a fresh view, on one point or another, of the dimensions of the universe.

Foremost among such new realizations (because it is the most tangible and spectacular) is obviously the recent appearance in the field of our experience of the infinitesimal and the immense in all sorts of *real* forms (numerical, temporal and spatial) which are closely associated: incredible multitudes of minute existences, often incredibly brief, within an incredibly vast universe.

In these few pages I shall try to draw attention to and to analyse a phenomenon which (because it is more elusive) has attracted less notice but is nevertheless much more revolutionary than these cosmic-scale changes: I mean the intellectual phenomenon as a result of which we are at this very moment awakening collectively to the consciousness of three movements – at once so slow that they had so far been overlooked by us – and so universal that they affect and involve what have hitherto been regarded as the most metaphysical, and in consequence, most unchangeable, depths of our being.

A cosmic movement (or cosmogenesis).

Which takes the more exact form of an organic movement (or biogenesis).

And is itself completed in a reflective movement (or anthropogenesis).

Three movements, let me repeat – or more accurately three

phases of one and the same movement – whose succession (taking them in the order of, simultaneously, decreasing obviousness and increased interiority) may be described as follows.

a. The cosmic movement (cosmogenesis)

Just as we should today have to do intolerable violence to ourselves in order to try to see in the stars in the sky anything but a dust-cloud of suns – so (without our realizing it) the impossibility has crept in of our regarding the world around us as a *ne varietur* construction, adroitly assembled in a single operation. In the space of two to three centuries, and under the converging influence of a number of factors (all connected with our growing awareness of the importance, in all fields of knowledge, of history) it has become impossible to present the world to us in the form of an established harmony: we now see unmistakably that it is a system in movement. It is no longer an *order* but a *process*. No longer a cosmos but a cosmo-genesis.

We hear much rather aimless talk nowadays, defending or attacking an evolution that is still understood in the restricted and out of date sense of 'transformism' (or even simply 'Darwinism'!). In the new and magnificent sense of the word, let us insist once more, evolution has become for science something very different – something much bigger and much more certain than that. It is an expression of the structural law (both of 'being' and of knowledge) by virtue of which *nothing, absolutely nothing*, we now realize, can enter our lives or our field of vision except by *way of birth*[1] – which means, in other words, the pan-harmony in space-time of the phenom-enon – and as such evolution has nothing in common with a hypothesis: nor (though one still hears such nonsense) has it had for a long time. On the contrary, taken in the general sense of 'cosmogenesis', it represents the only dimensional setting in

1. That is, as a function of antecedents which are themselves linked with the totality of earlier states of the universe.

which our capacity to think, to seek and to create can henceforth function. And for that reason (when considered, I insist, at this first degree – however vague it may be – of 'becoming conscious of a cosmic movement') not only must it be regarded as certain, but, further, one could only intellectually despair of every mind that did not see in it, now and henceforth, the stuff of which all that we are certain of is made.

b. *The organic movement* (*biogenesis*)

Of itself, and in itself, a cosmogenesis may have all sorts of forms. It could, for example, be conceived *a priori* either as an orderless turmoil in process of dissipation (pseudo-cosmogenesis) – or on the contrary as a *directed* process (eu-cosmogenesis): this latter again, in turn, might either spread equally in all directions (like a ray in an amorphous medium), or (as light in an anisotropic medium) become polarized along certain favoured axes.

In the experimental reality of things, the question is with which of these various types of evolution are we in practice concerned.

Although before long an answer must inevitably be found to this important question, it does not seem that science has yet *explicitly* come to any definitive conclusion. Implicitly, however, it seems to me that there can be no doubt that it is already coming down with its whole weight on the side of recognizing and admitting a *directed* cosmogenesis: this being later defined by a main axis of complexity-consciousness (or of 'corpusculization'), whose nature I would like once again briefly to make clear.

Merely to hear the phrase 'controlled cosmogenesis', the first reaction of our alert mind is to turn to that impressive 'mass-drift' by which in obedience to the laws of gravity a powdery matter first twists itself into galaxies and ultimately coalesces into distinct stars, within space. The main axis of the world in movement: why should it not be a line running from atoms to stars?

If I am not deluding myself, it is this 'astronomical' view of things which is gradually being so forcibly attacked by a very different outlook that it must soon be supplanted by it – by, that is, the 'biological' view of a movement not of gravitational coalescence but of organic complexification. At the beginning we still have the extremely simple, the extremely small and (perhaps) the extremely short-lived. Starting, however, from this common origin, we have another and quite different branch; this does not rise up towards the vast sidereal magnitudes but runs, through the building-up of ever more formidably polyatomic molecules, in the direction of the cell and of the multicellular, up to and including man. It is an axis, in this case, stretching not from the infinitesimal to the immense of density and mass, but from the elementary to the immensity of complexity.

For science to perceive this new directrix of the cosmos it had to negotiate two difficult steps. The first rung consisted in recognizing a genetic bond within the world of molecules on the one hand, and between living species on the other – which sums up, in fact, all the nineteenth century's work in analysis and systematics – and then, when that was done – to divine (and then make apparent) the possibility of laying the two segments of the curve end to end. The second rung consisted in becoming accustomed to the idea that an apparently so exceptional phenomenon as life could seriously be regarded as representing the extreme and specific term of universal physico-chemism.

In our present position, let me repeat, we cannot yet say that this twofold intellectual re-orientation has been expressly effected in the minds of all specialists in the study of organic or inorganic matter. While there is inevitably complete unanimity about the general existence of an evolution (otherwise we could neither understand one another nor get on with our work), it is equally true that there is still a certain indecision in the attitude of many scientists to the particular form assumed by this great movement. This, however, is much more, I believe, from the fact that they express their opinions with caution and reserve than from any fundamental lack of certainty.

In fact, and whatever may be said, the idea of a universe that is moving, principally and specifically, towards states of super-organization which can be measured, in terms of absolute value, by an increase of psychic interiorization and centration – the idea of such a universe is, I am sure, clearly gaining ground. And the reason for this is that it is constantly implicit in the irresistible movement which has first permanently welded physics and chemistry into one, and is now bringing together the two domains, external and internal ('objective' and 'subjective'), of matter and psyche – a process that, with each new impact of the facts recorded, it is carrying a little further.

So advanced is this development that the problem is quite naturally and logically shifting its ground, and the real question which is now raised for the scientific mind by the problem of evolution is a different one: and a vital and burning question it is. It is not to know whether, when reduced to its essence, cosmogenesis is a biogenesis, but to decide categorically whether it is possible to attribute to this same biogenesis a principal axis – an axis that runs through the phenomenon of man.

c. The reflective movement (anthropogenesis)

Let us consider, within our own selves and around us, the natural play of human particles – that is, of the most advanced corpuscles known to our science on the cosmic axis of complexity-consciousness. It calls for nothing less than the obliterating action[2] in our minds of ingrained habit to disguise from us the unique and amazing power displayed by these 'reflective molecules' of grouping together, under planetary pressure, in such a way as to form a system which is in a state of continual

2. Combined with the firmly rooted preconception, shared as much by the 'materialist' as the 'theologian' that the biological stops short at the frontiers of the human.

super-reflection. It is, true enough, an effect of socialization; in other words, a hominized extension of a property that is common to all organic matter – but it is an extension that amounts, quite simply, to a change of order (as does reflection itself in relation to the direct consciousness of the pre-human).

I am deeply convinced that it is by being confronted with this great event (*interpreted in biological terms*) of the totalization of man, that modern science will soon find itself inevitably obliged to take its third step; and this will be the most serious of the three, in the direction of an ever more closely reasoned and exact concept of the idea of evolution.

It is astonishing even for specialists in living forms and in palaeontology to observe how often man is still naïvely regarded either as a species that has come to a dead end and will never in future exceed its present ceiling – or, at the most, as some phylum which does no more than continue its linear development – as do horses and elephants.

It is, then, I maintain, this unenterprising and static view which is being demolished by the still youthful – but eminently vigorous – idea of a human zoological group which by no means represents a mere terminal branch, but corresponds in reality to an original rebound of evolution on itself – one that, by the crossing of a characteristic threshold, introduces a complete transformation. In that human group we see a higher type and stage of cosmic arrangement in which, through the specific properties of a reflective psychic milieu, convergence replaces the divergence of the evolving scales – so much so that the corpusculization of matter, at this level, comes to operate not merely by the grouping of atoms, molecules, or cells, but by ultra-reflecting synthesis of entire 'reflective individuals'.

I shall not examine here in detail the facts that in the eyes of science justify this hypothesis of an extension and generalization, through man, of the cosmic law of complexity–consciousness: individuation, expansion, and consolidation, continually more evident, of a terrestrial noosphere, accompanied by the ever more marked establishment within that noosphere of a regime of inventive auto-evolution – the effective passage, as an effect of the mutual reinforcement of minds, through new levels of consciousness (such as that mentioned above, for example, which introduces us to the general notion of cosmogenesis), etc.

What, on the other hand, I must emphasize, is the imminence and the gravity of the coming psychic mutation or sloughing of accustomed ways: for, by giving us a better appreciation of the phenomenon of man, it is going to lead us all, and soon, to the habitual perception of an ultra-evolution of life on earth towards states that are ever more organic and interiorized. Henceforth, there lies ahead of us, in time, not merely a greater number of men; not merely, even, a higher intensity of humanity; but the concentration of the whole of the human in a single co-reflective system, planetary in dimensions.

Anthropogenesis, the basic axis of biogenesis, extending itself like a cluster of convergent rays in the direction of some glowing centre – the human gradually in some way being 'mono-moleculized' by ultra-hominization . . .

I could not, of course, go so far as to say that this possibility is as yet commonly envisaged.

But, unless we are to be scientifically inconsistent, I do not see how we could in future escape it – nor, meanwhile, prevent the half-hidden accumulation of the evidence for this interfering, in the depths of our hearts, with the ancient and traditional influence of the forces of religion.

II. RELIGIOUS CONSEQUENCES OF THE EXISTENCE OF AN ULTRA-HUMAN: A CHRISTOGENESIS BY WHICH THE ABOVE AND THE AHEAD ARE RECONCILED

Inasmuch as it discloses ahead of us the possibility of as yet unknown physico-psychic arrangements, the recognition that the universe is moving evolutively towards a peak of consciousness, that it has a 'head', has more than a great physical importance: inasmuch, too, as the act of reflection ceases to be no more than an individual operation of mental dialectic and assumes the form of an historic process cosmic[3] in scope, it has more than a great metaphysical importance. Even – indeed above all – in the field of mysticism the newly acquired perception of a movement of ontological convergence inevitably arouses anxious questionings and necessitates profound reformulations.

The reason for this may be described as follows.

Hitherto, the idea of *spirit* had always, on the whole, been presented to the consciousness of men as linked with some *ascending* movement which carries the soul towards heaven through *denial* (or at least through *contempt*) of terrestrial values. Thus, whatever the form of the divine – personal or impersonal, immanent or transcendent – for the 'perfect' it always represented a sort of Above; and to attain it, it was 'by definition' necessary to escape from the determinisms and seductions of the corporeal things in which we are involved.

Now, it is precisely at right-angles (if I may so put it) to this traditional pole of sublimation and holiness that, as a result of the *cephalization* of evolution, our baffled minds see the emergence at this moment of a second centre of spiritualization and divinization: spirit no longer in discord, but in *concord*, with a super-arrangement of the phenomenal multiple. The issue, no longer above, into some transcendent supernatural, but ahead, into the immanence of an ultra-human.

In other words, there is now a conflict between two pictures of God, one vertical and the other horizontal.

In that diagrammatic form, I am daily more convinced, we can express the root source of the religious difficulties we are going through.

Mankind, in a world that has suddenly become too big and too organic, has for a moment lost its God.

In order to remedy the *rupture* of this situation, a certain intransigent supernaturalism would not shrink, I know, from

3. Thought, in consequence, being exchanged for noogenesis (just as cosmos for cosmogenesis, and man for anthropogenesis).

accepting the idea of a *bi-cephalous* universe, in which man would in reality be presented with the choice between *two* consummations of the world, the one natural and the other supernatural. For my own part, however, such a 'dynamic dualism' has so exaggerated an element of the arbitrary (not to say of the inconsistent) and involves so colossal a waste of energy, that it seems to me completely unviable and unacceptable.

We have, however, already admitted that the idea of a convergent cosmogenesis is destined tomorrow to form an integral and essential part of man's psychological heritage; and inasmuch as that is so, nothing seems to me more feasible and fruitful (and hence more imminent) than a synthesis between the above and the ahead in a becoming of the 'Christic' type, in which access to the transcendent hyper-personal would depend, as a condition, on the previous arrival of human consciousness at a critical point of collective reflection. The supernatural, in consequence, would not exclude but, on the contrary, call for, as a necessary preparation, the complete maturing of an ultra-human.[4]

One can readily appreciate the advantages for the future of human energy represented by such a transfiguration of anthropogenesis, now recognized as ultimately identical with a *Christogenesis*. On the one hand, there is an end to the anxious questionings of a capacity for worship that is unsatisfied and torn in two directions. On the other hand, there is an end to the torment of a reflective awakening into a world that is blind and closed. These grim shadows are replaced by a blaze of light.

This is something I have already said countless times, but I must repeat it once more.

4. Here Père Teilhard reproduces the teaching of St Irenaeus, of which he was so fond. God raises man up step by step in the course of history. 'It was necessary that man should first be created, then that he should grow up, then that he should become adult man, then that he should multiply, then gain in strength, then attain glory, and, having attained glory, that he should have the vision of his master' (*Demonstration*, Bk. IV, ch. 38). (Ed.)

What man is looking for now, and would die were he not to find it in things, is a *complete pabulum* to nourish in him the passion for fuller-being, in other words for evolution.

And, in a universe that is drawn and animated by a Christogenesis, it is this very passion which, through the according of a maximum value to the forces of arrangement and the opening of a maximum field to the forces of worship, is carried to its paroxysmal climax.

'In truth, the more one reflects on this remarkable harmonization and sympathetic resonance, along a humano-Christian axis, of the various major components (physical and psychic) of a cosmogenesis that no one henceforth can seriously deny – the more one comes to think that the characteristic event of our time is far from being (as is still often said) the decline of God *in our minds and our hearts*. On the contrary it is clearly apparent as an undreamed-of renaissance of God *in the universe, in the form of love-energy*, produced as the fruit of, and within, a matter that has become for us the home and the expression of *an evolutionary convergence*.

After a million years of reflection, there is a dynamic meeting in the consciousness of man between heaven and earth at last endowed with motion, and from it there emerges not simply a world that manages to survive but a world that kindles into fire.

Unpublished, Paris
Easter, 25 March 1951

The Convergence of the Universe

INTRODUCTION. NOTE ON THE NOTION OF 'COSMIC DRIFT'

FOR some time there has been much talk among astrophysicists of an accelerated movement, in all directions around us, of the galaxies – a movement that is evidence of a general expansion of the universe.

Whatever fate may tomorrow await this attractive theory,[1] one fact is now permanently established, and it is in a way more important than any particular hypothesis of the geometric configuration of the world. It is that in the course of the twentieth century science has gone beyond the simple notions of structures, of pressures, and of cycles, and finally awoken to the idea that there are certain general processes that, dynamically or genetically, affect the totality of the universe.

'An exploding universe' is a common expression nowadays, and a frequent subject of speculation: and it is used with the full realization that in doing so we are not leaving the field of facts and experience.

Why not, then – and with even more justification, I would say – 'a universe which, under the influence of an ever more advanced organic arrangement, concentrates and reflects psychologically upon itself'?

What I propose briefly to set out here, are the objective proofs and the subjective consequences of such a movement, which is no longer merely one of spatial expansion for the

1. Which is based, as we know, on the still arguable idea that the reddening of the galaxies in proportion to their distance is due to their own movement – and not simply to a fatigue (or ageing) of light.

   [By 'reddening' Père Teilhard means the shift of spectrum lines towards red. (Ed.)]

stuff of the cosmos but of psychogenic concentration: and this I shall do by dealing in turn with each of the three following points:

1. The positive evidence for an organo-psychic convergence of the world upon itself.

2. The vital necessity for us immediately to make up our minds about the reality of such a movement of convergence.

3. The main lines of attack that will enable us once and for all to verify the existence of the phenomenon and determine its behaviour.

I. THE EVIDENCE FOR AN ORGANO-PSYCHIC CONVERGENCE OF THE UNIVERSE UPON ITSELF

If we are to understand the nature and realize the probability of the particular movement of cosmic concentration referred to in this essay, we must first (and this is all we need to do) come to an agreement on two points. It is only rarely, as yet, that these are directly taken into consideration, but I believe that we must say that they are now due for a discussion and a decision of the scientific order. The first concerns the position of the human in relation to the rest of the living; and the second defines the significance of the social within the human.

a. Direct life and reflective life

Modern science has made us familiar with the idea that certain sudden radical changes inevitably occur in the course of every development, provided it be carried far enough and constantly in the same direction. When matter has reached certain extreme levels of transformation, then an extremely small modification in its arrangement (or in the conditions that govern the arrangement) allows it suddenly to modify its properties or even to change its state.

This notion of *critical thresholds* is commonly accepted today in physics, in chemistry, and in genetics.

The time, surely, has come for us to make use of it in order to reconstruct the entire fabric of anthropology on a new and solid foundation.

By pure 'anatomical' routine man is still, inexplicably, regarded by the majority of biologists as a mere filament (or sub-filament) in the fascicle of zoological forms: a 'sub-family' (no more than a few lines) in Dr G. G. Simpson's monumental catalogue of genera; an utterly insignificant leaflet on the impressive tree of life that illustrates Lucien Cuénot's scientific testament.

And yet, as a matter of sound science, is it not time for us to recognize that such a view is certainly mistaken?

Studied in his skeleton, it is true, man undoubtedly appears to be closely derived from the large primates; but this in no way prevents him from, in other respects, displaying certain powers which oblige us (if we wish to systematize the facts correctly) to place him in a distinct category, completely separate from the rest of life.

It is an amazing thing – in less than a million years[2] the human 'species' has succeeded in covering the earth: and not only spatially – on this surface that is now completely encircled mankind has completed the construction of a close network of planetary links, so successfully that a special envelope now stretches over the old biosphere. Every day this new integument grows in strength; it can be clearly recognized and distinguished in every quarter; it is provided with its own system of internal connexions and communications – and for this I have for a long time proposed the name of noosphere.

If one really wishes to accord to this extraordinary event the place it is entitled to in nature, I can, for my part, see no other interpretation of it than this.

About a thousand million years ago – at the beginning, that is, of the pre-Cambrian era – a 'mutation' (whose exact nature

2. We could even say, if we confined ourselves to the second and more rapid phase of the phenomenon, in less than twenty thousand years of the expansion of *Homo sapiens*.

is not clear to us) without any doubt vitalized at certain points the film of proteinic substances which (we must presume) was spread over the surface of the juvenile earth. And from this particular transformation there emerged the whole of the biosphere.

So: it is, I believe, by analogy with this primitive revolution of planetary chemism that we must judge the great phenomenon which intervened towards the end of the Tertiary (through neuro-psychic mutation) in the most highly cerebralized areas of the biosphere. By this I mean the transition to a form of *reflective* activity.[3]

A generation of investigators in the nineteenth century devoted themselves to the indispensable task of disinterring the animal roots of mankind – in order genetically to connect the human to the general evolution of matter. Today, however, with this preliminary work of connecting the two completed, it is the physical nature of the 'hominization leap' which is becoming the important aspect of the problem. From this latter point of view, then, it is no longer enough (indeed it would henceforth be anti-scientific and illogical) to continue to treat man as a mere compartment *inside* the animal kingdom. Physico-biologically, in virtue of his planetary situation, man transcends classic systematics, because he belongs to another level, another form, another species of life in the universe.

With hominization, it is indeed, at a distance of some six hundred million years, a *second* vitalization (a super-vitalization) of the cosmic stuff that was effected on earth. And since that time, in man and through man, it is evolution itself that gets off to a fresh start, rebounding upon itself.

However, if we are to understand this correctly, we shall have to take another look, from a new angle, at the true nature of the phenomenon, all around us, of socialization and its effects.

---

3. The animal, it would seem, only *knows*: while man '*knows that he knows*'. It is a case, as it has sometimes been described, of 'consciousness squared'.

b. The individual and society

Practically all of us, again under the influence of 'anatomical' preconceptions, live with the impression (and some scientists even develop, as a principle, the conviction) that the human individual is not organically affected by the multiple links that act upon him from all sides to associate him 'symbiotically' with his fellows. For more than twenty thousand years, we now know, there has been no appreciable change in the shape of his cranium; his elementary instincts have remained the same. Is not this a conclusive proof that civilization and culture produce in us no more than temporary and superficial modifications, from which primitive man would emerge unchanged if, by chance, the forces of collectivity were to slacken their grip on him?

'In nature, socialization is not a process that belongs to specifically evolutionary substance; biologically speaking, it is the individual who is everything; and, in man, the individual has for a long time been permanently stabilized as he now is.'

This is a proposition that we now hear and read almost everywhere – not only in literature but even in the most scientific of writings.

Has it, however, ever occurred to us that, reasoning in this way (if they were able to reason), the various atoms which make up a molecule of protein (or the various particles of protein united in a cell) would have to decide that this molecule or this cell had no specifically 'corpuscular' value: their argument being that, within the system, carbon is still apparently made of carbon, hydrogen of hydrogen, and so on?

In order to estimate the degree of organicity attained by an arrangement in the universe, we must now realize, it is not directly the variation of the constituent elements that we have to consider – nor even the rigidity of the links that ensure the permanence of the system. It is the irreversible appearance or growth, within the assembly, of certain fundamental properties, of which the most significant, in the organic series, is the gradual emergence of the effects of indetermination and preferential choice. In conformity with this rule, we must regard as possessing organic value in the living (whether we are concerned with a virus or with man) every arrangement[4] whose result is to cause a rise in the 'psychic temperature' – or, if the phrase is preferred, to increase the interiority – of the group in which the arrangement is found.

We cannot, therefore, fail to see that of all the living things we know, none is more really, more intensely, living than the noosphere.

Earlier, I said that what explains the human biological revolution is the organo-psychic threshold of reflection.

Is it not, then, precisely reflection which is now, as a result of the countless forces of socialization, freely and continuously rising to the surface of the earth? It is no longer the simple isolated reflection of an individual upon himself, but the conjugate and combined reflection of innumerable elements, adjusting and mutually reinforcing their activities, and so gradually forming one vast mirror – a mirror in which the universe might one day reflect itself and so fall into shape.

Collectivization may seem to us, in the detail of its manifestations, commonplace and superficial and tedious; however true that may be, it is ultimately, if I am right, nothing but, and nothing less than, the final form assumed by biological evolution in order to prolong itself in a reflective medium.

Let us accept this idea that there is in the forces of socialization a value that is specifically biological or even biological at a higher level; and let us connect it with the other idea, set out earlier, of a difference of order (or of nature) between the simply living and the reflective living.

If we do so, we shall experience the thrill of seeing that, in a direction for which we have never as yet had a name, and in which hitherto everything could appear completely immobile, it is now the whole universe that thus suddenly becomes animate and begins to get under way.

---

4. We shall call such a form of arrangement 'psychogenic'.

c. A new movement of the universe in relation to itself: the cosmic drift of complexity-consciousness

What, at this moment, most paralyses any advance in our vision of the world, is the habit we have formed (as being the less demanding of effort) of regarding life as something protean in its manifestations: something that can be indefinitely diversified to correspond to the multiple *phyla* of zoology, but which does not for all that change its nature. More the colourful blossoming of a firework display than the ascent of a rocket: more an explosion than a trajectory – it is as such (because this seems to us more simple) that we would like, maybe, to see evolution.

If I am right, however, it is precisely this stationary, if not static, view that is radically transformed by the discovery of an exact parameter (I mean the rise of reflection) which allows us to distinguish and estimate, in terms of absolute value, a certain drift inherent in life.

This is what I mean: if we use as abscissae the length in years of geological periods, as now determined for us by the study of radio-active bodies, and then approximately plot as ordinates a certain number of representative points in biogenesis, such as

a. The planetary origins of life

b. The appearance of the tetrapods

c. The appearance of mammals

d. The critical point of hominization

e. And finally (at the level of *Homo sapiens*) the starting point of the true noosphere

– and if, when we have done that, we draw the curve of planetary 'vitalization' as a function of time

– we cannot fail to see that, beneath the disconcerting multiplicity of the morphological branches continually developed within the biosphere by speciation, a fundamental trend[5] is unmistakably manifested around us by the phenomenon of man: a trend that displays the twofold character of

5. Exponential in form.

a. first, drawing us, at a speed that increases so rapidly as to become explosive, towards closely linked states of complexity and consciousness,

b. and secondly, of indicating, under the continued influence of planetary synthesis, the existence ahead of us of some critical and final point of ultra-hominization, corresponding to a complete reflection of the noosphere upon itself.

Moreover, I may add, we cannot fail to suspect, when we look at the graph we have produced, that by using the evidence of a particular case[6] we can distinguish in the hominization of matter on the surface of the earth, a certain fundamental law that affects the entire world.[7]

We no longer have in the universe nothing but that heart-breaking entropy, inexorably reducing things (as we are still constantly being told) to their most elementary and most stable forms: but, emerging through and above this rain of ashes, we see a sort of cosmic vortex within which the stuff of the world, by the preferential use of chances, twists and coils upon itself ever more tightly in more complex and more fully centred assemblies.

A world that is in equilibrium upon instability, because it is in movement: and a world whose dynamic consistence is increasing in exact proportion with the complexity of its arrangements, because it is converging upon itself[8] in as many sidereal points as there ever have been, as there are now, and as there ever will be, thinking planets.

II. THE VITAL NECESSITY, FOR OUR GENERATION, OF IMMEDIATELY MAKING UP ITS MIND ABOUT THE REALITY OF A COSMIC MOVEMENT OF CONVERGENCE

In the course of the sixteenth century, man found himself obliged to admit that the earth, far from being the immobile centre of the universe, revolved around the sun. The new thesis

6. The convergence of man.   7. A convergence of the cosmos.
8. Whether mono-centrically or poly-centrically, it is impossible to say.

was no doubt clumsily expressed, since, as much in the mind of Galileo as in that of his opponents, 'the heavenly bodies' were thought of as moving in an *absolute* space. Nevertheless, it was truly revolutionary inasmuch as, as a result of the blow dealt to geocentrism, the notion of cosmos began, both psychologically and logically, to vanish and make way for a view of the universe that was expressed in terms of cosmogenesis.

We can now see what happened. In Galileo's time, a decision had at all costs to be made (for all the persisting vagueness of contemporary scientific concepts) for or against a spatial revolution of the earth in the firmament. For a moment, the whole of the future of human thought (and activity) hung upon the answer to this question.

Nearly five centuries later, but in an even more critical way, we are, it seems to me, in the same situation now, according to whether we agree or refuse to recognize in the phenomenon of man the evidence of what I have just called a drift in which the universe converges upon itself.

Let me explain the reason for this.

It is unmistakably apparent (as all of us can see) that at this moment we are irretrievably involved in a rapidly accelerating process of human totalization.[9] Under the combined force of the multiplication (in numbers) and expansion (in radius of influence) of human individuals on the surface of the globe, the noosphere has for the last century shown signs of a sudden organic compression upon itself and compenetration. This is without any doubt the most massive and the most central of the events the earth has experienced in our day.

Now that life has placed us in this critical situation, how are we going to react to the test?

So long as we adhere to the cautious traditional concept and continue to say that mankind has come to a dead end, the compression and the consequent concretion of the human mass can be seen by us only as a ridiculous constraint or even evil: as ridiculous, in truth, as cramming passengers into a railway

9. A state, let me add, that is totalized but not totalitarian.

carriage. That is why we are so often horrified, or terrified, by the modern world: a machine for destroying the individual or mechanizing him.

If, on the other hand, as suggested by the indications mentioned above of a collective rise of reflection on earth, we admit that the hyper-socialization from which we are suffering is nothing but an ultra-vitalization (by ultra-arrangement) of the human mass which is forced gradually to shift its position in a convergent universe – we shall react quite differently.

In that case, while the process loses none of its peril or unpleasantness, it is completely transfigured. It takes on a meaning. And we see how we can effectively collaborate in its success.

I must, however, emphasize that if this is to come about, we must make up our minds and get down to work, *quickly*, *immediately*.

For, if it is really true that an ultra-human can be distinguished ahead of us, to be attained by ultra-evolution, it is equally true that this ultra-evolution, operating henceforth in *a reflective medium*, can only be (at least in its most seminal and central axis) an auto- or self-evolution: in other words, it must be *a consciously and passionately willed deliberate act*. If the totalization of the noosphere is to be biologically successful, it cannot be simply instinctive and passive. It looks to us for an active and immediate collaboration, for a vigorous drive, based on conviction and hope. For evolution will not mark time.

Do we see or do we not see, admit or refuse to admit, that as an effect of complexification and arrangement life is coming to rise more and more rapidly on earth, within a convergent universe? That is the precise point upon which mankind is obliged to divide itself (as, indeed, we can see for ourselves it is actually doing) into two irreconcilably conflicting blocs.

And, we can confidently predict, only that portion of mankind which has made the correct choice will survive – and super-live.

III. SOME LINES OF ATTACK THAT ALLOW US FURTHER TO VERIFY THE REALITY OF THE PHENOMENON

In order to verify the hypothesis of an explosive cosmos, the physicists have recently brought into operation a giant telescope, designed to reveal the existence of ever more distant galaxies and allow us to study their behaviour.

If the preceding considerations are correct, surely the most urgent task confronting the genius of man at this moment is to conceive and undertake the construction of another 'Palomar' – but this one would be designed to bring out not an expansion of the universe in space but a psychogenic concentration of the universe upon itself: and this by magnification and analysis of the phenomenon of man.

It is a story, this time, not of a sufficiently large mirror and sufficiently sensitive photographic plates: it is a matter of bringing together a large enough number of minds that are sufficiently open and in tune with influences of the cosmic order to perceive, record and amplify a movement of the noosphere in relation to itself.

Such an enterprise, it is evident, can profitably be undertaken only after a very considerable preliminary work of discussion and tentative inquiry conducted by expert physicists and biologists.[10]

Even so, it would seem possible here and now to enumerate some main lines along which the problem may be attacked.

1. From what I have already said, the ideal method of scientifically establishing the phenomenon of a convergence of the universe would be to be able, by some technique, at every moment to measure directly the psychic charge (or tempera-

---

10. This means, as a start, simply a working-party, made up of selected technical experts, which would produce a clear statement of the facts and provide a more or less official introduction into science of the problem of a shifting of mankind in relation to itself.

ture) of mankind – in other words, the degree or gradient of its reflection upon itself. This is an operation that is as yet hardly conceivable, but will not, perhaps, baffle the physics of tomorrow. Meanwhile, using a more descriptive method, may there not really be a way, for a scientifically alert observer, of detecting around us the signs of an ultra-evolution (we might say 'a wind of reflection') in a whole series of psychic phenomena, still incompletely identified and yet patient of statistical study? For example, the general rise, at this very moment, in the *most advanced* areas of human thought, of a certain distress – or, on the contrary, of a certain excited anticipation – both specifically connected with the gradual awakening in us of the consciousness that the universe is not only in movement but is carrying us with it.

2. In the absence of, or marginal to, these direct but as yet ill-explored proofs of a human drift towards some ultra-human, a vast field of indirect verification leading to the same result is indisputably open to us; it lies in the direction of a deeper analysis of *the structure of the noosphere*. One of the first tasks of the commission appointed to bring out and keep under observation the symptoms of a psychogenic convergence of the universe, would certainly be to design and forward the construction of certain characteristic curves (cf. above), which would express in terms of absolute value the chronological division of the levels crossed by life in order to become hominized, and by mankind in order to become planetized: a curve of speciation (or cerebration); a curve of expansion; a curve of population; a curve of planetary compression, etc. There can be little doubt but that such graphs would make abundantly clear to everyone the evidence of a process, at once qualitative and quantitative, of cosmic arrangement, whose explosive behaviour rules out the hypothesis that the movement into which we are born is now slowing down, and still less coming to a halt.

3. In consequence, we might say that at this moment, as in the

time of Galileo, what we most urgently need in order to appreciate the convergence of the universe is much less new facts (there are enough and even embarrassingly more than enough of these in every quarter) than a new way of looking at the facts and accepting them.

A new way of seeing, combined with a new way of acting – that is what we need.

From this we can draw but one conclusion, that the speculative effort of the new Palomar of which we are now dreaming cannot be conceived apart from an accompanying practical effort to readjust, within a universe that is recognized as convergent, the whole range of human values.

The admission that we have emerged from and are enveloped in a universal flux of centrifying complexification does not, indeed, have as its sole consequence the introduction of more meaning and coherence into the total fabric of our present experience than any former way of looking at things. More than any other, this new view, we must add, gives an orientation and an unlooked-for excitement to our need to act, at the very moment when we were beginning to be in two minds about the future.

We must recognize, then, the vital importance of a collective quest of discovery and invention no longer inspired solely by a vague delight in knowledge and power, but by the duty and the clearly-defined hope of gaining control (and so making use) of the fundamental driving forces of evolution.

And with this, the urgent need for a generalized eugenics (radical no less than individual) directed, beyond all concern with economic or nutritional problems, towards a biological maturing of the human type and of the biosphere.

Simultaneously, too, the necessity of drawing up as soon as possible the main lines of a spiritual energetics[11] devoted to the study of the conditions under which the human zest for auto-evolution and ultra-evolution – which at the moment is dissipated in any number of different forms of faith and love –

11. Or 'psychodynamics', on the analogy of 'thermodynamics'.

may be in a position to form a compact group,[12] to safeguard itself and to intensify – to meet the requirements, and through the influence of, the new regime we have just entered: that of a world in a reflective state of self-transformation.

Here we have a complete programme: in it, a momentary initial effort definitively to establish in men's minds the appreciation of a convergence of the universe, is gradually transformed into another and more constructive task, one that is capable of almost indefinite possible developments: it is the practical effort of industriously furthering this convergence, in our terrestrial sector, until it attains the term or centre (whatever it may be) of its fulfilment.[13]

Unpublished, Capetown, 23 July 1951

---

12. Sexual attraction; religious forces; the sense of man, based now not on the notion of a common origin (a centre of divergence) but on the idea of some consummation lying ahead.

13. This centre of complete reflection coinciding with what mysticism has since all time called the revelation of God.

The Transformation and Continuation in Man of the Mechanism of Evolution

Written for Huxley[1]

NOBODY today has any serious doubt that, speaking in terms of anatomy and psyche, man appeared towards the end of the Tertiary as a function of the general process of zoological evolution. However, since that initial emergence, has man continued, and does he still continue, to move and change organically in relation to himself? In other words, does man represent a threshold, or on the contrary a ceiling, in the progress of biogenesis?

It is curious to note the reaction of professional scientists when confronted by this fundamental question (which, nevertheless, is still so seldom explicitly formulated); they either evade it, on the ground that it lies outside their competence, or they take a completely opposite line, and adopting the 'common sense' attitude of the man in the street, decide that after all there is every possibility that man has reached a zoological dead end of evolution. For, they say, echoing a commonplace of moralists and writers, 'As long as we have known man, he has always been the same; or, if mankind is changing it is no longer doing so, as life does, in an organic field, but solely on a cultural and technical plane. Which is a completely different matter.'

At the root of this hesitancy, or even persistent refusal, on the part of anthropologists to recognize a biological value, properly so called, in human progress, there lies, to my mind, a strange forgetfulness of what one might call *the general law of transformation of physical processes* in nature.

1. The manuscript has this dedication (*Écrit pour Huxley*) to Sir Julian Huxley. (Ed.)

Theoretically, for a geometrician who deals with *pure* variables, any magnitude (length, volume, density, number, temperature, speed) may increase or decrease indefinitely, in accordance with a constant formula. However, physics teaches us that in the concrete realization of things it is quite a different story. Just as a river whose flow constantly changes as it makes its way to the sea, so any *real* transformation you care to study – because it depends on a complex cluster of inter-dependent factors – inevitably changes its form (or even its state) as it proceeds, *as a result of the unequal increase* in the different variables it includes. The physicists quote as an example the rapid increase in mass which occurs at very great speeds, until it makes any further acceleration impossible; or again (to take a case to which I shall be returning later) the ultimate transformation into airborne flight of the progressively accelerated motion of an aircraft along the runway.

What I hope briefly to make clear in this essay is how, when we are prepared to apply this general effect of *differential increase* to the particular case of the development of life, the zoological process of evolution does not weaken or even fade out at the level of man (as is so persistently maintained); on the contrary, it is unmistakably continued and even intensified in man.

The movement is there all the time, and the evidence stares us in the face – and yet we do not recognize it.

How, in the first place, as the appearance of man becomes imminent, the progress of biogenesis, without the least slackening of speed, so changes its aspect as to seem to us un-recognizable at first; and how, secondly, once the new mechan-ism of evolution has been distinguished all around us, there is a sudden metamorphosis, a sudden vivification, of the way in which it was until then still possible for us to look at the present and the future of mankind.

These are two points with which I shall deal in turn.

I. THE TRANSFORMATION, STARTING WITH MAN, OF THE PROCESS OF EVOLUTION

However little one may, by conviction or temperament, be 'Darwinist', it is impossible to deny the immense part (at least in the first stages of the phenomenon) played by chance effects in the appearance and intensification of life within our universe.

'Given a very large number of elements taken in a state simultaneously of agitation and compression (or, which comes to the same thing, of agitation and multiplication), experience teaches us that such a system tends intrinsically and automatically *to develop its arrangement additively* to an ever more marked degree: subject to the condition that, for some reason, certain types of arrangement can be considered as *specially favoured*. For once such a type of association has been effected by chance at one point for the first time (as an effect of the tentative gropings of large numbers and of agitation), then this "initial atom of arrangement" tends (through the selective influence of compression, that is, of competition) to take advantage of new chances and so grow and intensify in the favourable direction – and this continues indefinitely.'

Such is the first rough picture we can draw of the process of evolution, in its elementary and primordial essence.

Let us start from this approximate definition and try to press it further home – to approximate rather more closely to an accurate picture. We have just spoken of 'specially favoured arrangements'. What precisely should we understand by this expression – *on which everything depends*?

In the classic formulations of 'Darwinian transformism', this nice point is generally expressed as 'the survival of the fittest'. To my mind, however, the phrase is unfortunate and unsatisfactory, and for two reasons.

In the first place, because it is too vague and lends itself to no precise standard of measurement.

And secondly, because by expressing a purely *relative*

superiority among 'arrangements', it does not bring out that factor in the rise of life which, going beyond the effects of competition, gives unmistakable evidence of an exuberant tendency to expand and of a sense of absolute advance.

Supposing, on the other hand, we substitute '*most complex*' in our formula, for '*fittest*'.[2] In other words supposing we admit that, under the tentative play of chance, the *Weltstoff* behaves, by nature, as though by preference it fell into those forms of arrangement which are at the same time the richest, the most closely associated, and the most fully centred.

Let us look at the consequences and the advantages of this change of variable.

In the first place, we find, now that we have thought of it, that we at last possess the *absolute parameter* that is essential to us if we are to follow and scientifically appreciate the movements of life. For after all, historically, the biosphere did not spread out like a spot of oil simply through morphological diversification in every direction on the surface of the earth. On the contrary, along each of its rays (and more particularly along a very small number of principal axes) it has continually been increasing from age to age the number of useful components in its constructions: and it has never ceased, either, to secure in them the maximum of perfection and co-ordination (the phenomena of cephalization and cerebration). As an explanation (and, still more as a standard of measurement) of this so clearly oriented (or polarized) trend, to speak of 'the greatest capacity for survival in the organisms' is quite useless. On the other hand, the situation is clarified and can be seen with accuracy if we envisage, as the basis of cosmic physics, the existence of a sort of second entropy (or anti-entropy) which, as an effect of

2. I say 'complex' advisedly, and not '*complicated*': because, as we all know, if an organism (whether natural or artificial) is to be perfect, it must combine with the plurality and differentiation of its parts, a maximum of lightness and simplicity. Side by side with the complication which makes a thing unwieldy, there is *useful* (or centred) *complexity*: and here we are concerned only with the latter.

chances that are seized, draws a portion of matter in the direction of continually higher forms of structurization and centration.

By the introduction into biogenesis of the *notion* (or *principle*) of *greatest complexity*, let me emphasize, the general situation of life in the universe can be seen accurately in terms of energetics. At the same time, and further, another valuable piece of evidence is disclosed: and it is precisely the one that could be of most service to us in understanding what happens to evolution starting with man.

I referred earlier to the fruitful impact upon modern physics of the observation and admission of the fact that the acceleration of the real speed[3] of bodies was productive of mass.

In biology, a further fact (at once so glaring, so simple, and nevertheless as yet so little understood) cannot fail before very long to be equally revolutionary: I mean the fact that the organic complexity of beings (the true parameter, we have just seen, of evolution) cannot increase *concretely* without producing, at its core, a rapidly increasing quantity of indetermination and psychism. By its very nature, as the cosmic stuff's power of self-arrangement is realized more fully, so there tends to be a gradual *interiorization* of its driving force and the methods it uses. As a universal experience of things teaches us, the increasing complexification of matter, while in its origins principally the effect of chance, is gradually shot through and loaded with 'choice'. When the process first appears, in monocellular beings, it is forcibly imposed or automatic; but among highly cerebralized beings it tends irreversibly to become one of *active preference*.

We must, therefore, admit that an important correction must be applied to our first idea that once the movement producing the arrangement of matter has been initiated by the play of chance, it can and must continue to develop *as it is indefinitely* – that it must 'snowball'.

'Indefinitely': not precisely (cf. below, in the conclusion, the

3· 'Real speed', as opposed to the abstract speed of kinematics.

possibility in the future of a higher focus-point of ultra-humanization).

'As it is': most certainly not.

Just like the aircraft I spoke of at the beginning, which gradually lifts its tail and finally takes off as it gains speed – so evolution, from being initially *selective*, cannot but make itself *elective* in higher living beings, as a *direct effect of complexity*: until the time comes when, with the appearance of the faculty of *thought*, it reflects definitively upon itself and so 'takes off' and suddenly opens out into planned invention (technology) and higher co-consciousness (civilization).

And it is here, if I am not mistaken, that the true nature of the phenomenon of man becomes apparent in its full grandeur and simplicity.

II. THE CONTINUATION, THROUGH AND BEYOND MAN, OF THE PROCESS OF EVOLUTION

A better understanding of the degree to which *time introduces change* into the process of evolution, enables us to realize that the organizing forces of life do not become weaker in man nor superficial; on the contrary, through his industrialization and collectivization, they become interiorized and reinforce one another. From the moment we appreciate that fact, a radical transformation is clearly effected in the traditional, classic, view of a mankind that has biologically come to a halt.

A new form of complexification (arrangement *sought from within*) replaces the old type of evolution (in which arrangement was imposed *ab extra*). The artificial takes over from the natural and continues it. The social takes on the value of the ultra-organic.

As a result of this single transformation, as though by magic, our eyes are opened and we see a world that might have seemed to us permanently stabilized stir into movement.

Everything starts anew; everything is in movement; everything continues, in a higher way, to evolve with even more ably fated – *by the very operation of its countless individual preferences* – ever more rapidly and ever more fully to complexify and coalesce upon itself.

Faced with this factual situation, many minds, even with scientific training behind them, are still disconcerted by what seems to them to be a dangerous crisis (if not a retrogression or self-destruction) of evolution: evolution, through the mechanizing effect of large numbers, re-absorbing and destroying the individual centres of autonomy and reflection which, through the tentative gropings of large numbers, it had so patiently produced.

That is the great fear of today: that we may founder in the multitude.

However, once we have become familiar with the notion of the 'parameter of complexity' and its application, we cannot fail to see, on the contrary, that what we have to deal with in the totalizing trend we find so disturbing is not some antagonistic or parasitic by-product of evolution but a direct *super-effect*.

We cannot possibly, it is true, fail to be struck by the fact that the rise of the collective and of mass-man is accompanied by a first wave of slavery, of levelling-down, of ugliness and disaster.

But, looking further, beneath the froth of this wave we cannot fail to be aware of a fantastic increase in the flexibility and speed of inter-communication – of organization and penetrative power of research, of efficiency and forcefulness in action – and, finally, of breadth and depth in our view of the world around us.

It is a remarkable leap forward (involving, indeed, a change of order) in arrangement – one that is accompanied by another, no less remarkable, whether it be in the reduction of chance in the world (planned and co-operative invention) or in the biological interiorization of consciousness (all the individual reflective particles of the earth being impelled to associate planetarily in one single reflective system).

By this *twofold* evidence, in truth (the *combined* increase of complexity and consciousness), we are obliged to recognize that the progressive and irresistible technico-cultural unification now being effected in mankind is an event whose nature is specifically organic; and that in it the general process of cosmic biogenesis can not only still be distinguished but is attaining, in the field of our experience, a supreme degree of its development.

It is not only that in man, as Julian Huxley has said, evolution becomes *conscious* (that is, reflectively inventive); what is more, by the gathering together and concentration of all its forces and all its strands, from being divergent it is becoming *convergent*.

Such, reduced to a single word, would appear to be the full and authentic lesson of history: and also, maybe, the greatest discovery ever bequeathed to the natural sciences since that other discovery of the existence of *an* evolution.

In man, and starting with man, we have a folding back and a *general convergence* upon itself (both in its mechanism and in its products) of evolution's most axial nucleus.

If the scientific reality of this massive phenomenon (as massive, in truth, as, at the other extreme of things, the expansion of the universe) were to be definitively confirmed, a great light would certainly dawn over the world of tomorrow.

Intellectually at first, we would begin to understand once and for all what is going on all around us on earth at this moment. This zoological proliferation of mankind in which the phyla, continually being born from the prolonged activity of speciation, never cease to involute upon one another without ever succeeding in separating; this appearance of collective organisms (for the circulation of food-supplies and of ideas, for the promotion of discovery and its additive progress), in which, so disconcertingly (because in some way exteriorized and taken to a planetary scale) we meet again the fundamental processes which have for long been recognized in animate organisms by anatomy and physiology – all this confused and disturbing medley of relationships and differences between the living and the human, is readily explained once we have found, to lead us from one domain into the other, *the law of transposition and of transformation*.

But above all, affectively – hominization, instead of spreading out at random (as we had at first thought) would *be given a direction*; and in consequence we would awake scientifically to the idea that in the form of *some critical point of ultra-hominization* (or of complete and final reflection), some issue to – that is, some justification of – life may well be waiting for us at the term of existence: *because*, physically and biologically, *the process is convergent*!

And in consequence the zest for action, the impetus to action, would be re-born and re-bound in our hearts in step with the ever greater evolutionary effect we have to make in order to ensure the progress of a complexity whose burden becomes progressively heavier to bear.

This, we must never forget, is the dynamic condition essential to survival for a biogenesis that has definitively passed in us from the state of passively experienced evolution to the state of auto- or self-evolution.

Unpublished
19 November 1951

A Major Problem for Anthropology

Is there or is there not, in man, a
continuation and transformation of the
biological process of evolution?

INTRODUCTION

SINCE we have learnt to see the universe not as a *thing* but as a *process*, the age-old and exasperating question of 'man's place in nature' has become that of 'man's movement in nature'. In other words the problem is not so much to know what man is, or even how man, historically, appeared on earth, but rather to decide whether, in the framework of time, there is or is not, for us, something *ultra-human*, lying ahead of the human.[1]

The majority of anthropologists would still regard this question of the reality, as a present development, of an ultra-human (that is of the reality of a continuation beyond man of the process of evolution) as a verbal or metaphysical question. However, I hope to show here that a scientifically verifiable answer is in fact already possible, provided that we first adopt a certain highly probable interpretation of the fact (henceforth, to my mind, indisputable) that, taken in its organico-cultural totality, mankind represents a specifically defined *biological unit*.

I. THE ORGANIC STUFF OF THE HUMAN PLANETARY WHOLE

No one has still any doubt but that, under the network of demographic, economic, political and cultural forces which daily force us into ever closer mutual contact, man forms a group, terrestrial in scale, ever more closely welded together. It is still, however, seldom that anyone considers attributing a specifically 'natural' value to this evident totalizing upon itself

1. That is to say, that the appearance of man is not only the terminus of a long phase of evolution, but the starting point of a new phase. The progress of organization, which can be observed in the past, is now being continued in the noosphere. (Ed.)

of our species. Human civilization is spoken of as a secondary and superficial effect of social adjustment, not to be confused with the true biological phenomena of evolution.

No real progress, I am convinced, can henceforth be made in anthropology unless this antiquated, facile, belittling of the social phenomenon is abandoned, and we at last decide to accept once and for all (and with all its consequences) the position that is defined and established by the following chain of reasoning:

'In nature, every arrangement whose realization has the effect of producing a rise in "psychic temperature" (or, if you prefer, the "degree of consciousness") of the system, is, and must be accepted as, specifically organic and evolutive in its stuff.[2]

'Now, if there is one fact that can clearly be distinguished in the world around us, it is undoubtedly that man, under the influence of planetary totalization, is daily increasing ever more rapidly his collective capacity for thought and its collective intensity.

'We must therefore conclude that mankind, taken collectively, is certainly not (as is so often said) an aggregate or a *mixture*: scientifically, it can be included only among the products of synthesis. This means that henceforth we can make no further progress in biology without recognizing and distinguishing, in the spectrum of animate substances, at the other extreme from the ultra-microscopic living proteins, certain colossal units, planetary in dimensions.'

Thus, as I said earlier, experience clearly forces us to accept the physico-biological reality of what I have long been calling the noosphere.[3]

The whole problem is, with the help of some appropriate

2. This major premise does no more than express the most general experience we can have of the physico-chemical history of life.
3. The noosphere or 'thinking envelope' of the planet, as opposed to the biosphere, the earth's simply living (and non-thinking) envelope.

hypothesis, to bring out the consequences for our faculty of understanding and for our need for action entailed by this *fact* of the existence of a noosphere.

II. VITALIZATION OF MATTER, AND HOMINIZATION OF LIFE: A SINGLE GENERAL FORMULA FOR THE TWO FORMS OF EVOLUTION

In a more or less vague way, human thought has never, since its awakening, failed to note a certain persistent relationship between the psychic perfection and the organic complexity of living beings.

In this case (as in that of gravity, for example) it is interesting to see how successfully a mere commonsense intuition, if scientifically developed more profoundly, can be transformed into a general explanation of things.

Let us, then, decide to recognize not simply an occasional or accidental character in the link between complexity and consciousness that can be seen everywhere in nature, but one that is genetic and functional: in other words, let us hypothetically attribute to the *Weltstoff*, in virtue of a sort of anti-entropy, the property of directing itself *by preferential choice*, under the play of chance,[4] towards progressively more complicated and more fully *centred* arrangements – this increasing centro-complexification having the effect of producing a constant rise in the psychism of the system so arranged.

In this case, we have no difficulty in seeing that a chain process is initiated – one that includes, in the same formula, the complete unfolding of life on earth from its most humble precellular stages[5] up to the immeasurable reality of a human planetary organism.

This intellectual readjustment enables the human and the pre-human, as known to our experience, to be fitted together

4. Providing at the same time that it be subject to a certain compression which produces within the system effects of competition and selection.
5. Père Teilhard uses the English word. (Tr.)

without difficulty in the unity of one and the same mechanism: the only difference between the two domains being that at the level of man the extraordinary psychic faculty of *reflection*[6] emerges in the conscious as a critical effect of centro–complex-ification. This phenomenon of initial reflection has, by its nature, two principal effects:

a. The first is to ensure in man the gradual transition of life from the state of *passively experienced* evolution (*ortho-selection*) to that of directed evolution or self-evolution (*ortho-election*).

b. And the second is to secure, in the thinking layer of the earth, the predominance of *the convergent forces of hominization* over *the divergent forces of speciation* (or phyletization).

From this point of view the noosphere, instead of represent-ing a sort of isolated freak in the world, finds a well-defined place in a naturally determined series – *and one that is not yet finished*. Mankind is no longer what it is still too often said to be, *a dead end* of evolution; but, by the planned ultra-arrange-ment of its reflective particles it is coming to ultra-humanize itself through the total convergence of its powers and its elements in the direction of some 'ultra-reflection' – at the head of evolution and on its main axis.

III. VERIFICATION OF THE HYPOTHESIS OF AN EVOLUTIONARY CONVERGENCE UPON ITSELF OF MANKIND

The well-established recognition of an intensified continuation *of natural animal evolution* into *cultural human evolution*[7] is far from being merely metaphysical or verbal, or even productive of intellectual confusion; it would entail such consequences for

6. Reflection: the state of a consciousness which has become capable of seeing and foreseeing itself. *To think* is not only *to know*, but *to know that one knows*.

7. That is, the recognition of the fact that the universe is 'mono-evolution-ary'.

both our theoretical and our practical attitude to life[8] that we may well wonder why it is that science is not more actively devoting the best part of its resources to reaching a decision one way or the other on a question upon which everything else depends for us.

To effect this verification one would obviously do well to find out by all possible means whether there might not, by some chance, be some physical or psychic way of detecting and measuring at every moment (in such a way as to express it in a curve) the noosphere's degree of reflection (or, if we may use the phrase, its 'psychic temperature').

However, a second line of attack would appear to be more immediately possible in order to arrive at the same result. This would be quite simply to prove the reality of the biological convergence theoretically divined in man, by causing it to progress further, and so become apparent, *in operation*.

For the idea put forward here of a world that is psychologically convergent has, we shall find, a remarkable property.

Of such an hypothesis we may say not only that it works[9] to a first degree by explaining and co-ordinating for our intelligence, better than any other, the whole body of the known facts.

But, what is more, it works, to a second degree, by providing a definite plan of operation and an inexhaustible source of interest (an incentive)[10] for our power of acting.

The time, then, seems to have come when a small number of men representative of the principal *living* branches of modern scientific thought (physics, chemistry, biochemistry, sociology, and psychology) must come together in a concerted attack on the following points:

8. This it would do as a result of a complete transformation of our way of conceiving the significance of the deep-seated organic laws, the future, and the value of totalization of man.
9. Here, and below, Père Teilhard uses the English phrase: '. . . *elle réussit* (it works)'. (Tr.)
10. Père Teilhard uses the English word. (Tr.)

1. To affirm, and secure official recognition for, the proposition that henceforth the question of an ultra-evolution of man (through collective reflection or convergence) must be expressed in scientific terms.

2. To seek in common for the best ways of verifying the existence of the problem and tackling it scientifically, with all its consequences and on every plane.

3. To lay the foundations of a *technics* (both biophysical and psychological) of *ultra-evolution*, from the twofold point of view:

a. both of the planetary arrangements that should be conceived (in general research, for example, and in eugenics) with a view to an ultra-arrangement of the noosphere

b. and of the psychic energies that must be generated or concentrated in the light of a mankind which is in a state of collective super-reflection upon itself: the whole problem, in fact, of the maintenance and development of *the psychic energy of self-evolution*.

Unpublished, New York
30 December 1951

The Reflection of Energy

THE human 'species', like any other piece of living matter, has
an organic tendency to multiply itself to the maximum.
However, unlike what happens in a shoal of fish or a colony of
bacteria (and for a number of reasons which will be apparent
later), this multiplication does more than simply increase the
number of elements that make up the population: in addition,
it produces a system of ever more closely linked and more fully
centred structures in the totality of the group that is in a state
of expansion.

In itself, we should note, this phenomenon of concentration
and organization is absolutely indisputable. It seems difficult in
these days to deny that mankind, after having gradually
covered the earth with a loosely socialized living fabric, is now
coming to knit itself together (racially, economically and
mentally) at a rapidly increasing speed. Before we attempt any
explanation of the process, we must realize that the world of
man is being irresistibly driven to form one single bloc. It is
converging upon itself.

No one, I repeat, disputes this convergence because everyone
is subject to it. On the other hand, it is an odd fact that no one
seems to notice it (except to lament it); and no one seems to
suspect that, beneath the complex of historical accidents into
which the event may be reduced by analysis, a certain 'force'
is undoubtedly at work: a force as primordial and general as
nuclear forces or gravity, but one which tells us much more,
perhaps, about the physical nature of the universe.

We have here the massive fact, which is nevertheless completely disregarded (precisely, it may be, because it is too vast
and too obvious), of a gradual totalization of mankind on
itself which nothing can stop. What I shall try to do here is to
ensure that this fact is resolutely accepted and thought out, with

all its implications, in the scientific setting of energetics and biology; and in doing so, I shall deal with the following points:

1. The initial appearance (in the Pliocene) of the faculty of reflection.

2. The collective acceleration (in modern man) of the process of reflection.

3. Energy and reflection.

4. The irreversibility of reflection.

Each of these successive steps will oblige us to take a more definitive line in relation to the scientific interpretation of the phenomenon of man. It is hardly necessary to say in so many words, so clearly does it emerge from the context of this essay, that I am speaking here purely as 'a man of science'. Our inquiry lies on the plane of 'appearances' and does not touch the transcendent problem of causality.

I. THE INITIAL (PLIOCENE) STEP OF REFLECTION

For any clear-sighted modern observer, we have just seen, the 'phenomenon of phenomena' in nature is (or at least should be) the physical concentration and mental centration, now taking place, of mankind upon itself.

To this I must now add that, for any mind that has had even the least training in envisaging the past, this great modern affair of human convergence is simply the repercussion or continuation of another, much older, event (and just as much neglected, even though just as vast): this was the radical refashioning of life towards the end of the Tertiary period under the influence of 'hominization'.

Let us try, then, consciously to realize that there is something extraordinary about a state of the world – the world of man – that can seem quite 'natural' to us because we are born into it, but which constitutes for the palaeontologist a fundamental enigma.

Influenced by simplifying anatomical and phylogenic ideas, the layman has become accustomed to thinking of man as a more or less unbroken continuation of the Pliocene world. 'Man: an animal who has been more successful, though in obedience to the same laws, as the rats and the elephants' – and that is the whole story.

Objectively and scientifically, however, we must form another and a very different conception, if we are to respect the facts.

Between the animal world of the Pliocene period (so exuberant and open in the variety and dispersal of its forms) and the human world which succeeds it (so astoundingly closed, structured, and so predominant over, or exclusive of, every other form of life) – between these two, whatever may have been said, there is not simply a difference of degree: there is a change of order or (if the word is preferred) of state. However rooted in the pre-human the noosphere may be, just as the pre-human itself is rooted in the pre-living, nevertheless, in virtue of its properties, its methods of invention, and its autonomy, it is undeniably a *new* envelope, *sui generis*, appearing on the ancient biosphere.

Before any attempt at explanation, it must be accepted as indisputable that 'something' happened in between those two successive planetary states (before and after the kingdom of man); that 'something' intervened in the general process of the vitalization of matter: something so subtle that at the very beginning its coming produced no apparent stir, and yet something so violently active, fundamentally, that after several hundreds of thousands of years the face of the earth has been completely transformed by it.

What then, was that something, if not the birth of reflection?

Reflection – that psychological quality found in a being which not only *knows* but *knows that it knows*: I am quite sure that we do not sufficiently realize in our minds how amply – simply by the power it gives us of intellectually embracing the world, of foreseeing the future and even, up to a point, of controlling our own evolution – reflection by itself is sufficient to explain the sudden lead over all the rest of life achieved by the human.

There is a further, and even more important fact to which we pay too little attention – how naturally, in virtue of its genesis, this property (characteristic of a matter that has been taken to its maximum of arranged complexity) emerges from the most axial depths of the process – not (as was still thought in Darwin's time) the zoological but the cosmic process of what we call evolution.[1]

In science, two things are henceforth beyond discussion.

First, in virtue of some initial (and, because 'initial', inexplicable) disposition of the *Weltstoff*, matter coalesces or crystallizes (this is as a result of chances that are brought into play by the fantastic multiplicity and fantastic agitation of the particles into which it condenses); but, what is more, it also tends to organize itself 'centrically' in the form of ever larger and more complex particles.

And secondly, under the influence of this increasing organization and in step with it, this same matter becomes *interiorized* (here we meet the phenomena of consciousness) with an intensity that increases, in the higher living beings, with the development of the nervous system.

Supposing we arrange this series of observed facts in a continuous sequence: let us, that is, having allowed its full value to the evolutionary law of complexity-consciousness, study the rise throughout the geological ages, in conformity with this universal trend,[2] of the earth's 'psychic temperature'. And, in conclusion, let us see how at the term of this rise,

1. In the nineteenth century the theory of evolution ('transformism') was simply a problem of animal speciation. Today it extends to the general problem of 'the corpusculization of energy' throughout time, from the atomic elements up to the individual man, including (this is the whole point of my thesis) 'planetized' mankind.

2. A trend that in some mysterious way is inseparable, as we shall see later, from the entropy of the physicists.

thought, properly so called, suddenly bursts in, to dominate and transform everything on the surface of the earth.

Confronted with this whole body of experience, I do not see that it is possible, scientifically, to avoid the following conclusion:

'Towards the end of the Tertiary period, at one particularly cerebralized point of the biosphere, and in virtue of a general maturing of the latter, one of the countless organo-psychic rays (at once divergent and proceeding by tentative gropings) which make up the living world, succeeded, by the play of chances preferentially selected and accumulated, in crossing the surface-boundary which separates the reflective from the irreflective.[3]

'We cannot yet say to what sudden (and perhaps infinitesimal) shift in the arrangement of the neurones this psychological revolution may well have corresponded.

'But we can no longer be blind to the biological and dynamic value of the event.

'Man is not simply a new species of animal (as we are still too often told). He represents, he initiates, *a new species of life*.

'And this means that if we are to picture to ourselves the true dimensions of the human, we must conceive it as so rich and so capable of expansion as by itself alone to fill an "evolu-

3. And not 'intelligence from instinct' as the great Bergson said, and thus, simply by locating the dividing line in the wrong place, robbed the human stock of its value as the 'leading shoot' at the head of evolution. For reflection (the essence of hominization) does more than generate ratiocinative reason, by introducing a sort of dichotomy which impoverishes the being concerned: it recasts and transforms animal psychism in its entirety. What, in fact, is man's creative intuition if not an example of *reflective instinct*?

On the biological and historical mechanism of the biosphere's transition into the noosphere (a phenomenon which presupposes that life, when taken to its natural limits, *reflects itself*), cf. Teilhard de Chardin, 'La Structure phylétique du Groupe humain', *Annales de Paléontologie*, 1951; Eng. trans. in *The Appearance of Man*, Collins, London, and Harper and Row, New York, 1965, pp. 132–71.

tionary space" at least as large as that occupied by the whole of the pre-human.'

Thus the initial (Pliocene) hominization of life is the critical point – not simply terminal (and marking an ending) but initial (and introducing a rebound) – through which, as I shall now try to show, the cosmic wave of arrangement and interiorization gets off to a fresh start in a direction that we can accurately determine: and it is with that cosmic wave that henceforth the idea of evolution is identified in our minds.

II. CONTINUATIONS AND ACCELERATION IN MODERN MAN OF THE COSMIC PROCESS OF REFLECTION

One of the most pernicious illusions developed in the heart of man during the course of history is the pseudo-evidence of his completeness and fixity. Today, we have just come to realize that the atoms themselves, in their turn, are in motion, drawn, after life and after the stars, into a generalized evolutionary scheme: and yet even now one can still find good minds (even among philosophers and scientists) to maintain that even if everything around us in the universe, from the infinitesimal to the immense, is in motion, nevertheless we ourselves, at any rate, are always the same – because we are stabilized once and for all.

This alleged 'perennial' dogma of human invariance fades into contemptible insignificance, if only we realize the genetical relationship that connects the two elements or terms which emerge from what we have been saying:

1. Of a collective convergence (now taking place) of mankind upon itself,

2. Which succeeds a reflection (which took place in the past) of the living individual upon himself.

Placed side by side, we shall find, the two events have but a single explanation and a single possible significance.

It is *because* man reflected as an individual in the past that today he can no longer prevent himself from converging technico-socially upon himself. And, again, it is *because* he is converging, irresistibly and collectively, upon himself that he is forced to reflect ever more profoundly upon himself and upon all his fellow-men at the same time.

In other words, a convergent mankind is identical with an ultra-reflective mankind: and, conversely, an ultra-reflective mankind is identical with a convergent mankind.

From this point of view, and as though by magic, what seemed the most completely stabilized thing in nature – man – is suddenly seen to be the most mobile thing in the world – because it has been launched into a new compartment of the universe ('the domain of reflection') in which everything is still free and everything still has to be created.

A *completely new* space, lying open ahead.

And yet, at the same time, a space which is *structurally limited* in the future by the maximum state (or degree) of reflection that is theoretically attainable by the *human planetary quantum* when, through convergence, it has reached the biological term of its totalization.

Once we have woken up to this twofold realization, our first reaction is one of astonishment that so evident an ordering of the universe should have gone so long unnoticed. An extremely simple historical reason then becomes obvious to our minds, which explains and justifies this sort of blindness. The reason is as follows.

Although mankind has been potentially converging upon itself ever since its origins (in virtue of the reflective quality of its very stuff), nevertheless it was inevitable that it should go through a long 'distracting' period of spatial expansion before becoming conscious of its underlying unity: that period was the time mankind needed for invading and occupying the earth.

Just (as I have said elsewhere) as a vibration which penetrates a sphere through one of its poles, so the human wave (even though propagating itself in a 'curved' medium) was obliged at first to spread out and diversify, rather than coalesce. Now, it is from this phase of expansion and dispersion (which includes the whole of the Palaeolithic, the whole of the Neolithic, the whole of history) that we are now in process of emerging. In us, and around us, under the continued influence of hominization, the wave has just crossed the equator and suddenly entered into another hemisphere; and there, if it is to continue its advance, it must necessarily force itself into closer contact in a new climate.

In a mankind that has reached saturation point on the planet, a neo-socialization of compression is coming to replace the palaeo-socialization of expansion whose various vicissitudes fill – often so uselessly – our history books.[4]

This is, indeed, a massive event. For, in step with the gaining of preponderance by the phenomena of convergence in anthropogenesis, it is collective reflection that is beginning to grow vertically in the noosphere, while at the same time there rises over our horizon the hitherto hidden pole of a unification, both organic and mental, into which we are henceforth 'falling' at a constantly accelerating speed.

It seems to me inevitable that in the near future our scientific attention must be continually more attracted, even fascinated, by this extreme evolutionary point of our 'forward dive': the more so that it seems possible here and now to distinguish, as we shall be seeing, some of its essential characteristics or fundamental properties.

However, before we embark on this nice question of the upper limits of the phenomenon of man, I must first explain how, from the point of view I am adopting, we meet and how we can solve the problem in energetics presented by a reconciliation of the inexorable laws of thermodynamics with the appearance and development on earth of reflection.

---

4. The transition, I say advisedly, from a dispersed to a compressed phase of reflection, *and not* 'from a state of instinctive culture to one of intellectual civilization', as recently suggested by Roderick Seidenberg in *Post-historical Man* (University of Carolina Press, 1950).

III. REFLECTION AND ENERGY

What still makes contact between physics and biology impossible and in consequence delays the incorporation of the latter in the former inside a generalized physics is ultimately a problem of energy.

On the one hand, we have in physics a matter which slides irresistibly, following the line of least resistance, in the direction of the most probable forms of distribution. And on the other hand, we have in biology the same matter drifting (no less irresistibly but in this case in a sort of 'greater effort for survival')[5] towards ever more improbable, because ever more complex, forms of arrangement.

In order to solve this fundamental contradiction between physical entropy and biological 'orthogenesis' the nineteenth century vitalists had tried to develop the notion of certain (measurable) forces peculiar to organic substances: a position that was soon to become untenable, both experimentally and theoretically, inasmuch as it involved the co-existence of two independent energetics in the same universe: one for what was called inert matter, and the other for vitalized matter.

In our own day the too few scientists who have the courage to face the problem squarely[6] seem to be looking for a way out of their difficulties, and a compensation for them, by emphasizing the fact that life, when studied right down to its ultimate strands, is seen experientially to obey the laws of thermodynamics; and, moreover, that this same life represents quantitatively only an insignificant event in the totality of the universe.

5. This 'greater effort to live (or even to super-live)' being produced, moreover, economically, that is by the least demanding methods and the most direct roads.
6. Cf., for example, Harold F. Blum, *Time's Arrow and Evolution*, Princeton University Press, 1951, and Joseph Needham, *Time, the Refreshing River*, Fernhill, New York, and Allen and Unwin, London, 1943.

Surely, however, this answer evades the very basis of the problem while at the same time improperly minimizing its data.

It is undeniable, indeed, that life occupies an incredibly small volume of time and space in the field of our experience. It is undeniable, too, that it is born and develops in the very heart of the flood of entropy, precisely as an *eddy* – as the effect of a counter-current.

If, on the other hand, we do no more than study the case of the earth, we cannot dismiss this further series of evident facts:

a. First, that the eddies of life within entropy appear *as soon as* and *wherever* the chances allow it (the planetary birth of life).

b. Secondly, once these eddies have appeared, they grow more pronounced in their manifestations as intensely as they possibly can (the planetary reflection of life).

c. Finally, the phenomenon of the vitalization of large molecules, which we find so astonishing, is itself no more than the continuation of the moleculization of atoms, and ultimately of the atomization of energy – that is, of a process that affects, and defines, the universe in the totality of its substance and history.

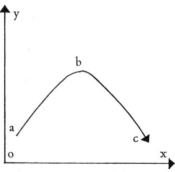

FIGURE I. Graphical representation of the energetics of evolution. (First approximation) OX, axis of greater probability (entropy); OY, axis (apparently of less probability): biological 'orthogenesis' of increasing complexity.

Cosmic energy, *un-arranged* (in tension) at *a*, passes through a maximum of *arrangement* in *b*, before becoming completely *dis-arranged* (release of tension) at *c*.

In fact, if we are graphically to express the energetic situation of the universe as it is presented objectively to our experience, it would appear that we must envisage a system (figure 1) in which, running at right angles to the axis OX of increasing entropy, a second axis OY expresses a remarkable fact: that, in order to pass entropically from an initial state of 'tension' to a final state of 'release of tension', cosmic energy is obliged, in its totality, to *follow a curve* which runs *through the complex* (atomization, moleculization, vitalization, reflection). Along this curve it develops arrangement before it ultimately discards its arrangement in conformity with the laws of less effort and greater probability.[7]

This means that in order to incorporate life (and, in a more general way, all the phenomena of corpusculization) a general energetics must necessarily be built up not on the single axis of entropy, but on two *conjugate axes, one of greater probability*, and the other of *greater complexity*.[8]

The whole problem, then, depends upon deciding:

a. On the one hand, whether the ascent of the curve *abc* along OY, towards the more complex, is or is not a mere *momentary by-effect* of the general downward trend of the world in the direction OX towards greater probabilities.

b. And on the other hand (if the answer has to be negative) whether, when the curve in question has reached its *highest point b* of maximum arrangement[9] it does in fact again descend

7. In classical thermodynamics this final state was conceived as a homogeneous distribution of the most simple molecules, which were considered as permanent. In modern physics, in which molecules and atoms are divisible, I must confess that I do not know in what form the theoreticians envisage totally entropized energy.

8. The axis OY of increasing complexity being precisely (if defined by its higher values) an *axis of reflection*.

9. This highest point *b* corresponds, on earth, to the higher pole of collective reflection we recognized earlier as the normal termination of the phenomenon of human convergence.

integrally towards the axis OX; or whether, on the contrary, when it reaches that point *b* it does not undergo some specific transformation.

At first sight, this group of related questions would appear to be impatient of experimental handling, and to depend upon each individual's intellectual preferences – or his philosophy.

I hope to show here that they are open to a scientific attack, provided that we are alive to the 'demand for irreversibility' that is inherent in the very nature of the evolutionary phenomenon of reflection.

IV. THE IRREVERSIBILITY OF REFLECTION

From the foregoing analysis of energetics, it emerges that in any case the evolutionary complexification and arrangement of matter (or, which comes to the same thing, the interiorization, followed by the reflection, of energy) appear to us experientially as a cosmic process just as determined, in its own way, as the entropy on which they are grafted. Along the axis OY, it is just as though as a result of the controlled play of chances[10] the *elementary indetermination* of the physicists necessarily accumulated and expanded within special structures (progressively larger and more fully living particles) until it ultimately assumed the form of '*reflective choice*'. And, once that peak has been attained, we cannot say (very much the opposite, in fact) that determinism tends to disappear from the rest of the operation. However 'free' man feels (or believes) himself to be, he cannot escape the need (at once economic and mental) which forces him individually and collectively, to reflect – and therefore to reflect *himself* – ever more and more. Because he has once begun to think, because he thinks, it is now to some extent impossible for him to stop thinking continually more and more.

While this is true, it does not, even so, prevent the generating movement of our curve *abc* (figure 1) from being profoundly

10. A play of chances, one might say, which are selected by a sort of polarity or preference inherent (like a sort of higher gravity) in the *Weltstoff* itself.

modified, starting from its initial point of hominization, in the *form or nature of the inevitability with which it continues.*

For in man, while evolution becomes both self-conscious and (at least in its main axis) self-operative, at the same time it automatically develops the power *to foresee its own future.*

This is all that is needed to disclose, over and above the questions of *structures* and *processes* which were hitherto sufficient to cover the economy of nature, the formidable problem of the *impetus of evolution:*[11] here we have a new type of biological problem which is silently making itself felt in our hearts as a preliminary to predominating tomorrow over the other more general problem (itself also becoming more important in our world) of at last building up *an energetics of man.*

We must try to understand this important event correctly, starting with a particular, and particularly obvious, case.

In the domain of large industrial enterprises (than which few could be less idealistic) the theoreticians of productivity have finally come to appreciate that the production of a factory is functionally dependent on the enthusiasm the workers bring to the execution of their work. Similarly, then, and on a scale whose gravity and scope is incomparably higher, we are obliged to recognize that, *from the moment when* mankind begins to appear to our experience not as a state that is reached but as *a work that has to be done* – one whose completion depends ultimately on the ingenuity and tenacity with which we pursue it – from that moment we must recognize that the future of man depends *much more on a certain passion for hard work than on a certain wealth of material resources.*

As I have often written (and as, it would be no exaggeration to say, everyone can see), the mankind of tomorrow, though standing on mountains of iron, of coal, of uranium, of wheat, would do no more than 'tick over', if, by some mischance,[12] there should be a weakening of its *zest* not simply for subsisting and surviving but for *super-living.*

11. What would be called in English 'the evolutive drive'.
12. Should one add, *per impossibile*?

If it is not to fall short of its natural maximum of convergence and reflection (and the attainment of this requires of us that *we pursue it with all our strength*) hominized evolution must henceforth include in its determinism, over and above the economic *vis a tergo* (or 'push') the 'pull'[13] of some *powerful magnetic force, psychic in nature.*

There, bluntly expressed in terms of relentless forces, we have the present energetic situation of the human mass.

But then – in what direction are we to look for, in what form are we to conceive, and by what general conditions are we to define the object or objective that is capable of arousing and fostering the magnetic pull which has become essential for the realization of our evolutionary possibilities?

In this connexion, two things (at the least) seem to me to be clearly dictated by an elementary psychological analysis: they both concern the nature of the mysterious *point b*, the peak of the cosmic curve of 'evolutionary arrangement' as represented diagrammatically in our figure 1.

1. First of all, now that man has (by reflection) become conscious of the future towards which the convergence of the noosphere is drawing him, he must, if he is not to feel a radical distaste of *action*, be able to say to himself this: that when he arrives *at b*, he is going, in some way, to escape the re-descent, towards the unarranged and the more probable, of the eddy of improbability within which he appeared and for whose ascent he now finds himself responsible. If it is not to smother itself, evolution, now that it has become reflective, cannot be conceived as proceeding within a 'cyclic or closed universe': it is incompatible with the hypothesis of a *total death.*[14]

13. Père Teilhard uses the English words. (Tr.)
14. To establish on solid scientific foundations the reality and the requirements of the first property of the reflective *Weltstoff* (a property that since all time has been 'sensed' by the philosophies and religions of immortality) should be the concern and task of a 'constructive psycho-analysis' devoted now to the study not simply of the disorders of human psychism but of its fundamental driving forces.

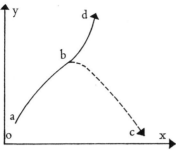

FIGURE 2. Graphical representation of the energetics of evolution (closer approximation).

bd, escape-branch for *reflective energy*, through *b* (higher critical point of convergence and reflection).

2. Secondly, if man is not simply to be rescued from his disgust at the prospect of exerting *his active powers to the maximum* but is to be *given a positive zest* for so doing (as he must be),[15] then, again, now that he has developed the sense of his ultra-evolution, he must be able to hope that if he does ultimately escape this re-descent he will do so not just as a survivor from a catastrophe but as the victor in a battle: in other words, that he will do so in a fulfilment of – as a paroxysmal climax to – all that he holds at the heart of his being of what is most essential, that is, most 'reflective'.

These two conditions are satisfied simultaneously if the peak of the curve corresponds not only to a culminating point in which 'the differential disappears' but also (1) to a point of bifurcation and inflexion, from which a branch *bd* (figure 2) breaks away, rising exponentially, or (2), which comes to the same thing, corresponds to *a higher critical point of planetary reflection* beyond which we can distinguish nothing more,[16] but

15. I recognize that here I am introducing a postulate: that, in virtue of its construction, the universe cannot disappoint the consciousness it engenders. But I maintain that if this postulate ('of the maximum activance of the conscious by the real') is not accepted, the world automatically comes to a halt.

16. Because we then find ourselves outside time and space.

beyond which, also, we can say that the universe still continues, though with other dimensions that we are as yet unable to represent.

Thus, as I promised, recognition of the *irreversible* character of reflection enables us to some degree to fill out the picture we can give ourselves of the relationship between life and entropy.

Broadly speaking, it is perfectly true to say that life appears in the universe simply as an effect of the play of probabilities.

Ultimately, however, it becomes clear that if the same life is studied in its 'reflective' form, it must, in order to be able to function, be conscious of its power to make the play of probabilities serve its own purposes, thereby escaping from the death towards which it would have been driven by a blind determinism.

From this point of view, it is now absolutely impossible to regard reflective psychism, within the cosmos, as a mere transitory *superstructure*. When life has become self-conscious, it manifests itself to our experience as self-evolving: but, further, it must necessarily be self-consistent, this essential self-consistence itself being, in its turn, explicable in two ways:

a. either because it is born *exclusively from the confluence* of reflective particles reflecting on one another,

b. or (and more probably) because it calls for and discloses the existence of a supreme centre – not simply potential, but *real* – of cosmic convergence.

SUMMARY, OR CONCLUSION

The substance of the various considerations presented above may be reduced to the following points.

1. Taken in its origin in each human element, reflection (or the transition, for a being, *from the conscious to the self-conscious state*) corresponds to a critical point separating the two species of life from one another.

2. Once reflective life has been initiated elementarily within

individuals (continuing the movement of non-reflective life and transposing it into a new domain) it never ceases to diversify and intensify, following a collective process which is closely linked to the technico-cultural convergence of man.

3. At the term of this process of ultra-reflection (operating on a limited planetary 'quantum') a pole of maximum convergence can be distinguished. As a result of the demands for irreversibility which are inherent in reflective life, this pole cannot be regarded as a transitory state (or 'flash'), but must be seen as a higher critical point (of reflection) beyond which the evolutionary curve of complexity-consciousness emerges, so far as our experience is concerned, from space and time.

4. Ultimately then, from the point of view of energetics, it is just as though the universe continued its development not just along a single axis but along two *conjugate* axes: one (entropy) of greater probability – the other (life) of greater complexity. Consciousness (in conformity with the requirements of thermodynamics) develops throughout as a function of entropy, but ultimately escapes 'dis-organization', as a specific effect of reflection, either as a separate energy 'of the second species' or as an interiorized fraction of the common energy.

5. This amounts to saying that in order completely to cover the evolutionary economy of the universe (including life) a third principle, the principle of the reflection of energy, must be added to and associated with the two that are already accepted, the principles of the conservation and of the dissipation of energy.

New York, 27 April 1952. Published in the
Revue des questions scientifiques,
20 October 1952

Reflections on the Compression of Mankind

AFTER thousands and thousands of years of slow expansion, the
human species, ever increasing in numbers, has just suddenly
entered a phase of compression. Along all their frontiers, the
various population groups spread out over the globe have come
into contact, and they are beginning to be ever more closely
forced together on the surface of an earth that is every day
becoming more restricted. And, unfortunately, the most
directly perceptible result of this compression would appear to
be, for our generation, a generally experienced agony – not to
say a general worsening of our situation.

For, in short, is it not under the influence – always the same
influence – of an extreme demographic pressure that a linked
series of disorders and evils is making itself felt, threatening
gradually to make the world uninhabitable for us?

This flood of sheer humanity which seeps up through every
fissure, drowning all the best of us, and, in virtue of its very
mass, one might say, escaping from the governance of selection –

This disappearance, so enervating both intellectually and
physically, of solitude and of nature, in favour of the factory
and the town –

This disagreeable closeness of intercourse, this continual
friction between individuals who become more alien or even
hostile to one another, the more numerous they are –

This mechanization of persons by enslavement to forms of
work that are inevitably collectivized –

This complication, this burden, this increasing insecurity of
daily life, which largely explains[1] the extreme nervous tension
(or even the disturbing neuroses) of our time –

1. The other (possibly the most important?) part of the explanation being

Not to mention the increasing danger of contagious influences and the exhaustion of resources in an over-populated setting –

– And all this because there are too many of us in too little room.

The truth is, it is just like a train in the rush hour – the earth is coming to be a place on which we simply cannot breathe. And this asphyxiation explains the violent methods employed by nations and individuals in their attempt to break loose and to preserve, by isolation, their customs, their language and their country. A useless attempt, moreover, since passengers continue to pile into the railway carriage.

Instead of being exasperated by these nuisances from which we all suffer, or waiting vaguely for things to settle down, would we not do better to ask ourselves whether, as a matter of solid experiential fact, there may not possibly be, first, a *reassuring explanation* of what is going on, and, secondly, an *acceptable issue* to it?

To answer this question is the purpose of these reflections.

II. THE SOURCE OF THE 'EVIL': A UNIVERSE THAT IS CLOSING IN

At first sight, what seems most alarming in the present excess of pressure upon the human layer is the sheer crude simplicity of the process that is taking place. We are witnessing the almost explosive proliferation of a part of the biosphere, which (through emergence into reflection) has suddenly been released from the rest of the living mass, and is now piling up, to the point of being crushed, on the *closed* surface of the earth: nothing could be less mysterious than this determinism and this geometric progression – and yet nothing could be more blind and more implacable.

---

the unvoiced anxiety experienced by a being momentarily lost in the immensity of a universe he no longer understands.

Man in his thousands and thousands of millions – simply the equivalent of a gas under pressure.

That is what we are tempted to say.

And it is precisely that which we find so disheartening.

– However, is it really true that in the case of the over-population of our planet there is no special feature for the physicist, backed up by a biologist, to reckon with? Something new appears in a gaseous mass whose volume is reduced: the temperature rises. Similarly, when the human mass is continually more compressed, does not some significant effect make itself apparent which, if we knew how to look at it correctly, would teach us the true nature of the phenomenon and show us how it really behaves?

In order to characterize – and condemn – the age in which we live – we are only too ready to point to the rise of the masses, the intrusion of the machine mentality, the trend towards totalitarianism . . . and heaven knows what else. But what is *science's* position in all this, and what use are we making of it?

A great deal has been written, for and against, about science – crediting it, as the case may be, with all the good things and all the bad things that happen to us. One more instance of the tree of good and evil. But how is it that, in the midst of this chorus of criticism and praise, no one thinks of going beyond the various planes of utilitarianism, of moral judgments, or of pure speculation, and pointing out a further fact: by that I mean, that, before being good or bad, the conquest of the world by man's intelligence is primarily and basically a phenomenon of an 'intensification of consciousness' closely linked with the historical progress of civilization. Precisely in so far as they are forced together, the thinking elements, which we all are, undoubtedly increase, under the influence of inter-reflection, their power of individual reflection. Brought together as one whole, they can understand what a single one of them in isolation could never have succeeded in understanding. That being so, surely in this perfectly clear case of a mankind that is being mentally ultra-humanized by self-compression, we meet again the same familiar linked couple of compression→consciousness: the couple which (as a consequence of the arrangements inevitably produced by compression in an organic medium) has been controlling all the progress made by evolution since its beginning.

If that is indeed so, then we must henceforth, where at first we saw nothing but the brutal clamping in a vice of the human mass, recognize the sign of, the driving force behind, and the price to be paid for, a new forward leap achieved on the earth by the cosmic forces of psychogenesis from which we emerged towards the end of the Tertiary. After a simple reflection, co-reflection – that is to say, super-reflection.

Thereby, too, in the flash of illumination cast by this shaft of light a whole new prospect emerges: that of a world not suffocated by, but elevated by, its internal tension.

From this re-adjusted point of view, it is true, the force which is compressing us is even more implacable than we thought: since instead of there being simply a planet which is contracting, there is the entire universe concentrating in the depths of our being.

On the other hand, as we can readily appreciate, this vast energy, by showing itself to be cosmic in order, changes its nature and ceases to be a burden to us: since, precisely in so far as it forces us into closer spiritual contact, it can tomorrow become the most active factor in our true and final liberation.

III. THE GREAT RELEASE: A CONVERGENCE AHEAD

Contrary to what happens so often in nature, the propagation of our species does not seem destined to regularize and limit itself automatically: for the more numerous men are, the more their ingenuity protects them and incites them to multiply even more.

In such an event, and in order to escape the asphyxiation which threatens us, the remedies habitually proposed are:

either a drastic restriction of reproduction, or, again (an ancient dream that is now, maybe, ceasing to be a dream?), a mass migration of human beings to some still uninhabited star.

But, with whatever skill such methods of decompression may be improved, surely their very nature is such that they are to some degree imaginary, precarious, and desperate. The idea, in particular, of a transplanetary swarm of migrants must undoubtedly be rejected as impossible to realize, simply from the fact that not a single visitor from another quarter of the heavens has ever come to find us.

To my mind (and providing, as I believe, that the world in which we live can be regarded as sufficiently coherent not automatically, when all is said and done, to suppress the life it engenders) we must look for the relief without which our zoological phylum cannot now survive, not in a eugenic reduction nor in an extra-terrestrial expansion of the human mass, but rather in what one might call 'an escape into time, through what lies ahead'.

Let me explain this important point.

Earlier, relying on the undisputed fact of the rise of science, I suggested the idea that there is a psychic trend in the universe – a trend that draws the human mass under pressure (and *because* it is under pressure) towards ever more reflective states of consciousness.

In virtue, we should note, of its convergent nature, such a movement, *if it does in fact exist*, necessarily determines, at a finite distance in the future, a critical point or peak of common encounter, which may be defined:

– either, in a first approximate definition, as an ultimate centre of co-reflection

– or, more completely, as a focus-point of 'conspiration'[2] of the thinking monads,

since, by psychological necessity, it is impossible for us to think actively and *completely* with another without tending to identify ourselves affectively with that other.

2. The expression is Edouard Le Roy's.

With that clear in our minds, let us consider the extreme point of reflection and union thus determined by extrapolation into time of the generating lines of man.

Is it not evident, in the first place, that simply by the fact of its appearance on our horizon, such a pole of attraction, if we should succeed in distinguishing its rays, would have the power to initiate a general intensification of the forces of hominization throughout the whole of the thinking layer of the earth?

And secondly, is it not certain that, just as a crowd is restored to order and flows through peacefully once the gates that held it back are opened for it, so the multitude of men, once it is so polarized and activated in the very fibres of its being, would immediately be restored to harmony and calm simply by the force of the call that summons it to press on ahead?

'By the very fact that it introduces arrangement and energizes, convergence brings a release of tension.'

The more one thinks about this elementary truth, the more one is convinced that our thinking earth, subjected henceforth to a pressure which nothing would appear to be able to prevent from rising from within, is biologically confronted with the following dilemma:

– of either remaining psychologically in its state of dis-ordered agitation: and of being crushed

– or of developing within itself a faith in the future precise enough and ardent enough, through very excess of compression upon itself, for it to emerge from the ordeal mentally and affectively made one.

New York, 18 January 1953
Published in *Psyché*, September 1953

On Looking at a Cyclotron

Reflections on the folding-back upon
itself of human energy

LAST summer I was admitted as a visitor to the cyclotrons of the University of California.

There you will already find a whole series of individual examples of these strange machines (which will no doubt become as familiar to our descendants as a turbine or a dynamo is to us), increasing in size as they follow one after another (or even, you might say, engender one another).

There are some (the cyclotrons properly so called) used to accelerate protons, deuterons and alpha particles.

Others (betatrons and synchrotons) which act upon electrons.

And finally a third type, the youngest of the family and at the same time the largest, the *bevatron*, so called because by means of its annular electro-magnet 40 metres in diameter (and weighing 10,000 tons) it is hoped that it will accelerate protons not simply to millions but to *billions* of *electron-volts*.

Picture to yourself, for each of these gigantic tools, a circular housing, built somewhat on the lines of a locomotive shed: and within these housings an annular vacuum chamber in which the atomic particles, whipped up by a periodic series of electrical impulses and at the same time forced into a circular orbit by the action of a powerful magnetic field, spiral at an ever increasing speed until they break away at a tangent, at a speed which approaches that of light: they are then, in virtue of this fantastic living force, capable of breaking up matter, of transmuting and soon, perhaps, even of creating it.

With that in mind, imagine to yourself, built up around these mysterious housings, a whole miniature city, with its closely guarded entrances, its many offices, its garages, its restaurant – and, of course, its human population, a motley, hand-picked body of scientists and technicians of all sorts.

And finally, situate this concourse among the eucalyptus

trees in the hills that look out on the bay of San Francisco and the Golden Gate.

Do all this, I say: and then you will come close to having a picture of Berkeley's famous Radiation Laboratory which today, in close alliance with the Atomic Energy Commission of the U.S.A., is one of the most vigorous centres in the world for the study and harnessing of nuclear energy.

I am no physicist, and so I shall say nothing here of what were my own reflections, in these high places, on the explosion or 'implosion' of atoms. On the other hand I am now a student of life of many years' standing: and in that capacity I would like, using the allegorical form of a phenomenon of 'second sight', to express and critically analyse a certain feeling of spiritual presence and energy which hit me like a blow when, for the first time in my life, I found myself standing face to face with one of our modern atom splitters.

II. THE OTHER, INVISIBLE, CYCLOTRON: OR, A LOCAL CONCENTRATION OF HUMAN ENERGY

When I visited the Berkeley cyclotrons they were either being overhauled or not yet completed. This meant that they could be approached without danger, and I was therefore allowed to pass through the thick concrete shell that shrouded them and study the working of their most secret organs.

Now, as I penetrated further into the inside of the monster, there occurred a sort of gradual change of plane and another group of images began to replace in my mind that of the atomic accelerator I was looking at. My guide went on talking about interacting fields, and all the time I could not help feeling and perceiving, beyond and around this electro-magnetic cyclone, the concentric inflow of another and no less formidable radiation: that of the human, sucked up over me in a whirlwind from the four corners of space.

A whole range of specialized knowledge and skills – a whole spectrum of energies, too – converging on the point where I stood – and running together to form something specifically unique, in a state highly charged with passion.

First, *a whole range of specialized knowledge and techniques*: mathematics, electronics, chemistry, photography, metallurgy, resistance of materials, architecture: these manifold sciences have to meet and work together, all simultaneously at the same degree of perfection, if a cyclotron is to be designed, built, and brought into operation.

And then, *a whole spectrum of energies*. Kilowatts upon kilowatts – that goes without saying – but coal, too, and oil, and uranium. Money, again – dollars in millions – money that it is easy for the righteous to condemn, but which is none the less – which every day is none the less *becoming* more – the life-blood of mankind. And further, to fuse together and finally give a soul to all this mass, an untiring will to build, drawn from all the sources of necessity and appetite.

For, when all is said and done, if the physical atmosphere surrounding a nuclear energy generator becomes dangerously active, what words can we find for the psychic voltage produced in the same place by the coming together of all that is most harassing or most inspiring in economic needs, in national aspirations, in the demands of war, in our hopes of conquering disease and (even more) in the control we anticipate over the very driving forces of cosmogenesis?

In truth, what impressed me much more than the millions or billions of electron-volts, what went completely to my head in the neighbourhood of a cyclotron, was to see how, when what are reckoned to be our most firmly established categories are taken to a certain degree of intensity and concentration, they tend to synthesize into some completely new psychic reality whose nature is as yet unexplored.

On the hills of Berkeley, the frontiers vanish between laboratory and factory – between the atomic and the social – and also, as I shall be showing, between the local and the planetary.

So true is this, that if a man who works there thinks about where he is and what he is doing, he is justified in asking himself whether he is still engaged in research, or in industry, in physics or metaphysics, in energetics or in medicine, in war or in peace – or even whether, carried along by a flood which outdistances him, he may not even now be arriving, perchance, at some hitherto unknown form of composite (or 'concentrated') humanity.

III. AN ALMOST UNIVERSAL PHENOMENON: THE MULTIPLICATION ON EARTH OF CONCENTRATORS OF HUMAN ENERGY

Then, like a wave that spreads out, it seemed to me that my vision widened to the dimensions of the earth. For, hardly had I become sensitive to the 'odour' of the ultra-human given off by the huge atomic turbines I was looking at, than I suddenly recognized in it the emanations which surround all the other great machines that for the last half-century have been continually growing up in every quarter, under our eyes, like so many giant trees.

Electronic microscopes and gigantic telescopes.

Rockets with inter-planetary potentialities.

Computers.

At all these nodal points of human activity, the same chain process can surely be clearly recognized beneath the extreme diversity of forms and procedures: a process of concentration and synthesis, leading in every case to the same result – man, *the worker*, at first sucked up by – made prisoner by – the object of his effort, and then finally transformed (ultra-unified) by the combined influence of *his working* and *his work*.

By his working, I say advisedly: inasmuch as it forces him to reach unanimity with his fellows and in himself.

And by his work, too, inasmuch as man inevitably at the term of everything he creates, finds man again, at a slightly higher level: a man who has always grown greater, either through sensorial penetration into the immense and the infinitesimal, or by geometrical invasion of space – or (which is per-

haps the most astonishing of all forms of progress) by direct multiplication and acceleration of his cerebral faculty of thought.

In consequence, the whole earth became like a fluorescent
substance exposed to a pencil of mysterious rays: under the
influence of the physico-spiritual emanations which surrounded
me, it gradually appeared to me to be dotted with luminous
points, each one of those 'stars' corresponding to some laboratory or some apparatus around which the human, through its
charge of energy and its union, was here and now being
transformed into some neo-human 'isotope'.

Now, while my fascinated mind lingered in wonder, noting
the number, the brilliance and the shades of colour in these
points of light that enveloped the earth, a supremely assertive
fact suddenly forced itself on my attention.

When first my eyes, at last trained to see, noted that the
hitherto dull face of the planet had begun to sparkle with ultra-
humanity, I could have thought that the only general law
covering this manifestation was the multiplication, the
intensification and the inter-connexion of the luminous centres
that were lighting up in turn over the continental masses.

But, now that my eyes were becoming still more used to
what they saw, I realized that this be-starred vault was stirring
into motion: not with the monotonous motion of a firmament
that revolves on its poles, but with the creative movement of
an involutive galaxy.

In a first phase I had realized that for the last fifty years we
had, though hardly noticing it, been witnessing the birth
practically everywhere on earth of what are true generators (or
concentrators) of human energy. Now, in a second phase, I
could distinctly see that these concentrators were inevitably
concentrating among themselves.

IV. THE GENERAL CONCENTRATION OF THE HUMAN
UPON ITSELF: OR THE WHIRLPOOL OF RESEARCH

Last century one might have believed (as there was no lack of people to say) that the great modern human event was the appearance of the machine and industry.

Today we are beginning to suspect that this estimate left the heart of the phenomenon still untouched. For, under the influence of an irresistible interior movement, machines and industrial processes, even as we handle them, are coming to be dominated by a still more powerful agent. As I said earlier, it is not only that in our society the differences between the laboratory and the factory are rapidly disappearing, but, what is more, that in the coalescence of the two it is clearly the laboratory that is dominant. When all the factors have been taken into account, what we have just entered is not an industrial age but rather an age of research.

Since all time, it is true, man has been a seeker. He has sought unremittingly and persistently both from necessity and for the delight of finding. But this effort was to a large extent diffuse – it made hardly any impression on the mass of mankind – was hardly put into words and justified by plain ordinary people – and was more or less abandoned as a *hobby*[1] to the initiative of a few eccentrics. Well into the eighteenth century, we should remember, the scientific investigator was still looked on as an oddity, or as a species of philosopher.

But now, in less than two hundred years we find that what research has done is precisely to engulf everything, like a tide: the thirst for understanding allying itself to the need to produce – man suddenly discovering that he could (or even that he must) assist scientifically in his own person the uninterrupted, though still incomplete, progress of biological evolution: in these days we have to reckon the number of research workers in millions – and they are not scattered at random, but so distributed as to form a system of integral, prolific, groups; moreover, no observer can fail to see in the growth, the differentiation and the complementary character of these groups a more powerful repetition of what happens elsewhere in the genesis of human cultures or in that of zoological species.

1. Père Teilhard uses the English word. (Tr.)

In short, there is every indication that, following upon a long and slow accumulation of physical and psychic energies in the human atmosphere (the whole of prehistory, and the whole of history), a sort of spiritual tornado has just burst upon us and swept us up.

And at this point let us make sure that we appreciate the exactness and the realism of the simile.

The whirlpool of research –

Not, like the 'whirlpool' of business enterprise, a mere restless to and fro in every direction –

Nor, like the whirlpool of animal species, simply a swarm of divergent forms carried into ever more widely separated orbits by the blast of evolution –

But a true 'maelstrom' that sucks everything it engulfs into its deep-rooted axis.

We still often hear it said of research that precisely as a result of its ramification into continually more numerous and more specialized branches, it loses contact with itself and has the consequent effect of inhibiting contact between the minds it enlists.

I wonder when this disheartening cliché will be treated as it deserves.

That, in particular instances, and during the formative phase we are going through, there does exist a danger of intellectual fragmentation, and that it even claims some victims, is true enough. But from the soundly scientific point of view, what does this wastage matter compared with the vast quantity of psychological unity effected in man by the force which inexorably impels him to discover and invent ever further?

Let us look once again at the array of devices of all sorts (machines to create or break down matter, machines for seeing, machines for communicating, machines for thinking) whose fantastically variegated fauna is beginning to populate the earth. Can we fail to see that, far from breaking away from one another as autonomous individuals, these incredible creations of man have a natural tendency to come together and interlock in such a way as to combine and multiply their powers?

If we look at these multiple elementary *vortexes* not simply one by one, each within the radius of its specific operation, but include them all simultaneously in one and the same survey, do they not manifestly run together to form one single, gigantic eddy of thought within which science does not *deploy* its countless branches nearly so much as *fold them in*?

Let us recognize this once and for all: in us men it is not simply that the tide of life is still rising; it is not simply that it has ceased to divide itself into divergent phyla – but, in addition, concentrated upon itself by its need to know, it has just been carried under the influence of convergence to a paroxysm of its characteristic power of causing a simultaneous and reciprocally effected rise, in the universe, of organization and consciousness, that is to say of interiorizing matter by complexifying it.

*

Before my bewildered eyes the Berkeley cyclotron had definitely vanished; and in its place my imagination saw the entire noosphere, twisted back upon itself by the wind of research, forming but one single vast cyclone, whose specific effect was to produce, instead of and in place of nuclear energy, psychic energy in a continually more reflective state: and that is precisely the same as saying to produce the ultra-human.

Now, what was so remarkable was that confronted by this gigantic reality which might have made my head reel, all I experienced, on the contrary, was a feeling of peace and joy, a *fundamental* peace and joy.

First, of peace: because precisely in virtue of its immensity and *in consequence of its security*, the movement I saw came to me as a reassurance for the terrified monad. The faster the whirlpool the less danger there was that the grain of sand I represented might be lost in the universe. Contrary, then, to what existential writers have been dinning into our ears for the last twenty years, it is only a general view of evolution (and not an ever more solitary introspection of the individual by the individual) that (as I experienced it once more in my own person) can save twentieth-century man from the anxious questionings prompted by life.

And of joy, too: for I saw then more clearly than ever before that if we were to explain the presence in and around us of a physical field sufficiently powerful to cause the totality of the human mass to fold in on itself, we should have to do more than cite the collective pressure of untold numbers of elements driven in the same direction by the need to survive. To create the current that is to draw us, with increasing intensity and probably for hundreds of centuries still to come, both towards the above and the ahead, the repulsive (or negative) pole of a death to be avoided must, by dynamic necessity, be matched by a second, attractive (or positive) pole – the pole of a super-life to be attained: a pole capable of arousing and satisfying ever more fully, with the passage of time, the two demands characteristic of a reflective activity: the demand for irreversibility and the demand for total unity.

And it was thus that, the more I tried to extend into what lies ahead, and to divine, the progress of the immense physico-psychic spiral in which I saw that I was involved by history, the more it seemed to me that what we still know by the too simple name of 'research' became charged with, became tinted with, became warmed by, certain forces (faith, worship) hitherto regarded as alien to science.

For the more closely I looked at this research, the more I saw that it was forced, by an inner compulsion, ultimately to concentrate its efforts and its hopes in the direction of some divine centre.

Published in *Recherches et Débats*, April 1953

The Energy of Evolution

IN a way that is somehow paralleled by the dominance in the fields of pure thought of the *ens* of the metaphysicians, the *energy* of the physicist operates as something against which there is no appeal in the domain of experience: energy, the prime, multiform stuff of all phenomena; and energy, again, the standard by which is measured what is, or is not, achievable in practice.

'*A priori*', says the philosopher, 'only that can exist which is thinkable'.

'*A priori*', says the scientist, 'only that can appear which is in conformity with energy'.

On the strength of his energetics, the scientist, it is true, no more claims to explain (or foresee) the particular configuration assumed (or to be assumed) by the universe, than does the thinker on the authority of his ontology.

But the scientist, too, in his own way and on his own level, recognizes that he is capable of deciding, even in advance, under what conditions an event is possible – and in what general direction, once it has been initiated, the course of things must inevitably develop. And this, moreover, applies *in all departments of the real*; because, running through the rigorous laws of physiology and production, for example, the decrees of thermodynamics extend even into zones as apparently 'spiritual' as the psychology of the individual and of society.

Here, nevertheless (I mean in the case of the biological extension of energetics) we must take careful note of what happens.

While in metaphysics the notion of *being* can be defined with a precision that is geometric in type, *energy*, for its part, presents itself to the physicist as a magnitude that is still open to all sorts of possible corrections or improvements. No one has any doubt about its properties of conservation, transformation and dissipation. But in addition to this sharply defined and firmly established thermodynamic nucleus, should we not recognize in the *Weltstoff* the presence of certain structural elements which, though negligible for physics and physical chemistry, take on a rapidly increasing importance in the case of the extremely complex assemblies with which the biological sciences are concerned?

It is the reality of an additional term such as this that I would like to bring out here, in a brief study, not just from a morphological or qualitative point of view, but from that of energetics, of the great phenomenon of evolution: this being considered, moreover, not as one whole but exclusively in that part of it which is the most advanced and the most characteristic – by that I mean the social evolution of man, or, in the widest sense of the word, *hominization*.

I. THE OLD AND THE NEW EVOLUTION

When we hear people speaking of evolution the idea that comes naturally to our minds is that of the origin and transformation of living forms – that is, the idea of an operation which is essentially phyletic and divergent – based on chromosomic heredity – and maintained by the combined play of chance and selection. A '*transformism*', corrected, of course, and improved by genetics, but nevertheless still essentially the transformism of the nineteenth century, with its fully homogeneous mechanism extended to no more than a strictly limited field. Nine times out of ten that is the picture the *word* 'evolution' calls up for us.

We have only, however, to reflect for a moment to realize that it is something very different from, and something much more than, a mere 'genesis of animal species' that the *phenom-*

enon of evolution, both as an over-all process and in the forms it assumes, is now tending to become for science, and indeed has already become.

On the one hand, below 'living matter', that is, in the vast domain of the inorganic, physics is now disclosing to us a veritable genesis of 'simple bodies'. True, it is an 'a-phyletic' type of evolution, in which each particle is formed, coalesces or disintegrates on its own account (without yet, that is, going beyond the boundaries of an ontogenesis); but it is nevertheless a true evolution since, in one way or another,[1] we can henceforth be certain, atomic *additivity* exists from nuclear elements and electrons onwards.

On the other hand, right in the heart of the organic world an illuminating cleavage in our view of vitalization is in process of being effected at the level of the human. We are gradually coming to see that anthropogenesis is specifically distinct from the rest of biogenesis. Would it be a great mistake to see in the perception of this threshold and this leap one of the most decisive steps taken by modern scientific thought? After Galileo and Darwin man came to question, or even to cease to take seriously, the feeling he had always had until then of occupying a privileged position at the summit of nature. Was not anthropocentricism a mere optical illusion, like geo-centricism? But now the whole breadth and depth of the phenomenon of man has been analysed more fully; the present rebound it is effecting has been appreciated; and there can be no doubt that our minds have come to realize that there is a distinction between 'man at the centre of a static cosmos' and 'man at the head of a universe in a state of complexification and interiorization'. For ultimately, when every allowance has been made for subjective effects of outlook, it is evident that man (and more particularly social man) behaves, objectively, like a life 'of the second species' in nature: a life that has acquired the faculty of foresight, of invention, and, by deliberate skill, of

1. Whether gradually or in leaps – by explosion or 'implosion' – hardly matters.

associating in an ever more marked process of planetary co-adjustment and co-reflection.

In these circumstances, a perfected form of evolution over-laying and incorporating the 'old' zoological evolution, which was mainly automatic, chromosomic and divergent, is making itself apparent in a *reflective* living medium: and it is a truly 'new'[2] evolution, defined by the three properties:

a. of self-direction in arrangement (by invention)

b. of additive transmission of the acquired (by education)

c. and finally of convergence upon itself (by socialization and 'planetization').

Although there is not yet complete agreement on a number of secondary points, it is true to say that to all appearances, following this new line of thought, the decisive intellectual step has already been taken by the specialists in biology and in biogenesis. Of that practically nobody engaged in either has any doubt. Whether it be in the form of a derivative lateral branch, or on the contrary,[3] in its main current, the cosmic energy of evolution, already remoulded for a first time in its passage from the mineral to the living, is transformed for a second time by entry into the domain of the reflective psyche. Biological evolution is not only prolonged, in the strict literal sense of the word, in the socialization of man: what is more, it noticeably lengthens the range of its inner attributes.

– And this produces a remarkable result, as yet insufficiently exploited by science: now that evolution has become in each one of us to some extent master of its movements and at the same time reflectively conscious of the forces which animate it, it offers itself to our minds as an object not only of external observation but of *introspection*.

Let us, then, as a first approach, make use of this sort of 'spectroscopy' of the energy of evolution 'from within'.

2. The adjective is borrowed from the epilogue to G. Gaylord Simpson's *The Meaning of Evolution*, Yale University Press, 1949.

3. The more coherent and more rewarding and, in consequence, more probable explanation.

II. ACTION AND ACTIVATION, OR, ON THE DYNAMIC ROLE OF FORESIGHT IN THE NEW EVOLUTION

One of the most distinctive characteristics of living substance in action is undoubtedly the predominant importance assumed in it by the fact of being (or of not being) appropriately *responsive to a stimulus* and *stimulated*. Theoretically, the physicist may well be able to calculate (in calories, for example) the quantity of energy that can usefully be employed by any animal at a given moment. But what quantity of this store of energy is going, in each case, to be effectively released – and in what direction – and at what speed? That is something we cannot determine without introducing a whole series of imponderables which are tied up with the psychism of the individual in question. The animal (one *particular* animal) behaves in an entirely different way, according to whether he has a full belly or is starving, is left in peace or hunted, and so on.

This means that, even in the case of very imperfectly cerebralized beings, no one who compared it with what happens in ourselves can have any doubt that, in order fully to express the dynamic state of a living mass,[4] we must, as I pointed out at the beginning, use a formula that includes at least two terms: the first measuring in figures a certain thermodynamic magnitude, and the second expressing a certain capacity given to this energy of expending itself, more rapidly or less rapidly, in the direction of survival, of multiplication, or of some super-arrangement of organic matter.

Precisely, no doubt, because it rests upon imponderables, this second term (which we shall here call '*activation*') may well be neglected by bio-energetic specialists. Nevertheless two things are immediately apparent:

1. First, that throughout the animal series (from the protozoon

4. Whether taken individually – or considered statistically in its power of speciation.

to the most highly developed mammal) the operation of evolution has invariably consisted (for an approximately constant quantity of energy stored up in each cell) in progressively increasing and sensitizing to a higher degree the stimulation-area of organic beings.

2. And secondly, that in man, by harnessing forces that stem from the future, this general process of activation of living matter has entered a critical phase, characterized by an increasing predominance of the effects of fear or hope allied to the formidable gift of foresight.

Let us concentrate more particularly on the study of this second point, for in it can certainly be found the ultimate driving force of the mechanism of the new evolution.

For an over-all reserve of physical energy that is more or less equal to that of the animals of the same size around him, man displays an amazing power of acting as a leaven in the whole of his natural environment: and, to explain this unusual 'activity' of our species, we may rightly, as a start, emphasize the co-existence in the human individual of an extreme perfection of the nervous system and a sort of universality of knowledge – so that a very great number of objects and objectives are continually being presented to a vibrant sensibility. This, indeed, is sufficient to cause a sharp increase in the importance of the part played by the effects of activation in the general balance sheet of human energy.

But what precisely would have been the value of this two-fold biological advance in the response of the subject to stimulus and the extension of the object, if man had in this respect resembled the other animals and his perception of time had continued to be restricted to a narrow fringe of duration ahead of him?[5]

Not only, needless to say, would the power to 'project', that is to say, to invent, never have been caused to develop in him;

5. An absurd hypothesis, of course, since reflection necessarily entails foresight.

but, further, there would have been a radical difference, for his fundamental affectivity, in the degree of attractive power the world exerted on him.

With the magnetic pull of the future gradually replacing for us the mere effort to survive, we know how much larger a part is progressively coming to be played in our personal ideas and affections by the unfinished, the unexpected, *the ideal*.

In, that case, is not what is happening in each one of us a miniature reproduction of what is happening in the whole species?

Let us look on the one hand at mankind as it might have been in its beginnings, in the Neolithic, for example; then, on the other hand, at mankind today; and then let us try to determine the relationship, in terms of energetic value, of the two.

The difference, expressed in thermodynamic units, between each of these two mankinds is obviously considerable: and it is due both to the sheer increase in numbers, and to the fantastic enlargement of the natural forces that have been tapped and hominized by collective technology in the course of the last thousands of years. If, however, we now look at it from the point of view of the 'activity' of the system, surely the leap is seen to be very much more vigorous and more significant? For we have to realize that what is holding, paradoxically 'cantilevered' on entropy, this vast mass of improbable arrangements constituted by twentieth-century man, is ultimately the awareness (still vague, but already infinitely more developed than in the Neolithic) that 'something' is waiting for us in the depths of time to come. No longer is there simply (as there is to all appearances in animal species) the sting of death to be avoided: there is the passion for outdistancing ourselves and reaching a peak we can glimpse through the clouds.

On this point, which physics itself cannot neglect, our own examination of our power to act gives us a categorical answer:

'Starting with man, the activation of energy necessary for the maintenance and furtherance of evolution is secured by a stimulus which proceeds from a focus-point of attraction lying continually higher and further ahead in time: which means that it gradually takes on the characteristics and the dimensions of *a faith*'.

There we have a principle that must be borne in mind whenever we venture to speculate on the future of the human species.

III. THE ENERGETIC FUTURE OF THE NEW EVOLUTION

As biologists come to see more clearly that the course of evolution is authentically (if not even axially) continued in the socialization of man, so they become more open to the temptation to extrapolate into the future the curve of hominization.[6] Judging from the past history of the earth and of life, what is going to happen to man in one million, or *n* million years?

In this order of ideas, it would obviously be infantile to try to give oneself any sort of positively determined *picture* of the shape of things. In no more than two or three centuries, what is going to be the state of our economic world, our political or our religious world? This is something it is utterly impossible to envisage. If the study of man's future is left to the imagination it collapses into absurdity. On the other hand, entrusted to science, it becomes meaningful if we adopt a purely functional point of view and simply ask ourselves what conditions of energetics mankind must, from compulsive necessity and in every case, satisfy in order to continue to move ahead and possibly (should such a thing exist) reach the natural term of its development.

And it is here that the laws, outlined above, of a dynamics of evolution can be applied.

There is a first inescapable fact which in a general way

6. See, for example, C. Galton Darwin, *The Next Million Years*, Rupert Hart-Davis, London, 1952; Julian Huxley, *Evolution in Action*, Chatto and Windus, London, 1953; G. Gaylord Simpson, *The Meaning of Evolution*, Yale University Press, 1949, etc.

dominates the whole problem of the 'human energy of evolution'. It is that the further the socialization of man progresses, the more the mass of physical energy absorbed by the operation tends rapidly to increase. In the quantity of heat or electricity expended, in the number and variety of the substances employed, the average consumption of each human individual is decisively coming to follow a sort of exponential curve moving towards the vertical. And since this staggering rise would seem, when all the factors are weighed, to represent not a wastage but what one might call a 'specific energy of totalization' of the human mass, there is no ground at all for thinking (all being well) that the curve is ever going to bend back and sink down again.

But if, by dynamic necessity, we find that we have to admit that for hominization to continue the thermodynamic force is bound continually to increase in the thinking envelope of the earth – and in geometric progression – then, in virtue of what we were saying earlier, it is even more urgently necessary for us to accept exactly the same conclusion in relation to the general *activation* of the system.

Thus we find, in fact, that we have reached the heart of the difficulties raised by the problem of knowing whether, and up to what point, it is physically (planetarily) possible for man to trans- or ultra-hominize himself.

There was a time when the chief danger threatening a biological future for man seemed to lie in the order of astronomy. For some catastrophic reason (collision with another star, deterioration of the atmosphere, and so on) might not the earth prematurely disappoint our hopes?

Today we have ceased to worry on those lines. So slow, we now know, is the evolution of the solar system in comparison with the average duration of animal forms[7] that a catastrophic clash between the two processes seems to be, absolutely speaking, improbable.

7. Particularly if, as in the case of man, the development of the latter appears to be produced at an 'explosive' speed.

And while we men will not lack the time we need to complete our evolution, neither, in spite of certain pessimistic prophecies, is it any more probable that we will lack material energy. In his recent short book *The Next Million Years*[8] Charles Galton Darwin lucidly restated the paradoxical thesis that the economic prosperity of our generation, largely based on a destructive exploitation of the earth's resources, was no more than a flash in the pan. Once we have burnt our capital of coal and oil, accumulated with geological slowness in a few privileged zones of the earth, nothing, he believes, will enable us to maintain the way of life of which we are so proud – neither hydro-electric power, nor solar radiation, nor the paltry reserves of uranium scattered about the ancient continental masses. The golden age of the nineteenth and twentieth centuries will be followed once more by shortages, by the threat of famine and the necessity of cutting down the population.

While I am far from being as informed and competent in this field as the author, I cannot manage to take his terrifying prophecies very seriously. It is only twenty-five years since we began to consider the possibility of nuclear energy and, theoretically, our resources in that quarter are boundless. By analogy with what happened historically in the past in the case of steam and electricity, surely we may once again rely on the progress of a science whose inventive powers have been fantastically enlarged.

To my mind, what is our prime concern in connexion with the ultra-evolution of man is not to know how, for perhaps hundreds of thousands of years to come, we are going to feed an ever growing population and fuel machines that are becoming ever more complicated and voracious. It will be to discover how man can maintain and increase, without check, throughout these vast periods of time, a passionate will not only to subsist but to press on: as we said, without that will

8. See note 6, p. 368 above.

every physical or chemical force we dispose of would remain heartbreakingly idle in our hands.

When all is said and done, if hominized evolution is to be continued into the future without any loss of speed, an extraordinarily powerful *field of stimulation* is dynamically necessary – one that itself, as an absolute necessity,[9] presupposes the emergence sooner or later in our consciousness of an objective with a completely and inexhaustibly compelling magnetic power.

To reassure us about the thermodynamic future of the new evolution, a way out has just opened up for us in the direction of the atom. But, in what concerns the psycho–dynamic aspect of the operation, to what quarter are we to turn if we are to perceive at least the first rays of the star for which we are looking? Is the horizon completely clouded over in that quarter? Or cannot we, rather, distinguish a glimmer which is a continuation of what we spoke of at the beginning as a biological concentration of mankind upon itself?

There can be no doubt, we said then, provided that 'socialization' is not arbitrarily divorced from 'speciation', that in the field of our experience man represents the single magnificent example to be found of a phylum which, instead of branching out, folds back its branches ever more closely – and of this the most immediately evident consequence is the rise in us of the phenomena of co-invention and co-consciousness.

We no longer find anything surprising in the *present* manifestations and rate of progress of this great biological fact of *human convergence*, which we are at last beginning to face squarely as an object of science. On the other hand, are we paying sufficient attention to the *unique possibility* that this *unique phenomenon* offers us of correctly extrapolating in direction (and at the same time explaining dynamically) a continued forward advance of hominization?

Since everything that converges must necessarily have, at a

9. Provided, of course (which is the essential postulate), that the universe is accepted as evolutively *viable*.

distance that may be greater or may be less, some place of meeting and confluence; and since mankind, on the other hand, disposes biologically of no more than a limited number of thousands of millions of years for the completion of his evolution – for these two reasons we cannot avoid the conclusion of envisaging, *at some finite distance* ahead of us in time, the existence of *an ultimate point* or culminating peak of organic co-ordination, of intellectual co-reflection, and finally (step by step) of unanimity. And if such a point does exist, does it not represent precisely, in just the form we want, the permanent centre of stimulation, the impelling end that we still lack in order to satisfy the physical conditions required for a fulfilment of the human species?

Of this there can be no possible doubt.

And thus we find that the mystery of the energetics of hominization is cleared up and its fundamental mechanism is exposed.

'Convergent by nature, the new evolution functions by nourishing its increasing zest to evolve into a progressively more vivid consciousness of its actual convergence'.

This, it must be admitted, is a particularly elegant solution of the problem; but it is primarily a solution that finds a universal practical application at all times.

And this is because, in order to define at every moment (both in position and in its properties) the mysterious pole towards which we are gravitating through time, our faculty of thought and of action disposes of a simple and certain rule of energetics: to know how constantly to direct ourselves – in what we choose, in what we build, in what we believe – along those lines in which the universe, through the opportunities it offers for the unification and union of its elements, displays a *maximum activation*.

Unpublished, New York
24 May 1953

The Stuff of the Universe

S o, once again, I want to try to get more completely down to, and to express more fully, the ever elusive fundamentals of what I feel, of what I see and what I live. Once again, in the first place, because for some time it has seemed to me that I have succeeded in narrowing down more closely the ultimate essence of what envelops me, of what draws me along, of what I am. And once again, also, because at this further degree of the compression of things, there seems to me to be a leap produced in the coherence and simplicity – and so in the likelihood and appeal – of a certain structure of the world: a structure whose gradual discovery will have been the history, the strength and the joy of a life that is drawing to a close.

To the reason of the metaphysician it is 'being' (*ens*) which first appears in its widest general form, later to be dialectically differentiated, in the universe.

To the intuitive emotion of the mystic, it is the 'divine' that is immediately revealed, as a sort of common stock, in which, however, the multiplicity of things and their activity may well be lost.

For my innate 'materialism' (as I now clearly recognize) it was from a starting point in the tangible layers of the universe that, in my eyes, all reality was lit up and transfigured.

As an initial approach, the physicist sees the elementary stuff of the world as a flood of measurable physical energy, more, or less, corpusculized in 'matter'.

The secret and the mainspring of my spiritual drive will have been to see that, underlying this outer envelope of the phenomenon (and yet in genetic continuity with it) there stretched another domain. In this, which was no longer a domain of the *tangential* but of the *centric*, a second species of energy (not electro-thermodynamic but spiritual) radiated from a starting point in the first: and this could be divided, in ascending order, into three successive zones of increasing interiorization.

– First, the zone of the *human* (or of the *reflective*).

– Secondly, the zone of the *ultra-human* (or of the *co-reflective*).

– Finally, the zone of the *Christic* (or of the *pan-reflective*).

In the course of three successive phases, one and the same evolutionary flux extends to the full dimensions of the universe; and, by convergence upon itself, is personalized.

Without for once being concerned to respect any orthodoxy (whether scientific or religious) in the way I express myself – though at the same time in the consciousness that I am simply acting out of loyalty, carried to its extreme limit, to my two-fold vocation as a man and as a Christian: this is the astounding panorama that, simply by adjusting our vision to what we can all see, I would like to bring out for you with unmistakable clarity.

This is not a thesis, but a presentation – or, if you like, a summons. The summons of the traveller who has left the road and so by chance has arrived at a viewpoint from which everything is bathed in light, and calls out to his companions, 'Come and look!'

I. THE HUMAN (OR THE REFLECTIVE)

Governing the whole make-up of the universe, as it now finally presents itself to my experience at this moment, there stands a particular way of seeing the human. I say 'the human' and not 'man' advisedly in order to emphasize to what a degree, at this level of fundamental understanding, what most influences my vision when I look at mankind is not man's social concentration nor man as a zoological species but the perception (almost as a physico-chemical fact) of a certain extreme attained in its thinking element (as one might say, in its 'uranium') by the stuff of the universe.

At the level of scientific knowledge no less than at that of common sense, we all have an instinctive tendency to picture matter to ourselves as slackening, as losing tension, in a progression from the atom towards the molecular and the living; as though the *Weltstoff*, considered in its highest forms of arrangement, gradually lost some part of its primordial stability and cohesion.

Well, then, my view of the world has gradually been developed and has ultimately come to be fixed in direct opposition to this too widespread feeling of a cosmos that dissipates, or at any rate becomes more tenuous, as it becomes to all appearances progressively more fragile. By that I mean that my views changed as I accepted the evidence (which I had at first rejected) that our minds can divine a solution, at once general and genetic, of the universe, not in an entropic dissipation of energy nor in a rhythmic rise in atomic numbers, but rather in an inflexible trend inherent in corpusculized energy towards progressively higher states of *complexity-consciousness*.

If the fantastic mass of granular energy which we see as having in the past formed the primitive substance of the cosmos is left to the play of chance and to itself for a sufficiently long time, it has a natural tendency to associate in groups and to concentrate upon itself (wherever it can, and as much as it can) in systems of the highest possible complexity and centricity: this 'centro-complexity', which soon becomes extremely marked, coinciding with the appearance of progressively more luminous centres of consciousness.

If we finally decide, in order to judge the direction and absolute value of the progress of cosmogenesis, to accept (as I did) the truth of this fundamental formula – and it can be verified more than amply – then two facts become apparent. First a remarkable identity can immediately be seen between the mechanisms that, at one extreme of things, produce the atom of hydrogen and, at the other, the 'molecule' of man: but, further, it becomes evident that, in the transition from one of these forms of particle to the other, there is effected a strengthening (and not a slackening) of the cosmic ties. For, from one of the two extremes in question to the other, the radial nucleus of consciousness never ceases to become individualized within its (peripheral) electro- or thermo-dynamic envelope, until it reaches the point of reflecting upon itself and, in consequence, of insisting, in order to subsist, on the awareness of being *irreversible*.

For a long time, just like everybody else, I came close to being bogged down in the antiquated habit of looking on man, in nature, either as an inexplicable and ephemeral anomaly – or as the product of a physico-chemical evolution strictly confined to our planet – or, again, as the result of some miraculous extra-cosmic intervention.[1]

Now, on the other hand, that my eyes have been opened, I have come to understand that in the totality of itself, and at every point within itself, the *Weltstoff* tended to reflect upon itself[2] – now, in other words, that I can no longer regard the terrestrial human except as the natural and local, and for the moment the most advanced, product of a trend that embraces the totality of matter, and time, and space: now that that is so, I can say that I have found my bearings, and I can now breathe freely, in the feeling, vindicated at last, of forming but one with all the rest.

II. THE ULTRA-HUMAN (OR THE CO-REFLECTIVE)

Even if it is true, as I have just been saying, that the great opportunity in my life will have been that I was so situated existentially that the 'spirit' of the philosophers and theologians was seen by me as a direct extension of universal physico-chemism, I must nevertheless hasten to add that the discovery of this prime relationship would have been of no use to me if it

1. i.e. an intervention dissociated from the universal process. (Ed.)
2. Cf. *The Phenomenon of Man*, p. 169 n., 'I confine myself here to the phenomenon'. In connexion with the 'underlying causes controlling the whole process', see 'Cosmic Life' in *Writings in Time of War*, in particular pp. 46–71. (Ed.)

had not automatically been accompanied by a further apparent fact: that, on earth, in mankind considered globally, the cosmic process of psychogenesis (contrary to what one is told) is far from being halted at this moment: we can only say that it is accelerating.

In order to recognize in the human the quintessence of the *Weltstoff* I had had to do no more than allow an innate understanding of energy and matter to develop in me to the full. In order to see that this same human, taken as one whole, formed but a single galaxy in process of concentration, I shall have had to do no more than re-interpret and arrange in sequence, expressed in the same terms and on the same natural scale, the two great facts, both unmistakably evident, of the combined rise we are now witnessing of science and society.

Let me explain.

In our interpretation of human civilization, we are still, rationally speaking, adopting an illogical position.

On the one hand we all see and know by experience that, technically and economically, mankind is every day becoming more completely totalized upon itself. *But*, we are at pains to add, this does not mean that this irresistible trend towards the more organic has the least specifically biological value.

On the other hand, at the same time each of us fully appreciates that *in step with* a progress in our material dispositions, our perception of the universe is rapidly increasing in depth and coherence. *Even though*, we are again careful to point out, this does not mean that this added knowledge contributes anything new and permanent to 'human nature'.

In other words, while explicitly recognizing that the complexity-rise-of-consciousness couple operates just as evidently in the human mass as it does in any other department of the real, we still refuse to recognize that in this particular case its appearance points to and signifies, as it does elsewhere, a movement that is cosmic in dimensions and value.

It was against this refusal to treat the facts on an equal footing that I rebelled; I refused to accept a divorce between 'natural' and 'artificial'; and, further and even more important, I became alive to the sense of the creative, additive, and hereditary element in the common outlook (Weltanschauung) slowly developed in the mind of man by all forms of research: and so it was that in the end I was confirmed in the view I am now presenting.

Because we fail to relate ourselves to precise axes, and because, further, as we look at the curve of the phenomenon of man, we do not take in a sufficient length, we still, in a vague and sentimental way, discuss the notion of human perfectibility and the reality of a 'progress'. Now, in this field, we have only to apply appropriately the general parameter of *complexity-consciousness* for there to cease to be, I maintain, any remnant of doubt – for anyone whose eyes are opened. If you tell me that as time goes on man is getting 'better' or 'worse', I hardly know or care what the words mean.[3] But if you tell me that mankind can be regarded, at this moment, as a species that is disintegrating or has reached its ceiling, then I deny it absolutely. And this for the very good reason that in virtue of the power and the actual method of operation of its technico-mental unification, twentieth-century mankind, so far from trailing behind or falling back, presents itself quite clearly to our experience as a system in the full vigour of *co-reflection*, which is exactly the same as saying of *ultra-hominization*.

In truth, the great new tidings of joy that has to be published abroad in these days, if we are to allay the anxieties of the thinking earth and galvanize its energies, is undoubtedly (and here we see an unexpected aspect of the ancient gospel) that the horrors of the totalization phase we have just entered are not the symptoms of an imminent death: rather are they the signs of a further folding-back upon itself, that is, of an ultra-vivification, of the stuff of the universe.

3. Whether man be 'better' or 'worse' is in fact an ambiguous question. In any event, for Père Teilhard, as for every Christian, a man's moral value is a mystery of which God alone is the judge and to penetrate which is outside the competence of the scientist. (Ed.)

Happily for us, not only is mankind, considered experientially in its organic wholeness, still constantly in motion: what is more, unlike all the zoological species (divergent in type) which have preceded it, it is converging upon itself. And this irresistible biological folding-back (planetary in its scope and urgency) suggests to our minds the wild idea and the wild hope that perhaps there really does exist an ultimate centre of reflection (and hence of beatifying consummation) ahead of us, at the upper term of evolution.

III. THE CHRISTIC (OR THE PAN-REFLECTIVE)

Elsewhere I have told (in *The Heart of Matter*)[4] how, when all is said and done, the great event of my life will have been the gradual identification in my spiritual heaven of two suns: one of these stars was the cosmic peak postulated by a generalized evolution of the convergent type; and the other was constituted by the risen Christ of the Christian faith. And I see nothing to add here to the psychological history of that conjunction.

On the other hand, what does belong to my present theme, is to emphasize, more forcibly today than ever before, the astonishing energetic properties of the *divine Milieu* which is generated in the utmost depths of human consciousness by this truly 'implosive' meeting between a rising flood of co-reflection and a second, descending, flood of revelation.

The final and complete reflection of the universe upon itself in a meeting between the above of heaven and the ahead of earth – in other words, proceeding from the same movement, a God who makes himself cosmic and an evolution which makes itself person.

What more do we need, and what better could we imagine in our dreams, than this lightning flash, for all our active potentialities and all our possibilities of worship to be simultaneously realized in the highest form, *as they must be if we are to super-live?*

4. An autobiographical essay, to be published in a subsequent volume. (Ed.)

At last we are beginning to appreciate this. By the very fact that, in reflecting upon itself, cosmogenesis is coming more and more rapidly, starting with the human, to take on the characteristics of a *self-evolution*, every later advance of the universe in the direction of *maximum complexity-consciousness* henceforth requires that man feel himself to be interiorly supported by an ever more resolute will to press on: a will no ultimate prospect of a total death may intervene to discourage – but a will, on the contrary, which, from its very deepest roots, is spurred into action by an overpowering passion.

It is not in a dark (because closed) universe, nor in an ice-cold universe, nor in a merely lukewarm (because faceless) universe, that it is physically possible for the forces of co-reflection to remain alive and so reach their common pole.

But the open universe, the incandescent universe that our action demands if it is to function to the end – surely it is just that which the world of modern physics becomes for us, from the moment when, in Christic form, a *real* centre of irreversible personalization blazes out at the supreme pole of its concentration?

Here, as always, no doubt, action entails reaction. It is impossible to think of Christ as 'evolver' without at the same time having to re-think the whole of Christology.[5]

A functional completion of the one and the multiple takes the place of the creative paternalism we habitually envisaged.[6] The twofold notion of *statistical evil* and *evolutionary redemption* correcting or completing the idea of catastrophic sin and reparatory expiation. The final parousia more akin to a maturing than to a destruction.

In return for a valorization and amorization of the stuff of things, a whole series of readjustments must be made, I am well

5. In relation to, and on the scale of, the universe. (Ed.)
6. 'Paternalism' is used here as opposed to 'paternity', of which it is a distortion. It designates a mistaken concept of providence that relieves man of all responsibility for the evolution of the universe. Cf. above, 'The Evolution of Responsibility in the World'. (Ed.)

aware (if we wish frankly to Christify evolution), in a number of representations or attitudes which seem to us to be definitively fixed in Christian dogma. In consequence, and by factual necessity, one might say that a hitherto unknown form of religion – one that no one could as yet have imagined or described, for lack of a universe large enough and organic enough to contain it – is burgeoning in the heart of modern man, from a seed sown by the idea of evolution. God is no longer sought in an identification with things that annihilates personality, nor in an escape from things that de-humanizes man.[7] God is attained (and this is infinitely more energizing and brings infinitely truer communion) by entry into the centre of the total sphere that embraces all things – a centre that itself is in process of formation.

Far from being shaken in my faith by such a revolution, it is with irrepressible hope that I welcome the inevitable rise of this new mysticism and anticipate its equally inevitable triumph.

For if in the end nothing, absolutely nothing, can prevent man from ultimately coming to rest in the form of belief that activates the cosmic forces of convergence in him *to their maximum* – then, indeed, we have the finest proof of the transcendence of Christianity. We see it in its remarkable and unique power to find within itself, and present to us at the very time we need it, what at this precise moment in history is absolutely indispensable to our nature if it is to develop its power to act and to worship to the full: and that is a Christ who can be and is commensurate with the universe, in other words a God – the God we look for – of evolution.

> Unpublished, in sight of St Helena, on passage from New York to the Cape, 14 July 1953

---

7. Christian salvation, the resurrection of the flesh, is not an escape from the world but a transformation of the world in Christ. Cf. *Le Milieu Divin*, epilogue. (Ed.)

The Activation of Human Energy

I. DEFINITION AND UNIQUE VALUE OF HUMAN ENERGY

BY 'human energy' I shall mean here, as a first approach,[1] the sum total of physico-chemical energies either simply incorporated in, or (at a higher degree of assimilation) cerebralized[2] in, the human planetary mass at a given moment: the mass in question being considered in its linked totality, not only of its biological constituents, but also of its artificially constructed mechanisms.

Expressed in figures (which would be theoretically possible), this hominized quantity of energy would appear ridiculously small in comparison with the floods of thermodynamic power brought into operation by any other of the great phenomena of nature. On the other hand, considered qualitatively, it displays the power, by reason of its vast structural complexity, of creating within the universe[3] a progressively deeper and wider centre of indetermination and information. So true is this that one could define the human (considered from the point of view of physics) as a unique domain of the world, in which cosmic energy is caught up in a sort of *vortex* of self-arrangement and so concentrates and differentiates itself 'exponentially'.

What, then, are the absolute importance and value of this process of hominization (or reflection) of energy,[4] which as yet we find only on our earth, but which certainly represents a general and fundamental property of matter? Purely as a

1. For a fuller definition, see the conclusion.
2. Could one, perhaps, say 'cyberneticized'?
3. Like every type of life, moreover, but with an extreme intensity due to the two specifically human phenomena of individual reflection and co-reflection.
4. Cf. *Revue des Questions scientifiques*, 20 October 1952.

scientific problem, we cannot give too precise an answer. Nevertheless, without entering into any metaphysical considerations, it is surely unmistakably evident to our minds that if such a dynamic trend (from the non-arranged to the arranged) does exist in the universe, it must be a matter of supreme importance – as much to us as individuals, produced by that trend, as to the universe in which it originates – that the movement continue, and become more pronounced, and reach as perfect as possible a consummation in the future.

Let us try, then, to determine, in their most general form, the conditions that govern this continued existence and this fulfilment.

II. CONDITIONS GOVERNING THE INCREASE OF HUMAN ENERGY

In these days, when man is spurred on by a growing consciousness of forming part of the evolution which carries him with it, he cannot but ask himself, with ever increasing urgency and in ever clearer terms, what is his biological destiny: and it is only natural that his first concern should be to examine the soundness and the equipment of the vessel in which he is travelling.

We have ceased to worry about the threat of an earth that might suddenly be destroyed by collision with a star or that through continued cooling or poisonous infection or desiccation might gradually become uninhabitable. In comparison with the few paltry millions of years required (at the most) for the completion of the process of hominization, the rhythm of astronomical changes is so slow that we may reasonably dismiss, as affecting us, any deterioration of physico-chemical conditions within the solar system or even on the surface of the earth that carries us.

On the other hand it is fashionable nowadays, and not without reason, to emphasize the rapid diminution of the stocks of food and fuel miraculously made available to us by nature. For about the last two centuries, not only has there been a sudden, almost vertical, rise in the population of the globe; but, what is still more serious, each individual's requirements of an ever increasing number of different substances and forms of energy, are continually – as a direct result of the totalization upon itself of the human mass – rising at a fantastic rate. With such a pattern of consumption, how long have we before the coal and oil we use are exhausted, and not only those necessities but all sorts of substances which we already cannot go without if we are to remain alive – not to mention the chemical exhaustion or erosion of the soil? Only two or three hundred years more, we are warned, of this unbridled consumption[5] and the flame of man will, quite simply, die down for lack of fuel.

Although I have no special competence in such matters, I must confess that I cannot manage to take so tragic a view of the danger of famine with which they threaten us. It is true enough, indeed, that *in order to get started*, the technical exploitation of the earth will, in a first phase, have called for a reckless consumption of the treasures of energy accumulated in the bowels of the continents, and in a form that can be used immediately, by hundreds of millions of years of epirogenesis and biogenesis. But, without being naïvely optimistic, may one not think that the 'atomic age' is no dream for a second phase? I mean that everything that has been happening in physics for some time gives us ground for hoping that it will be possible for all forms of energy to continue to be distributed indefinitely to our descendants, and even more generously than ever – because we shall most probably have learnt by then how to draw it directly from an inexhaustible source.

No, there is no serious danger of any lack of time, measured though it be in centuries, nor even (whatever may be said) of calories for our species as it presses on in its effort to reach the end (whatever it may be) of its evolution.

Physical resources will not fail us.

5. Cf. for example, C. Galton Darwin, *The Next Million Years*, above, p. 368, n. 6.

But what, on the other hand, about courage? What about drive? What about *psychic* resources? Shall we always have enough of these?

We are now, quite rightly, concerned about our material reserves. But may not that concern make us forget the role and cardinal importance in energetics of the phenomena of *activation*?

If a living (or even a non-living) substance is to release, to 'actuate', its potentialities, it must, as we all know and feel, be appropriately capable of stimulation and be in fact stimulated. Theoretically, the physicist can express in figures the quantity of energy that can be usefully employed by an animal at a given moment. But what proportion of this potential is going, in each case, to be brought effectively into action? and in what direction? and at what speed? That is something which it is quite impossible to determine without introducing a whole series of imponderables which are tied up with the *psychism* of the individual in question. The animal (one particular animal) behaves in an entirely different way, depending on whether it has a full belly or is starving, is left in peace or hunted, and so on.

Among the very lowest living beings, this response to stimulus of organic matter is to all intents and purposes indistinguishable from an elaborated system of physico-chemical reactions from which consciousness would appear to be excluded. At a higher level, however, with the appearance of nervous systems, the reality of an energizing function exercised by knowledge becomes evident. The activation of the living being – the more living it is, and in virtue of what is most living in it – calls ever more insistently, if it is to become effective, for the intervention of some fear, some repugnance or (most of all) for some *attraction*.

And it is here that we find, in its most specific modes of conditioning, the hidden mechanism of hominized energy.

As a result of his extreme cerebration, man is not only the most responsive to stimulation of any living being known to us; but he is also the only one for whom the stimulating impulse without which there can be no action, is not confined to the perception of an immediate end, but comes from *a confrontation with the whole of the future.*

Earlier, I raised the question of where man is to find not simply the time and the physical powers but above all the *heart* to carry through thoroughly and to the end the ever more demanding task of his co-reflection.

The answer to this question must be that everything ultimately depends on the degree of activating power in the properties (that is to say the more, or the less, attractive characteristics) which our faculty of foresight can recognize in the totality of time that lies ahead of us.

And this, unexpectedly but most logically, leads us, along lines of pure energetics, from a simple question of Darwinian survival to the ancient, and to all appearances so para-scientific, problem of 'immortality'.

III. THE CONVERGENCE AND IRREVERSIBILITY OF HUMAN ENERGY

An open world? or a closed world?

A world that ultimately opens out into some fuller-life? or a world that in the end falls back, with its full weight?

It is becoming increasingly difficult for a true science of man (that is to say, an 'anthropology of movement') not to make a choice between the two terms of this dilemma, which is still left to professional metaphysicians and moralists. *And the reason for this is* that from the moment when man recognizes that he is in a state of evolution, he can no longer progress (as we have just seen) unless he develops in himself a deep-rooted, passionate zest for his own evolution: and there is the further reason that it is precisely this dynamic zest that could be vitiated beyond repair and annihilated by the prospect, however far ahead it may lie, of a definitive and total death.

No: if the world is not automatically to destroy its own

dynamic drive in step with its hominization, it cannot be of the 'closed' type. Every law of energetics insists that it shall 'open out' ahead. But by what mystery can this be effected? By what inexplicable exception to the general conditions of irreversibility from which, it would appear, nothing in the universe can be dispensed?

Let us try to suggest how this may be, even if we cannot make it completely evident.

On several occasions earlier, I referred to the effects of co-reflection in which the biological value of the progress of human socialization is expressed: man who cannot think without his thought being involved in and combined additively with that of all other thinking beings.

Sometimes, it would seem, this process of coalescence is described and interpreted as the reduction of the consciousness of all to one natural equality, which gradually imposes uniformity on intelligences within a sort of 'common basis' at a mean level.

What is happening, however, is in fact something very different.

The recognition that in virtue of his very nature man tends to co-reflect himself, is precisely the admission that in evolving he *converges* upon himself. Now, *to converge* entails two things for human energy. The first is that it never ceases to intensify and differentiate, with the passage of time, through concentration upon itself. And the second is that it can distinguish, at a certain finite distance ahead of it, a *peak*.

This can only mean that hominization, as witnessed by us in its operation, can only end (provided it wins through) in a *paroxysm* – and that can hardly be defined other than as a higher *critical point* of reflection – and of this again (precisely because it is *critical*) we are perfectly free to suppose that it might well be a *point of escape* from space and time: in other words that it may be exactly the *issue* which we found we must have if we are to have the heart to press on.

This, I realize, seems to leave us faced with the physical

monstrosity of a human energy that is at the same time reversible (as an effect of entropy) inasmuch as it is energy, and irreversible (as required by activation) inasmuch as it is hominized.

However, it may well be, perhaps, that this contradiction is a warning to our minds that we must completely reverse the way in which we see things. We still persist in regarding the physical as constituting the 'true' phenomenon in the universe, and the psychic as a sort of epiphenomenon. However, as suspected (if I understand them correctly) by such coolly objective minds as Louis de Broglie and Léon Brillouin,[6] surely, if we really wish to unify the real, we should completely reverse the values – that is, we should consider the whole of thermodynamics as an unstable and ephemeral by-effect of the concentration on itself of what we call 'consciousness' or 'spirit'.

– An interior energy of unification (true energy) gradually emerging, under the influence of organization, from the superficial system of actions and reactions that make up the physico-chemical.

In other words, there is no longer just one type of energy in the world: there are two different energies – one axial, increasing, and irreversible, and the other peripheral or tangential, constant, and reversible: and these two energies are linked together in 'arrangement', but without nevertheless being able either to form a compound or directly to be transformed into one another, because they operate at different levels.

We may well wonder whether, if we refuse to accept such a duality (which is no dualism!) in the stuff of things, it is scientifically conceivable that a universe can function, from the moment when it *reflects itself upon itself*.

Unpublished, New York, 6 December 1953

6. Cf. Louis de Broglie, 'La Cybernétique', in *Nouvelle Revue Française*, 1 July 1953, p. 84.

The Death-Barrier[1] and Co-Reflection

or, the imminent awakening of human
consciousness to the sense of its
irreversibility

1. By analogy with 'sound-barrier'.

mean, *without any change* in the empirically known genesis of spirit, as revealed historically in the course of the physico-chemical transformations of matter, let us imagine that evolution finally settles down into equilibrium not on its multiple and spread-out base but on its psychologically interiorized apex. In other words, let us make up our minds that it is not in the form of dispersed physical energy but in that of the conscious (and, more particularly, of the reflective-conscious) that the consistence of the universe is progressively distilled and accumulated.[2]

Then, as if by magic, every trace of contradiction between the physical and the psychic sides of the world is wiped out. For in this *spiritual* view of evolution (in which the philosophy of spirit is reduced to the *principle of the additive conservation of the reflective*) death, immediately, in spite of the terrifying transformations it entails, is in very truth neutralized: its poison has vanished from the heart of all things.

To my mind, there can be no doubt that it is in the direction determined by a transposition of this order that can be found the only psychologically possible road to mankind's self-development-to-the-end.

But how exactly are we to conceive that such a mental inversion can legitimately be effected while hominization is vigorously proceeding, and actually through the continuation of its influence?

IV. THE SENSE OF THE IRREVERSIBLE

The real difficulty (or at any rate the most worrying feature) of this whole matter is that at the present moment no one would seem to feel with the same acuteness the impossibility, in energetics, of co-existence which makes 'reflective evolutionary activity' conflict with 'anticipation of a total death'. Thus we

2. Assuming (as is conceivable) that as the conscious centres upon itself, so it is gradually released from the framework of complexity that was necessary to initiate and maintain its convergence.

find Norbert Wiener saying in his recent *The Human Use of Human Beings* (p. 45)[3] that the fact that the human species is inevitably doomed to death should no more make us relax our effort to discover than does the absolutely certain brevity of our individual lives.

Perhaps this de-activation of self-evolution by the threat of the complete annihilation of one's work is simply a matter of temperament. Are there perhaps two psychological species of man: of which one can enthusiastically pursue what is no more than 'temporary', while the other cannot commit himself (like Thucydides long ago) to anything that will not be 'for ever'?

Such a duality, on so fundamental a point, seems to me most unlikely – not to say 'cosmically' illogical. As an interpretation of the facts, I prefer to dwell on the idea that even if unanimity has not yet been achieved among men in what concerns the evolutionary consistence of spirit in its passage through death, it is at least *coming to be achieved*: the materialists of today are in fact (as I have often had the impression when listening to them or reading them) simply 'spiritualists' without realizing it.

And here it is important that I should be correctly understood.

While I envisage in the near future a human 'consensus' on the fact of the evolutionary irreversibility of the reflective (that is, I repeat, on the principle of the conservation of consciousness), that consensus has nothing in common with a practical contractual agreement (the sort of thing that is decided in an international congress), nor even with a blind or desperate act of faith. It must be conceived as the luminous attainment of *a new psychological stage*.

In the course of his history man has on several occasions crossed certain well-defined thresholds in his conscious appreciation of the universe: as, for example, when he discovered that the earth was round – or that it revolved – or,

3. Eyre and Spottiswoode, London, 1954.

again (and this was the most important of all), that, from top to bottom, the universe was no longer a cosmos but a cosmo-genesis. It is only reasonable, then, that this same man should reach certain stages or steps in the perception not simply of the external structure of things but also of the very nature of his spiritual stuff. In other words, why, in becoming adult, should he not awake to the knowledge of this or that primary 'de-mand' which until then had, for lack of stimulus, remained dormant in the depths of his being?

Today, ninety-nine per cent of men, perhaps, still fancy that they can breathe freely this side of an unbreakable death-barrier – provided it is thought to be sufficiently far away. Tomorrow (and of this I am certain because, like so many other people, I am already experiencing it) mankind would be possessed by a sort of panic claustrophobia simply at the idea that it might find itself hermetically sealed inside a closed universe.

All this is because deep within us (without, perhaps, our suspecting it) reflective being has since all time been orientated, in its very substance, towards a super-life to which there can be no end: but also because we could not have a 'mass-perception' of this primordial polarization until, all around us, co-reflection had attained a certain critical value.

And who can say how many other similar thresholds our species has still to pass over before it reaches the natural term of its evolution?

APPENDIX: SCIENCE AND REVELATION

From the preceding analysis it follows that when biological evolution has reached its *reflective* stage ('self-evolution') it can continue to function only in so far as man comes to realize that there is some *prima facie* evidence that the death-barrier *can* be broken. This evidence, however (as defined earlier) – which is a quasi-negative evidence, in short, and based mainly on the impossibility, in energetics, of its contrary – represents, it is evident, no more than a *minimum* accorded to the demands of our action. It was all very well for Leverrier to have discovered the planet Neptune, but Neptune began to exist for us only when we had actually *seen* it. Similarly, it is a great deal for man (even the essential thing) that he can be certain that the conscious, regarded along its principle axis of reflection, cannot fall back into the unconscious. But how much more comforting and 'electrifying' for our effort would it not be if some signal or some sign (some summons or some echo) should come to us from beyond death and give us *positive* assurance that some centre of convergence does really exist ahead of us!

And it is here, again by way of energetics, that there makes its way into physics and comes out into the open, not simply the 'philosophical' problem of immortality but (something much more unexpected) the question, in appearance completely 'theological', of a revelation.

Revelation – for greater clarity and simplicity I am taking the word and the notion here in its Christian sense – revelation: the beyond making itself manifest 'personally' to the here-below. It will have taken time, a great deal of time, for us to have appreciated that certain ways of conceiving such a phenomenon were disastrous and impossible. Throughout a long initial phase (from which we are hardly emerging) did we not look in the Bible for answers to the questions asked by astronomy, by geology, by biology?[4] As though in the field of experiment we could use (from the same stand-point and for the same facts) two different sources of light, that of the discovered and that of the taught.

Following on repeated setbacks, we have had to yield to the evidence. There is no domain, and no point, in which science and revelation encroach on one another – nor do one another's work. In return, however, an extremely remarkable double

A phase that the author later calls 'revelation that *duplicates* scientific research': cf. below. (Ed.)

relationship between the two (one that is both complementary and dynamic) is beginning to become apparent – without our perhaps paying sufficient attention to it.

First, if it is to make itself fully explicit and to develop fully, revelation needs ever more urgently the new contributions that scientific research is gradually making to human consciousness. Our Christology, for example, would certainly be in the doldrums at this moment if new (and, moreover, completely incredible) horizons were not opening up for our modern way of understanding and worshipping him 'in quo omnia constant'.

Secondly, however, can scientific research, on the other hand, if it is to be able fully to carry through its effort to discover, really be content (as we had earlier admitted) with a minimum – must it not on the contrary, by physical necessity, have a *maximum* of stimulation? And in that case will not faith in some revelation (correctly understood, of course)[5] in no way conflict with science (as some still, in all good faith, accuse it – through failing to understand it)?[6] Will it not, rather, some day become for our descendants – more distant, perhaps, or less distant – not a substitute, indeed, for, but an essential *activant* of research?

– Science and revelation being unable each to subsist functionally except in the movement which brings them together:

– Or (and this comes to the same thing) the terrestrial noosphere being unable to complete its evolution without

5. That is to say, the sense of a direct reaction on our thought, from within, of a peak of life beyond death.
6. Khrushchev decree of the Central Committee of the Communist Party, 10 November 1954: 'The essential opposition between science and religion is undeniable . . . Science cannot be reconciled with fictitious (revealed) concepts concerning nature and man. Religion dooms man to passivity . . . it fetters his creative activity'. It would be hard to find a franker and more typical example of intellectual failure to distinguish between the old and the new notion of revelation: that is, between a revelation that *duplicates*, and a revelation that *animates*, scientific research.

there being reflected on its co-reflective surface, ever more distinctly, the already present and actual centre of its complete reflection.[7]

It is in that quarter, it seems to me, that the definitive solution will soon be found to the conflict between science and religion.

Unpublished, New York, 1 January 1955
The appendix is dated the 5th

7. A progressive illumination which has been going on ever since the origin of mankind: the Word was the 'light, which enlighteneth every man that cometh into this world' (John 1 : 9). (Ed.)

Index